THE AMERICAN PRESIDENCY
AND THE
SOCIAL AGENDA

THE AMERICAN PRESIDENCY

AND THE

SOCIAL AGENDA

BYRON W. DAYNES

Brigham Young University

GLEN SUSSMAN

Old Dominion University

Prentice
Hall

Upper Saddle River, New Jersey 07458

Library of Congress Cataloging-in-Publication Data

DAYNES, BYRON W.
  The American presidency and the social agenda / by Byron W. Daynes and Glen Sussman.
     p. cm.
  Includes bibliographical references and index.
  ISBN 0-13-082632-4
  1. Executive power–United States. 2. Presidents–United States. 3. United
States–Social policy. 4. Social problems–United States. I. Sussman, Glen.

JK516. D394 2001
363'.0973–dc21   00-039139

VP, Editorial Director: *Laura Pearson*
Project Manager: *Merrill Peterson*
Prepress and Manufacturing Buyer: *Ben Smith*
Cover Director: *Jayne Conte*
Cover Photo: *AP/Wide World Photos*
Director of Marketing: *Beth Gillett Mejia*

This book was set in 10/12 Palatino by Progressive Information Technologies
and was printed and bound by Courier Companies, Inc.
The cover was printed by Phoenix Color Corp.

© 2001 by Prentice-Hall, Inc.
A Division of Pearson Education
Upper Saddle River, New Jersey 07458

Printed in the United States of America

10 9 8 7 6 5 4 3 2 1

ISBN   0-13-082632-4

PRENTICE-HALL INTERNATIONAL (UK) LIMITED, *London*
PRENTICE-HALL OF AUSTRALIA PTY. LIMITED, *Sydney*
PRENTICE-HALL CANADA INC., *Toronto*
PRENTICE-HALL HISPANOAMERICANA, S.A., *Mexico*
PRENTICE-HALL OF INDIA PRIVATE LIMITED, *New Delhi*
PRENTICE-HALL OF JAPAN, INC., *Tokyo*
PEARSON EDUCATION ASIA PTE. LTD., *Singapore*
EDITORA PRENTICE-HALL DO BRASIL, LTDA., *Rio de Janeiro*

We dedicate this volume to our spouses—

Kathy Daynes and *Elizabeth Masten*

whom we thank for their love, patience,
and long-suffering understanding
of the varying demands of academic life.

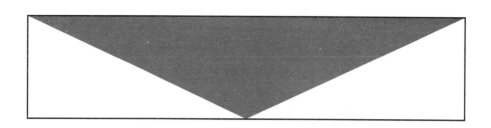

CONTENTS

5 | **THE CHIEF DIPLOMAT/COMMANDER IN CHIEF AND THE SOCIAL AGENDA *120***

6 | **CONCLUSION: PRESIDENTS AND THE SOCIAL AGENDA *154***

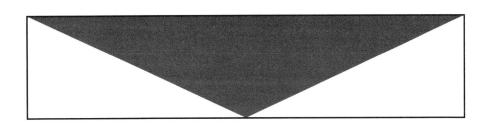

PREFACE

This book brings together two relatively recent areas of academic interest, namely, **presidential research** and **social policy research**. It may surprise many students of politics to realize that scholarship in both fields is quite recent. *Presidential research*, the earlier of the two fields, looks to 1960 as its origin, the same year that Richard Neustadt wrote his now classic *Presidential Power: The Politics of Leadership*. The American Political Science Association, however, did not sanction presidential studies until 1981, when it first established the Presidency Research Group as an organized section. Since that time, American presidency research has enjoyed a rapid growth and diversification into multiple speciality foci.

Social policy reserach likewise remained obscure during the years that scholars preferred to study economic policy. Moreover, when they did begin taking social policy seriously, none could agree on how to separate this subject from other public policy areas, nor could they agree on what term to use to refer to it. Thus, social policy has been called *emotive symbolization*, it has been collapsed in with *regulatory policy*, it has been examined as a special type of regulatory policy—*social regulatory policy*—and it has more recently been christened *morality policy*, a term that designates a category for these social policies.[1] All those researchers who contributed their insightful pioneering studies were in essence writing about the same phenomenon— namely, policies that consistently elicit vigorous responses based on strongly held beliefs. Now, while it is true that elite responses and public concerns toward social policies have long had political and social consequences in society, only recently have they been recognized as important in presidential politics. Yet most of the studies looking at the interaction between the two phenomena have either focused on one or two social issues or have dealt so briefly with them that it has been difficult to see patterns of response in the American executive and develop useful generalizations.[2] Hence it was our belief that the time was right to examine extensively the modern American presidency as our most visible federal institution, determining how the occupants of this office have dealt with the type of policy that frequently challenges our policymakers, often creates serious conflict in society, and remains an issue with great staying power on decision-making agendas. The six issues examined in this book share a similar characteristic found in previous research about social policy by Raymond Tatalovich and Byron W. Daynes—namely, that they continually evade "compromise and resolution."[3]

Our next challenge was how to organize this volume. We have relied on *presidential roles* as an integrating framework to examine how presidents respond to social issues and build their agendas. We have organized the book into chapters based on five presidential roles: *commander in chief, chief diplomat, chief executive, legislative leader*, and *opinion/party leader*.[4] We discuss the two most important roles,—*commander in chief* and *chief diplomat*—in one chapter that reflects the similar characteristics within each role. The *opinion/party leader* is a combined role suggesting a linkage between the president and the public because the president tries to build support among Americans not only for the office of the presidency but also for the particular president occupying the office, for those policies advocated by that president, and for the president's own party. Most social policy will fall within the domestic sector under the jurisdiction of the three roles that deal with that sector: *chief executive, legislative leader*, and *opinion/party leader*. We will discuss those few social policies that *do* have international significance in one chapter dealing with the two roles that focus on foreign affairs—*commander in chief* and *chief diplomat*.

After an introductory chapter, we explore how presidents in each of these roles handled the challenges of six social issues, including *abortion, pornography, gun control, affirmative action, homosexuality*, and *the environment*. In our concluding chapter, we explore a series of propositions that summarize our findings, allowing us to make meaningful generalizations about the American presidency and the social agenda.

It is obvious that such an undertaking requires the assistance of many who help move the ideas, the statements of the presidents, and their records of achievement and failures from draft form to final book form. Among those who must be thanked are our research assistants Suzanne McConkie, Emily Christensen, Kathleen Updike Strickler, Jaya Tiwari, and David Benson, without whom data would not have been collected. We so appreciate all of their efforts. We also wish to thank our wives and families for their

understanding of academia and its demands of researc
wish to thank Prentice Hall and, in particular, Beth Gillett .
science editor, astute critic, and friend, for her encouragem\
with us in recognizing that there are many demands in lif\
edge with gratitude the reviewer of this book, Daniel Ponder,
Colorado—Colorado Springs. We would also like to give spec   ..\s to
the late Ed Artinian for suggesting the title for this book. Finally we wish to
thank the American Political Science Association's Small Research Grant
Program, which provided some funding in support of this book.

ENDNOTES

1. For *emotive symbolization*, see the pioneering work of T. Alexander Smith, *The Comparative Policy Process* (Santa Barbara, CA: CLIO Press, 1975), esp. pp. 90–126. Theodore J. Lowi used the term *regulatory policy* to cover this policy in "Forward: New Dimensions in Policy and Politics," in Raymond Tatalovich and Byron W. Daynes, eds., *Social Regulatory Policy: Moral Controversies in American Politics* (Boulder, CO: Westview Press, 1988), pp. x–xxi. Raymond Tatalovich and Byron W. Daynes used the term *social regulatory policy* in Tatalovich and Daynes, *Social Regulatory Policy*, pp. 1–4. Christopher Z. Mooney and Mei-Hsien Lee used the term *morality policy* to refer to these issues in "Legislating Morality in the American States: The Case of Pre-*Roe* Abortion Regulation Reform," *American Journal of Political Science* 39 (1995): 599–627.
2. A recent book edited by Raymond Tatalovich and Byron W. Daynes examined eight social policies including abortion, affirmative action, death penalty, gay rights, religion in public life, gun control, English-only, and pornography. In each instance some brief treatment was devoted to how the modern president has responded to and been affected by these issues. See *Moral Controversies in American Politics: Cases in Social Regulatory Policy* (Armonk, NY: M.E. Sharpe, 1998).
3. See Raymond Tatalovich and Byron W. Daynes, preface, *The Politics of Abortion: A Study of Community Conflict in Public Policy Making* (New York: Praeger, 1981), p. v.
4. These roles were originated in Raymond Tatalovich and Byron W. Daynes, *Presidential Power in the United States* (Monterey, CA: Brooks/Cole, 1984) and were further refined in a 1998 book on the presidency by Daynes, Tatalovich, and Dennis L. Soden, *To Govern a Nation: Presidential Power and Politics* (New York: St. Martin's Press, 1998).

1

THE PRESIDENCY, ROLES, AND POLICY

INTRODUCTION

The Nature of Social Policy

Although social policy has been referred to in various ways—as policy of *emotive symbolism*,[1] as *social regulatory policy*,[2] and as *morality policy*[3]—it can simply be defined as *public policy that possesses legal authority having the potential of influencing or changing moral practices, including individual standards of behavior as well as community values*. In this book, we will use the more generic term—*social policy*—to avoid confusion and enhance the understanding of those who read this analysis.

Social policies, of course, may include, but should not be limited to, issues of abortion, pornography, affirmative action, English-only demands, prayer in school, gay rights, church and state issues, and gun control. Environmental policies are also included among the social policies since, as George McKenna recognized, the political dynamics of environmental issues also evoke "moral questions" as well as directing our thoughts to "social concerns."[4]

While most of these social policies are as old as politics itself, they have become increasingly important in the last several years in presidential politics[5]—even as significant as economic issues, by one estimate.[6] This should have been no surprise to anyone familiar with the social analysis of Ronald Inglehart, who argued that as our culture has changed from materialistic to postmaterialistic, "belongingness" and "self-actualization" have replaced industrialization.[7] Accompanying the postmaterialistic period, then, are new social cleavages emerging to replace economic ones that take the form of civil rights, the environment, abortion, and lifestyle concerns. These new cleavages are particularly important since they always have the potential to challenge lifestyles, disrupt social status and norms, and elicit strong responses from those directly affected.

Social policies, then, can pose an unending challenge to our established institutions making it difficult for them to handle and control policy results. The U.S. Defense Department's 1997 effort to establish guidelines for the punishment of adultery in the military services illustrates the point. The department found it perplexing even to define terms, let alone structure regulations and determine how they were to be applied and implemented.[8] A similar observation was made a number of years ago by Raymond Tatalovich and Byron W. Daynes regarding the difficulty of resolving the disharmonies and disagreements caused by the abortion debate: "Here is an issue [abortion] that consistently generates conflict, an issue that refused to disappear from the agendas of our governmental institutions, an issue that has continually evaded compromise and resolution."[9] The same, of course, can be said of all social policies.

How Social Policy Relates to the American Presidency[10]

Presidential scholars have all but ignored social policy in their research on the presidency. Several reasons may account for this oversight. To begin with, despite the attention paid to social issues during the presidential election of 1996[11] followed by the expected focus on religion and the so-called "V-words—'values' and 'virtues'" during the presidential election of 2000,[12] no social issue has ever been a determining factor in a presidential campaign. Not until 1992, moreover, was abortion—one of the more visible social issues—considered to be even a contributing factor to a presidential election outcome.[13]

Nor can one always find social policy to be a part of a president's agenda. Presidents recognize that the politics that often surround social policy can often result in a no-win situation for them because presidents may lose as many votes and as much support as they gain in taking a policy position. Moreover, when a president has become involved with social policies, it has not always been of his own choosing; but frequently the result of a position forced on him—as occurred with Presidents Gerald Ford and Jimmy Carter, both of whom reluctantly took a position on abortion only after it became evident that they could no longer delay speaking out on the issue in their respective presidential campaigns.

Some presidents have been forced to take positions on social issues as a result of a crisis or unusual circumstances, as occurred after the Supreme

Court's decision in *Engel v. Vitale* (1962), in which the justices ruled against prayer in schools. To alleviate the concerns of those persons who saw the Court's decision as a threat to their personal values and lifestyle, President John Kennedy, a Catholic, while reluctantly supporting the Court's position against prayer, at the same time encouraged Americans who opposed the Court's decision to continue to pray in their homes and in their churches. As he stated: "I would think that it would be a welcome reminder to every American family that we can pray a good deal more at home, we can attend our churches with a good deal more fidelity, and we can make the true meaning of prayer much more important in the lives of all of our children."[14]

For those presidential scholars who have taken social policy seriously, a common conclusion seems to pervade their work: that the *politics* that attends these policies places the president in a less than commanding position in terms of other political institutions. Both Theodore Lowi, in describing regulatory policy,[15] and Tatalovich and Daynes, in examining social regulatory policies, indicated that the President would more than likely play a less dominant role in fashioning these sorts of policies than one might expect of the Congress or the Court. Lowi, in his early examination of "arenas of power," indicated that as far as regulatory policy was concerned, the president has only a "moderate" level of influence over the legislative process.[16] Tatalovich and Daynes, in considering the president's contribution to social regulatory policy, maintained that one could expect only "modest leadership from the White House" in regard to these policies.[17]

The problem with these observations, of course, is that they treat all presidents alike. They do not explain why some presidents have exerted energetic policy leadership in handling selected social policies, while others have largely ignored or even rejected these same policies. What does seem clear, though, is that not all presidents fit one behavioral pattern. A Bill Clinton or a Ronald Reagan feels quite comfortable in strongly asserting views on abortion, for example, while a Gerald Ford or a Jimmy Carter is less convincing in his policy stance on abortion, publicly supporting a woman's right to choose while being personally opposed to it.

Such different reactions to social policy by presidents might be explained by a number of political considerations. To begin with, the *role* a president assumes in responding to social policy might help explain why a given president appears strong or weak in handling them; or a president's position could also depend on *party* preference or whether involvement with social policy strengthens or weakens his constituency base.[18] Lyndon Johnson, for example, found important support for his presidency coming from African Americans after he took a firm stance in support of civil rights; Bill Clinton found the support he had in the homosexual community encouraged him to issue the executive order that overturned a ban against gays in the military. Finally, a president's reactions to social policy could also result from personally held beliefs and values that would guide a president's interest in such policy.

For all of these reasons, we think it is safe to say that social policies have affected presidential policies, politics, and administrations, if only indirectly. Even if social policies have strengthened activist constituencies, encouraging them to work for the election of members of Congress who will ultimately constrain presidential activity, or have influenced presidential agendas, or have solidified presidential support, then this is reason enough to carefully examine the relationship of social policy to the American presidency.

METHOD OF ANALYSIS

The Presidents and the Time Frame

Several years ago, Barbara Hinckley stated that "work comparing presidents and the repetition of events over time should have the highest priority."[19] For our examination, we will limit our in-depth assessment of presidents to the contemporary presidency beginning with Franklin Roosevelt. In suggesting this time frame, of course, we are aware of arguments by such scholars as Fred Greenstein, who maintain that the modern presidency should begin with Dwight Eisenhower rather than Franklin Roosevelt.[20] In response to this position, we can say that we will also be paying attention to the presidency of Dwight Eisenhower but believe that several presidents prior to Eisenhower were also important to our understanding of how presidents have dealt with social policy.

More serious arguments are those propounded by such scholars as David K. Nichols, who believes that the roots of the modern presidency were first established in the Constitutional Convention and in the administrations of those early presidents;[21] and those of Sidney Milkis and Michael Nelson, who argue that scholars of the modern presidency need to examine the contributions of nineteenth-century presidencies, in particular those of Theodore Roosevelt and Woodrow Wilson as presidencies that contributed important bases for the modern institution.[22]

We understand these arguments, but in a limited study such as ours choices had to be made. Recognizing that there were fewer social issues in the public arena during the pre-Roosevelt period, we chose to concentrate our efforts on those presidents who confronted the greatest number of these issues. Thus we are comfortable in directing attention to the modern period, beginning with Franklin Roosevelt. Additionally, we feel assured that any generalization coming from our examination of presidents and their social agendas may also be applicable to all presidents, even those early presidents as they responded to social issues.

The Issues

In addition to the many presidents we could have examined, there are also a number of social issues on which we could concentrate. We have limited our investigation to six: *abortion, pornography, gun control, homosexuality, affirmative action*, and *environmental policy*. Each of these issues has been a visible focus of concern for many of the modern presidents. Moreover, they have generated interest group activity in support of or in opposition to them; each has also had congressional spokespersons as well as persons in executive agencies and departments of many of the contemporary presidential administrations encouraging their adoption or rejection as public law. Some of these issues have also been the focus of court decisions that have helped to guide presidential responses.

We recognize, of course, that in limiting our examination to these six social policies, other issues will be absent from our analysis; nevertheless, we are convinced from our prior research on social policy[23] that policymakers respond similarly enough to any social policy to enable us, despite our focus on six distinct issues, to form some general conclusions as to how presidents handle social policy.

The Roles

In addition to an examination of the six social issues, the theoretical framework we will adopt revolves around the role approach first developed by Raymond Tatalovich and Byron W. Daynes in *Presidential Power in the United States*.[24] The definition of *role* we will use in this book is the same definition that later appeared in 1998 in Daynes, Tatalovich, and Soden's *To Govern a Nation: Presidential Power and Politics*: A role is "the set of expectations by political elites and the citizenry that define(s) the scope of presidential responsibilities within a given policy area."[25]

Role theory is not new to presidential research. Notable researchers of the past such as Clinton Rossiter, Louis Koenig, and Edward Corwin, to name but a few, used a variant of role theory in their own research on the presidency. These theorists, moreover, all saw roles as part of the president's function or work.[26] All not only included the one role specifically mentioned in the Constitution (commander-in-chief), but also roles tied to the normal practice of governing, such as legislative leader and chief executive. Role is an important concept because decision makers are often inclined to adopt the behavior prescribed and norms sanctioned by the particular role in question. Roles can help to explain why a president succeeds or fails in a particular situation; why a president has an open field in which to operate; or why there is little room in which a president might negotiate with a coalition of interests. A role can also help explain why a president appears assertive or passive in response to social issues.

Given the apparent importance of roles, the next question really becomes: Which roles should we pay attention to? In this inquiry we will examine each of five presidential roles, including (1) *commander-in-chief*, the only role specifically listed in Article 2 of the Constitution, referring to a president as the nation's highest military leader; (2) *chief diplomat*, the role that defines a president's position as spokesperson to other nations and allows the president to define our nation's relationship to other countries; (3) *chief executive*, a role involving a president's relationship with the bureaucracy, his administrative staff,[27] and domestic policymaking; (4) *legislative leader*, a role pointing to the president's important relationship to the Congress; and (5) *opinion/party leader*, a combined role linking the president to the public through the political party and public opinion.

In looking at these five roles, the strength of each depends on the roles's *formal authority* and such political resources as a president's ability in a particular role to make unimpeded *decisions*, the public's potential to *disapprove* presidential actions, a president's individual *expertise* in exercising the role, and conditions of *crisis* that may enhance and enlarge the power of the president in a particular role.

Based on these variables and the political resources normally attending these roles, then, the president's five roles can be distributed along a power continuum as noted in Figure 1.1, from the strongest two roles—the commander-in-chief and chief diplomat—to the weaker two roles—the legislative leader and opinion/party leader—with the chief executive role falling in the middle.[28] While there are exceptions to this distribution of roles—such as when a president like Lyndon Johnson appears to strengthen a normally weak role like that of legislative leader, or where a Franklin Roosevelt or a Ronald Reagan mesmerizes the public in his role as opinion/party leader—one can normally expect these roles to distribute themselves in this fashion for any president. The exceptions just mentioned are based on individual skills of a president, but they remain exceptions that cannot be routinized or passed on to succeeding presidents.

For this book we will devote a chapter to each of these roles—with the exception of the first two roles, commander-in-chief and chief diplomat, which both deal with foreign affairs. In this case we will examine both of the roles in one chapter.

Figure 1.1   Presidential Roles and Their Relative Strength

Most powerful				Least powerful
Commander-in-chief	Chief diplomat	Chief executive	Legislative leader	Opinion/Party leader

THE ISSUES AND THE PRESIDENTS—A MORE EXTENSIVE LOOK

In this section we will examine in detail the six issues to be scrutinized throughout the book. These issues are, in effect, the measuring rods for presidential involvement with social issues in general.

Abortion

Abortion was an issue without regulation during the early 1800s. It was not until 1821 when Connecticut, a state with a large Catholic vote, became the first state to outlaw the procedure. Missouri soon followed in 1825, as did Illinois in 1827. In 1829, New York added an exception by allowing for therapeutic abortions when a mother's life was threatened. New York's approach served as the pattern for the states that revised their laws into the early 1900s.

Abortion has been one of the country's most prominent and divisive social issues. The American political landscape has been characterized by conflict on this issue, as witnessed by the current cleavages between pro-choice and pro-life groups. There were disagreements between those supporting abortion and those opposing it about what those first anti-abortion laws were designed to protect. Those favoring abortions—the *pro-choicers*—felt that those laws were established to protect the mother from uncertain surgery.[29] Those opposed to abortion—the *pro-lifers*—argued that the original laws were designed not to protect the mother, but to protect the fetus, suggesting that the fetus had rights that needed state protection.[30]

In the 1960s, however, physicians and the health care community began the movement to reform the abortion laws. Their primary concern was the illegal abortions being performed to avoid state restrictions. By 1966, some fourteen states had altered their original restrictive state laws, allowing therapeutic abortions for medical reasons. These states included, in order of repeal: Mississippi (1966), Colorado (1967), California (1967), North Carolina (1967), Georgia (1968), Maryland (1968), Arkansas (1969), Delaware (1969), Kansas (1969), New Mexico (1969), Oregon (1969), South Carolina (1970), Virginia (1970), and Florida (1970). In addition, Hawaii (1970), Alaska (1970), New York (1970), and Washington (1970) went beyond these fourteen states to make abortion an elective option.

But it was the decision in *Roe v. Wade* (1973), wherein the Supreme Court ruled that privacy governed a woman's right to end her pregnancy, that granted women in the United States a constitutional right to abortion. This decision gave impetus to both the pro-abortion and anti-abortion movement as we know it today. With it, forty-six states—some of which had had the same anti-abortion laws on the books since 1800—and the District of Columbia found it necessary to rewrite their own abortion laws.

As Raymond Tatalovich states: "*Roe* outstripped public opinion on abortion and disrupted an emerging consensus in favor of abortions for 'therapeutic,' or medical reasons. Finally, *Roe* caused a massive political backlash."[31]

It does not appear that the abortion controversy will become less important to twenty-first-century political decision makers than it is today; the debate over abortion is as polarized as it was in the 1970s; there are still two conflicting sides to the debate, and they even speak different languages. Both have their own terms, for example, to refer to potential life—pro-choicers use the term *fetus*, while pro-lifers use the term *unborn*. Both sides seem to be irreconcilable as to any consensus that might come out of their clashing views.

Ironically, most Americans are in neither of these two camps, holding a position in support of therapeutic abortion[32] that allows abortion to protect a mother's life and to terminate pregnancy that was caused by rape or incest or one where the infant might have severe deformity. Yet because the Court decided that abortion was now a woman's constitutional "right," the consensus in support of therapeutic abortion is somewhat weaker than it was before *Roe*. Politicians all but ignore this central position, placating instead the pro-life or the pro-choice advocates.

Presidents' General Response.   Although abortion was not a prominent public issue from the Roosevelt through Johnson administrations, the issue did gain prominence during the reelection campaign of Richard Nixon and has remained a divisive national issue. The *Roe v. Wade* decision was announced on January 23, 1973, at about the same time Richard Nixon took office for his second term. Abortion had already become a campaign issue in 1972 because of a report issued from the President's Commission on Population Growth in support of abortion on demand.[33] Nixon, however, courted the Catholic vote for his reelection bid and chose to side with New York's Catholic Cardinal Cook, who countered the report's findings and advocated a pro-life position. George McGovern, Nixon's Democratic opponent, was less successful in supporting abortion as a private matter between a woman and her physician, arguing that no state law should interfere with this relationship.

In 1976, Gerald Ford was not comfortable with the position the Republican party had taken on this issue that advocated a "human life" position;[34] Ford preferred that decisions about the abortion issue be restricted to the subnational level, where citizens and public officials would engage in decision making in the political setting of the fifty states.[35] That same year Jimmy Carter tried to placate both the Catholics and those supporting *Roe v. Wade*. Unfortunately for Carter, he ended up losing both the pro-lifer vote as well as offending the National Organization for Women (NOW), who refused to support his position on abortion.[36] For Carter, a born-again Christian, the abortion issue raised important challenges because he personally opposed abortion but refused to oppose the *Roe v. Wade* decision.[37]

A decade or so later, the next Democrat to occupy the White House assumed an important public role on the abortion issue. According to one observer, the 1992 election of Bill Clinton meant for the first time that a ". . . pro-choice president with a pro-choice agenda sat in the White House."[38]

In seeking the least controversial position on abortion, presidents have often chosen to hide behind their own party's platform position on the issue. This strategy allows a pro-life Republican candidate like Ronald Reagan or a pro-choice Democratic candidate like Bill Clinton a sort of built-in acceptance for their stance on a no-win policy like abortion. Republican George Bush, who also shared the Republican position, wasted no time in making his thoughts known on the issue. Three days after his inauguration, he told a group of right-to-lifers, "I think the Supreme Court's decision in *Roe v. Wade* was wrong and should be overturned. I think America needs a human life amendment."[39] It is interesting to note, however, that prior to becoming part of the Reagan-Bush ticket in 1980, Bush had maintained a pro-choice stance on the abortion issue.[40] Nonetheless, during his campaign for the presidency, and once in office, Bush sought support for his presidency among the pro-life movement in his public opposition to abortion.

Since 1973, most presidents have found abortion to be the sort of issue they try to avoid altogether because of the intense emotions and political dangers it promises. But, given the public's involvement with it, most have been unsuccessful in turning away from it. The 1980s and 1990s found pro-choice and pro-life groups gaining favor or opposition to their cause as they directed their attention to the White House. The pro-life movement found strong support during the Reagan-Bush years, while the Clinton administration generally aligned itself with the pro-choice movement. Although Ronald Reagan was unsuccessful in his attempt to take the Republican nomination away from Gerald Ford in 1976, he became the Republican nominee four years later. Unlike his fellow Republicans before him, Reagan took a decidedly anti-abortion public position during his presidential campaign, which was later reflected in his presidential politics. In his political rhetoric, Reagan was unequivocal in his support for a constitutional amendment to prohibit women from obtaining an abortion.[41] Reagan maintained this position throughout his presidency. In 1988, George Bush assumed the presidency and continued to pursue the Reagan philosophy of protection for the "unborn child." Thus abortion becomes a social issue prototype that has touched, in one way or another, each of the presidents since 1973.

Pornography

This social issue is more difficult to define than abortion. The issue represents, however, a fundamental conflict between the constitutional guarantee of free expression and the goal that society should defend a sort of moral order. While there are a number of types of *pornography* (or *obscenity*, a term that will be used interchangeably with pornography), here we will use the term to refer to materials that are sexually explicit and that cause sexual arousal.

Some persons believe that pornography should be a matter of privacy; most people, however, believe that possession of pornographic material should be subjected to some type of restriction, particularly if it is in the possession of minors or if the material, referred to as *child porn*, depicts minors as the objects of the pornography.

Some of the first restrictions on pornographic materials came in 1815, when a Pennsylvania court made it illegal to exhibit pictures of nudity for profit. After this decision, Vermont in 1821 became the first state to enact anti-obscenity laws. By 1842 the *US Code* had a federal statute preventing the importation of pornographic pictures. While government has confronted obscenity and pornography since the eighteenth century, it was not until a series of Supreme Court decisions in the 1960s and a presidential commission report in the 1970s that the issue really became politicized and a focus of public attention.[42] Controlling pornography has always proven difficult. Questions regarding the effectiveness of federal law regulating the importation, transportation, dissemination and sales of pornography can certainly be asked, given the enormous American market for pornography and the worldwide market (estimated at $56 billion in 1999).[43]

One reason for the possible ineffectiveness of anti-pornography laws, however, has been the conflict with First Amendment provisions protecting free expression. Another reason has been the lack of coordinated responses from policymakers, leaving it up to the individual policymaker to operate on his or her own definition of what pornography means. Illustrative of this problem is the well-documented approach of the late Associate Justice Potter Stewart, who stated in the *Jacobellis v. Ohio* (1964) case: "I shall not today attempt further to define the kinds of material I understand to be embraced within that shorthand description [hardcore pornography], and perhaps I could never succeed in intelligently doing so. But I know it when I see it, and the motion picture involved in this case is not that."[44]

The Internet has further complicated the problem of controlling information because it provides an unlimited exchange of ideas within a worldwide network where standards differ on what is and is not obscene. At present, the means of restraining expression on the Internet has been limited or nonexistent. Potter Stewart's solution to the problem of pornography, however, will have to be improved upon before Web restraint becomes a reality in the twenty-first century.

Presidents' General Response.   Generally speaking, Democratic and Republican presidents and candidates running for office have been more united in their responses to pornography than in their responses to other social issues, since it has been rather easy to be *against* pornography and quite difficult to take a stand in support of it—even if, in supporting it, the purpose has been to uphold a First Amendment right against censorship.

For this reason one would think that presidents would have had more to say about the issue than they have. Yet only a few contemporary presidents have been major advocates of limiting expression to control potential obscenity. Eisenhower was one of these. While generally supporting free expression, Eisenhower would only go so far. As he stated: "The other limit I draw is decency. We have certain books we bar from the mails and all that sort of thing; I think that is perfectly proper, and I would do it now."[45]

Two other presidents—Republicans Richard Nixon and Ronald Reagan—made obscenity and pornography campaign issues. Nixon focused public attention on his antipornography legislation as a means of dramatizing congressional inaction on his domestic program. For Reagan, antipornography was one issue objective in his broadbased conservative social agenda. That Democrats Kennedy, Johnson, and Carter did not exploit this issue politically shows the more liberal constituency base of the Democratic party and its traditional concern with civil liberties.

Another trend of interest has been the move since the 1970s for presidents to come out in opposition to child porn. Because child pornography is all but universally disapproved of, a president can do this without having to prove that the material in question is obscene. Failing to question whether child porn is obscene avoids many of the constitutional complications in limiting expression. Although most citizens generally oppose rigid censorship of books and films,[46] there exists a consensus against absolute free expression, particularly regarding minors. In the Clinton years, legislation to curb child pornography did find sympathetic public opinion.[47] Even groups representing authors, presses, and distributors—firm defenders of unrestricted information—want to limit minors' access of these materials while arguing at the same time for open access to the materials for adults.

Gun Control

Gun control as a social issue has been one of those longlasting concerns that encourage a great deal of movement and debate on both sides.[48] Those opposed to gun control seek the legitimacy of gun ownership in the Second Amendment, which gives them a source of moral strength despite their rather restrictive reading of this amendment, concentrating on "the right to bear arms" clause to the exclusion of the context in which this phrase appears. The entire amendment reads, of course: "A well regulated Militia, being necessary to the security of a free State, the right of the people to bear Arms, shall not be infringed." Those who support gun control pride themselves in reading the entire amendment and find statements of support for their position in the speeches of George Washington and other early patriots such as Sam Adams,[49] who issued warnings against "standing armies" while proposing the idea of arming state militias to protect citizens from the standing armies.[50] The National Defense Act of 1916 converted the old citizens' militias into the states' National Guard units. After 1916, states could maintain their militias against the uncertain federal army or against other states taking advantage.

Today the debate has not changed much except in the firepower of the weapons possessed. There are individuals and interest groups on both sides of the debate, but few as powerful as the National Rifle Association (NRA),[51] which pressures Congress to oppose any gun control at all. However, reading the Second Amendment in a way that would grant individuals the right to possess weapons is in opposition not only to the early debates on the issue that linked individual rights to state militias but also to such Court decisions as *U.S. v. Miller* (1939),[52] *U.S. v. Nelson* (1988),[53] as well as more than thirty lower federal and state court cases.

Presidents' General Response. Presidents in general have found themselves on both sides of the issue finding it safest and easiest to support their own party position. One of the first presidents to become so involved with guns was Theodore Roosevelt, who, as governor of New York, had helped to organize an association of marksmen. He was also an active member of the National Rifle Association while he was serving as president.

The central issue of government regulation of firearms remains at the heart of the national debate. From the 1930s to the 1960s, very little effort was made by presidents to secure substantive gun control legislation. Although President Franklin Roosevelt has been identified with early efforts toward gun control, little was done until the late 1960s, when modest gun control legislation was passed in the wake of the assassinations of civil rights leader Martin Luther King, Jr., and Democratic presidential candidate Robert Kennedy. With the support of President Johnson, who spoke on behalf of gun control, Congress passed legislation in 1968 to curtail the sale of mail-order handguns.

Republicans like Ronald Reagan—with a great deal of support from the NRA—generally supported free access to guns and opposed any gun restrictions. Reagan did not even change his position after the assassination attempt on this life.

While Presidents Reagan and Bush publicly opposed gun control, following a killing spree in California Bush issued an executive order that prohibited the importation of semi-automatic assault rifles.[54] Early in his first term in office, Bill Clinton publicly proclaimed his support for legislation that restricted the importation of semi-automatic weapons as well as the 1994 Crime Bill, which prohibited the manufacture and sale of a variety of assault weapons. Moreover, Clinton had actively campaigned for the Brady Bill, which mandated a waiting period for the purchase of handguns.[55] The increased frequency of shootings at schools around the country heightened the tension between President Clinton and many members of the Congress over the extent to which handguns should be regulated.

Though presidents have had a great deal to say about the issue, Robert Spitzer reminds us that presidential involvement with gun control has not really gone beyond the "symbolic level"; indeed, while presidents have made themselves heard on the issue, they have not been in the active forefront on gun issues.[56] In 1999, however, quite a different scenario presented itself, when thirteen Columbine High School students were gunned down in Littleton, Colorado, by two other students who also killed themselves.[57] It was President Bill Clinton who took the lead in calling for a White House conference to decide what to do with the problem of violence in the schools.[58] Clinton also insisted on introducing legislation to control access to weapons, to encourage safety locks on handguns, and to restrict the importing of certain assault weapons. The Republican Congress was not supportive of passing these strict gun restrictions.[59]

Homosexuality

Homosexuality is not a new issue, either, but it is one of the newer social issues to involve political decision makers. For years there has been a serious clash between those who see the homosexual community as one that should not be a recognized minority; instead, say those who advocate this position, it should be considered a deviant group and be denied traditional protections.[60] Others, however, sensing that this segment of society has for too long been discriminated against, see it as a minority needing full civil rights and liberties protection.

Until the last twenty years or so, sexual orientation was not frequently talked about or broadly exhibited in the United States. It was certainly not a viable political issue that candidates had to deal with. But when reaction to sexual orientation begins to interfere with basic civil rights protections, most people believe that something should be done to remedy the situation. Those advocating this position feel, as Margaret Ellis maintains, that "the immorality in this issue is the discrimination itself."[61] The feeling in the United States, even regarding groups most disdained (and with the possible exception of crisis conditions that focus attention on such a group, as occurred with Japanese-Americans during World War II), is that all persons deserve the protection of a citizen's basic rights.[62]

Presidents' General Response.   Homosexuality has been the most recent social issue of public concern for presidents, it was first made public during the 1980 campaign, dividing political parties and members of parties alike. Democrats appeared more likely to support the homosexual agenda, while Republicans appeared resistant to this agenda. Ronald Reagan was particularly assertive in the 1980 presidential campaign in condemning homosexuality, shielding himself behind quotations from the Bible and doctrine of churches. The other Republicans that year—George Bush and John Connally—could not compete on the issue and turned, instead, to the protection of the legal rights of homosexuals.[63] The Republicans' position on the issue made Democrat Jimmy Carter, running for reelection, appear to be the homosexuals' candidate for the presidency.[64]

Homosexuality became very visible in 1992 when Bill Clinton attempted to change military policy by executive order, dropping the ban against the military exclusion of homosexuals that had been the policy since 1982. Homosexuals had never been fully accepted in the military; during World War II, they had even been labeled as mentally ill. Clinton saw such a policy against homosexuals as depriving them of their civil rights,[65] though Clinton's critics charged that the president was merely placating a constituency that had contributed some $3 million dollars to his own campaign.[66] On January 28, 1993, a U.S. District Court declared the ban on homosexuals to be unconstitutional. A day later, President Clinton partially lifted the ban on homosexuals in the military; in what he considered a moderate policy, recruits would not be asked whether they were homosexuals and would not have to tell anyone their sexual orientation.[67] Clinton was convinced of the linkage between homosexuality and civil rights, but his "Don't ask, don't tell" policy pleased no one, being neither satisfying to homosexuals, since it did not go far enough, nor to the military—since it went too far.

Nor did this policy unify public opinion. In fact, in July 1993, Gallup found that the public was split down the middle, with 48 percent supporting the policy, 49 percent opposing it, and 3 percent having no opinion.[68] Within the military ranks, "Don't ask, don't tell" was not a popular policy. Among military personnel, however opposition to the policy stood in stark contrast to public opinion, reflecting the 74 percent of military enlistees opposed to the lifting of the ban against gays.[69] Of the president's change of focus toward homosexuals, Kevin Phillips noted: "No one should underestimate the political importance of this shift in political imagery . . . America now sees a Democratic President sympathetic to the gay cause, but an undercurrent suggests silent opposition."[70]

Affirmative Action

Affirmative action, one of the oldest social issues, is also one that touches every aspect of society. Harvey C. Mansfield, Jr., observed about a decade ago that affirmative action is "perhaps the most interesting policy issue of our day because it reveals how we understand our Constitution."[71] New York was the first state to institute an affirmative action program protecting African Americans from employment discrimination. By 1964, encouraged by Lyndon Johnson and the passage of the Civil Rights Act of that same year, twenty-five other states had laws protecting fair employment.

Although we may primarily associate this social issue with African Americans and their drive for equal employment and equal opportunities in education and transportation, it may also cover protections for women's rights and the rights of such minorities as Native Americans, Hispanics, and Asian Americans as well as the disabled. In this political system, affirmative action has become a focal issue for attracting disparate opposition that people have against certain races, economic and social groups, and gender differences. As they see this policy, it represents "preferential treatment" for minorities or "reverse discrimination" against the majority. This is why affirmative action is still debated today.

Presidents' General Response. While affirmative action has been an issue for all the modern presidents,[72] presidential involvement in affirmative action/equal opportunity practices has overall been rather limited. In most cases, presidents have spoken symbolically about "equal opportunity" for all Americans. Most presidents, Democrats and Republicans (with some exceptions) have followed Franklin Roosevelt's lead in encouraging the fair employment and fair labor practices in the workplace. Presidents Roosevelt, Eisenhower, and Truman issued a series of executive orders all geared toward addressing in a modest way the problems of equal employment opportunities for all Americans.[73] These efforts were generally limited in scope and tended to focus on encouraging voluntary action from employers who were engaged in seeking federal contracts to avoid practicing discrimination in their hiring procedures. Harry Truman did just this in creating the Committee on Government Contract Compliance as the federal arm to enforce integration. Truman also insisted in 1948 that the military be fully integrated.

Eisenhower created the President's Committee on Government Contracts in 1953, asking that all companies having a government contract adhere to the standards of affirmative action and do away with discriminatory practices. From Kennedy to Clinton, the issue of equal opportunity has evolved into affirmative action procedures as the federal government became increasingly involved in the compliance of companies to ensure fair hiring practices; if they failed to do so, the federal government reserved the right to cancel its contracts with federal contractors. Democrats Kennedy, Johnson, Carter, and Clinton used the power of the presidency to make modest changes in fair employment practices. During the early part of the Kennedy administration, the federal government maintained that companies with federal contracts must use "affirmative action to ensure applicants are employed without regard to their race, creed, color, or national origin."[74] John Kennedy also encouraged fair employment from contractors with federal agencies. In addition, he created the Committee on Equal

Employment Opportunity with the primary responsibility of seeing that standards were complied with.

Lyndon Johnson and Jimmy Carter, in particular, demonstrated their commitment to expanding equal employment opportunities by engaging in more vigorous efforts to gain the compliance of federal contractors to ensure fairness in their hiring practices. Johnson's 1965 executive order granted the secretary of labor authority to create regulations to implement the order. Johnson also encouraged the compliance of those goals that would assist women and minorities. During his run for the presidency in 1992, Bill Clinton proclaimed his support for promoting affirmative action to assure equal employment opportunities but his overall economic and budget plan as well as his health care initiatives were essentially the centerpiece of the early years of his presidency.

One of the more unusual affirmative action plans to come from a Republican president was the Philadelphia Plan, introduced first by Lyndon Johnson as Executive Order 11246 in 1965, and then revised by Richard Nixon. The plan, to encourage minority employment, was first devised in 1966 but was reintroduced by Richard Nixon in 1968. The Nixon version was an affirmative action plan that came very near being a quota system, despite Nixon's intention to stay away from quota plans. It was originally devised to cover only those employers in the construction industry working on federal contract, but by 1971 it was expanded to cover all businesses and all employees—men and women—on government contract. Minority workers were assured that they would be hired in proportion to the demographic makeup of the community in which the work was to take place. Employers were asked not only to integrate their businesses, but also to guarantee training for employees. Unions had to integrate their particular ranks as well. By 1974, affirmative action under Nixon reached its peak with an executive order that indicated that the goal for contractors would be "full utilization of minorities and women at all levels in all segments of its work force."[75] Coming up with such a plan was also a brilliant political move on Nixon's part to attract two critical constituencies from the Democratic party, African Americans and labor union members, into the ranks of the Republican party.[76] He was, however, criticized by trade unions and civil rights groups alike for promoting this policy as a means to drive a wedge between the two movements.[77]

Second only to Lyndon Johnson was Jimmy Carter, the next president to stand behind the goals of affirmative action. Some of the advances during the Carter years, however, were reversed by Ronald Reagan, who did as much to halt affirmative action advances as any president. Reagan not only reduced the authority of the Equal Employment Opportunity Commission,[78] he also reduced the number of employees who would fall under affirmative action standards as well as cutting budget allotments for federal employment. Although Reagan weakened affirmative action and attempted to undercut hiring goals, some of his efforts were slowed by two 1986 Supreme Court decisions.[79]

Bill Clinton was largely supportive of the goals of affirmative action, committing himself to working for the improvement of affirmative action when he indicated that the country should "mend it, don't end it."[80] This goal was embodied in his executive order of June 7, 1999, in which he established a special advisory commission on Asian Americans and Pacific Islanders within the Department of Health and Human Services to encourage more members of these two minority groups to get the health services they deserved.[81]

Overall, most presidents have moved in incremental ways to expand equal opportunity practices. However, Ronald Reagan contrasts with his predecessors in his effort to reverse the progress made. To a lesser degree, George Bush followed in Reagan's footsteps in his vocal opposition to quotas as a means to improve equal access for women and minorities,[82] while Bill Clinton has followed a "Mend it, don't end it" public approach.

Environmental Policy

While some readers might be surprised that the environment is listed as one of the six social issues, it became clear to those who observed President Clinton in September 18, 1996, when he set aside the 1.7 million acres as the Grand Staircase–Escalante National Monument in Southern Utah, that the resulting controversy this act produced among unsuspecting Utah residents raised the same moral questions and made residents focus on social concerns in the same way that the other social issues have.[83]

One striking characteristic of this issue is its diversity. Whereas environmental concerns from the 1930s through the 1970s tended to focus attention on clean air and water, forest conservation, preservation of natural resources, and public land use, today environmental concerns direct our attention to safe drinking water, overpopulation concerns, preserving species, chemical pollution of agricultural lands, Earth Summits, and the governmental structures that would handle these issues. Moreover, the issues can range from a local concern to a multinational development and all subunits in between. Thus, of all the social issues we are considering, environmental policies have perhaps the broadest reach.

Presidents' General Response. Given this broad reach, it is difficult for presidents to avoid involvement with one or another environmental issue. Their response to the issue can either clarify it for the voting public or further cloud the issue. A president's involvement with an environmental issue is, however, critical to the issue's success since it is essential for achieving funding.

Franklin Roosevelt is considered the president who introduced the so-called "Golden Age of Conservation" to America.[84] Much of his interest was tied to the critical concerns of the time, such as the Dust Bowl problems and other issues related to the Depression. Roosevelt used his interest in forestry and national parks, for example, to relieve some of those critical conditions of unemployment by establishing the Civilian Conservation Corps (CCC) to put the unemployed to work in the national parks and forests.

The period from Roosevelt through Nixon was a most productive time for the protection of the environment and its natural resources.[85] Some of the advancements include programs to protect coastal zones and sea mammals, restrict ocean dumping and water pollution in general, and restrict pesticides. Important structural extensions like the Environmental Protection Agency (EPA), OSHA (Occupational Safety and Health Administration) and the Consumer Product Safety Commission also were established by successive presidents.

Ronald Reagan slowed much of this progress during the 1980s by cutting environmental budgets. As Michael Kraft observed: "Virtually all environmental policies were to be reevaluated [by Reagan], and reversed or weakened, as part of the president's larger political agenda."[86] Reagan faced public opposition to his stance on the environment as well as opposition in both houses of Congress, where there was bipartisan consensus for environmental protection.

Some recovery took place under George Bush, who encouraged the passage of the Clean Air Act of 1990. Bush even pledged in 1988 to be a "Republican president in the Teddy Roosevelt tradition. A conservationist. An *environmentalist*."[87] He did not keep this focus, and at the end of his presidency he was lashing out at "environmental extremists."[88]

Bill Clinton had every intention of becoming another FDR on the environment. In terms of his priorities, the environment ranked high for Clinton and extended worldwide. His main problem was his inability to get environmental legislation passed by the Republican Congress. The 104th Congress—perhaps the most difficult Congress for Clinton—was called by the League of Conservation Voters the Congress with "the worst environmental voting record of any Congress in the past 25 years."[89] As a result, environmentalists were again disappointed with this president's efforts.

PRESIDENTIAL ROLES — A MORE EXTENSIVE LOOK

Since each chapter in this book will examine presidential efforts to deal with the six social issues from a presidential role perspective, the concluding portion of this chapter will examine these five roles in greater detail.

The Commander in Chief/Chief Diplomat and Social Policy

The two roles that focus a president's attention on foreign policy are commander-in-chief and chief diplomat. These are a president's strongest roles in terms of authority and resources. Moreover, commander-in-chief is the role that has been most expanded in power by presidents since George Washington. Originally only a military title, it has been transformed into a role that former Associate Supreme Court Justice Robert Jackson described as "the most dangerous one to free government in the whole catalogue of powers."[90] In this role the president can determine when and whether troops are committed overseas, call up reservists and National Guard personnel, set war strategies, and determine when the hostilities begin and end—all without a declaration of war.

The strength of this role is impressive. Because of the commander-in-chief's authority, decision making tends to be very centralized and major decisions may only involve the president and a select number of key advisers, including the joint chiefs of staff, the National Security Council, and a select number of cabinet members.

As a further strength to a president in this role, there is a natural well of support for presidents involved in hostilities, particularly at their beginning. The public's input in foreign affairs is necessarily limited and so gives the president great leeway in decision making. Because public opinion in this role is relatively imprecise, a president may choose to ignore it. Further, a president in this role has the advantages of enjoying both access to information and the opportunity to monopolize it and can also rely on such agencies as the CIA and FBI. A final area where the president enjoys dominance is expertise and control over information, which can be vital to diplomacy. Contemporary presidents have even tried relying on inherent or plenary power based primarily on tradition, as did George Bush when he ignored Congress' constitutionally granted war powers during the onset of the Persian Gulf War, making it quite clear to concerned Congresspersons that he was the commander-in-chief and completely in charge.[91]

Checking a president's power as commander-in-chief has at times proven difficult. For instance, Congress can force a president to give it progress reports or can hold the president accountable, but Congress finds it difficult to check a president in this role if a president is engaged in defending American forces.

World conditions can, however, constrain a president. Richard Rose indicated that the "postmodern president" may have insufficient resources to meet the challenges in the international arena and may be forced into an interdependent relationship with other nations.[92]

A president as chief diplomat occupies almost as powerful a role. Constitutionally, the powers of foreign affairs is shared with the Congress, but custom, judicial decision, and statutory law have favored executive dominance. George Washington set many of these precedents, including executive privilege, the recognition of other governments, and limiting the Senate's "advice and consent" powers.

But it was the Supreme Court and Chief Justice John Marshall who argued on March 7, 1800, that "the President is the sole organ of the nation in its external relations, and its sole representative with foreign nations,"[93] granting the president added leverage in foreign affairs. In addition, a century later the Court gave the president an inherent power in foreign affairs in its decision in *U.S. v. Curtiss-Wright Export Co.* (1936), wherein it supported a broadened meaning of presidential power in diplomacy, granting the president the receptor of nation-state authority.[94]

Because George Washington initiated executive agreements and set treaty precedents by putting the Senate's power of "advice and consent" in treaty making as an after-the-fact power, the president in foreign affairs has the advantage over the Congress. In addition, the president has use of executive privilege, another traditional power attending his role as chief diplomat. Presidents have used this power in refusing to give information to Congress or in preventing others from having to testify before Congress and giving information. Executive privilege has been used by most every modern president at one time or another.

Appointments allow a president to nominate ambassadors, with the approval of the Senate, or the president can appoint his own personal agents to conduct diplomacy without the approval of the Senate. As chief diplomat, the president can make decisions much as when he operates as commander-in-chief. Decisions are also centralized, involving only the president and a limited number of personal advisers, typically including the Secretaries of State, Treasury, and Defense and the Attorney General. In addition, the chairman of the Joint Chiefs of Staff, the CIA, and other department heads can be consulted. Finally, crisis can encourage public support for the president in this role, again reducing Congress's role in oversight. Thus in the area of foreign affairs, policymaking is shaped by the president and his advisors. Congress's role has become increasingly eroded over the years.

The primary check that Congress has over the president in his roles of commander-in-chief and chief diplomat is its control over finances which can force a president to comply with some of Congress's demands if Congress is insistent. Intelligence is also often shared between the two branches, although problems and distrust have also arisen.

Despite the fact that these roles are the president's most powerful ones, they also probably have the least to do with social policy. Yet issues of abortion, gun importation, the environment, and pornography are increasingly becoming more susceptible to international pressures. For those issues that do have international consequences, constitutional authority in this combined role puts the president in a very strong decision-making position. While a president does not have frequent occasion to exercise this role in implementing social policy, social issues have at times been companion issues of foreign relations. Both George Bush and Bill Clinton, for example, have spoken of their concern for environmental protection in the context of national security.

When social policy has reached beyond national borders—as in the case of abortion, gun control and environmental policy—the president's powers have been felt. In the future, presidents as chief diplomats may be called upon to resolve the controversies posed by indecency of communications on the Internet. As one American lawyer in Germany suggested, "The Internet created a universal jurisdiction so that once you are on the Internet you are subject to the laws of every country in the world. . . . The Internet gives rise to jurisdictional problems that never happened before."[95]

The Chief Executive and Social Policy

The chief executive may seem quite a powerful role for the president since the Framers determined that a chief executive should not share power with any advisory body. Yet the president in this role is often frustrated in establishing a social agenda because the Constitution fragments control over the bureaucracy, making it difficult for the president to exert any meaningful control over the executive branch. The president *can*, however, determine the direction of social policy through the use of executive orders, as Ronald Reagan and Bill Clinton did in enforcing their own perspectives of abortion.

Government's size and complexity can also be frustrating to an administration. As Harry Truman once exclaimed, after showing some visitors a wall chart that pointed out more than 100 offices that were to report to him: "I cannot even see all these men, let alone actually study what they are doing."[96] Given the multiple number of federal employees who interrelate with the chief executive, one would think that the president would need powerful tools to handle the workload. In truth, he has few resources and little constitutional authority.

Appointment is a key to presidential success in this role. Once an administrative post becomes vacant, the president must find appointees who are not only loyal to the party and to the president, but also possess the necessary experience for the job. Some presidents have had difficulties in staffing their administrations, as Bill Clinton proved as he stumbled through a series of missteps and miscalculations in his early appointments during his first term.[97]

Most presidents confine their search for persons to fill vacancies to their own party, but even here they may be limited in whom they can appoint as a result of political constraints imposed by special interests, voter blocs, policy focus, or their own ideologies. Many of those appointments must also sustain Senate approval, which can further complicate staffing. One thing that makes this role somewhat weaker than the first two roles is that multiple decision makers are involved in the day-to-day decisions that presidents must make. These include the president, his advisors, other federal bureaucrats, state political leaders, and on occasion congresspersons and the Court.

Structurally, it is the bureaucracy—the agencies, the departments, the bureaus, the federal employees—that is fashioned and organized by both Congress and the president. Congress creates the subunits initially, and then the president and Congress staff them. The president can, through reorganization, help to shape the bureaucracy, but Congress has oversight authority to make sure that a balance of powers is maintained. A president needs to be cautious in dealing with the bureaucracy because those agencies and bureaus that are strong enough to stand on their own may give him difficulty. Moreover, the terms of office for bureaucrats most often will outlast that of the president. Again, their longer tenure gives these offices an advantage.

The cabinet is the oldest advisory body associated with the president. The cabinet as a collective whole, however, has never been very important in strengthening the president's social agenda; individual secretaries, however, have been. The vice president has on occasion been an important advisor and supporter to the president if selected for this reason. Walter Mondale was, perhaps, one of the first "activist" vice presidents, serving as a trusted and close adviser to President Jimmy Carter. As Frank Kessler has said, Mondale "remade the much-maligned graveyard of the executive branch into an office to be sought after."[98] Vice president Al Gore, for example, has been one of the most visible vice presidents and has taken much of the responsibility in the administration for the advancement of environmental policy.

The advisory system really began with Franklin Roosevelt in 1939, when he established the Executive Office of the President. As one structural manifestation of the advisory system, presidents have frequently turned to *task forces* or *advisory commissions* to study particular issues and recommend remedial action. Both Lyndon Johnson and Ronald Reagan used presidential commissions to investigate the impact of pornography on society. Because the expertise of a president in this role is often limited, presidents have looked to private or public institutional sources to gather data needed to confront the Congress.

Both authority and influence are critical to the role of chief executive and have had an effect on the president's ability to establish a social agenda. While a few presidents have been able to use this role to enhance social values, overall the role has not been extremely productive in reinforcing a president's social agenda since no president has been able to master the "institutionalized presidency."

The Legislative Leader and Social Policy

Success as a legislative leader is important to a president since his overall accomplishments in office are quite often determined by his achievements in this role. The role suggests an active relationship between the president and Congress, with policymaking at its core. It is a role in which

Congress has a substantial advantage if not dominant influence,[99] thus, a successful legislative leader must rely on external political resources, creativity, and political persuasion to facilitate the administration's social agenda.

For a president to be effective as a legislative leader, he must assertively use all his individual skills as a negotiator and persuader, since a president has little real authority to exert over Congress. Article 2, section 3 of the Constitution specifies that a president has the authority to give to Congress "Information of the State of the Union, and recommend to their Consideration such Measures as he shall judge necessary and expedient." A president may also call Congress into special session and adjourn Congress when there is disagreement between the chambers about when this should occur.

Veto power is probably the clearest of the powers in Article 2 and the one that gives the president greatest leverage in the legislative process. In terms of social policy, the veto has most often been used by liberal Democrats protecting the First Amendment from rigid social policy proposed by the opposition party. Nonetheless, a presidential veto may be even more effective when it is not actually used but merely threatened. If Congress becomes aware of the president's wishes, they may well change the legislation so that the president will not use the veto, given the success rate when a president does use it. Here a president can succeed in garnering altered legislation as he would like to see it without ever actually using the veto.

Despite the veto power of the president—even if only threatened—Congress normally has most of the advantages when it comes to passing legislation. Article 1 gives Congress many more specific enumerated powers for shaping public policy than it gives the president. The success of Congress as it confronts the president has been documented in several early studies. One examined how Congress was the primary initiator of legislation between the years 1880 and 1940 despite the fact that during this time a number of strong presidents were elected, including Woodrow Wilson, Theodore Roosevelt, and Franklin Roosevelt.[100] A later study by Moe and Teel of the period 1940–67 also concluded that Congress had an important impact in each issue area.[101] While this might not be as true in foreign affairs, in domestic policy[102] Congress clearly tends to have the advantage over the president in most issue areas.

A legislative leader must constantly be on guard to counteract influences from public opinion, social movements, and interest groups that can work to shape legislation. The very organization of Congress allows for this influence through access points allowing ethnic, religious, racial and other minorities to bring their grievances before the legislative body. The two primary factors affecting the likelihood that presidents can exert some power in the legislative process—decision making and public inputs—work to the disadvantage of a president as legislative leader. No president can monopolize information and expert opinion as a legislative leader. The president is helped somewhat by using staffers who may specialize in legislative liaison and by manipulating the information sent to Congress by the executive branch. Presidents who are able to use the Office of Congressional Relations are helped in routinizing legislative leadership.

Despite the fact that some strong presidents have been assisted by crisis as legislative leaders, it is an uncertain variable. What is necessary for a president to take advantage of crisis, as Daynes, Tatalovich, and Soden maintain, really depends on a "collective feeling of urgency, a common definition of the situation as a crisis, and a Congress ready to answer the president's initiatives."[103]

It thus seems clear that a president as legislative leader does not have the power to force Congress in a particular direction, not even when the president's own party is in control, as it was in the 103rd Congress. In this case Bill Clinton had great difficulty in securing passage of his high-priority programs in both the House and Senate. Nor can a president rely on many political resources, since the role does not have many. The State of the Union address is one of those resources, as are special messages, the executive budget, and the veto as other resources a president can use. While a president can also expect more votes from the members of his own party than from the opposition, he cannot depend on unified support from his party. This phenomenon became clear in the 103rd Congress. While Clinton, in relying on the Democratic leadership and the Democratic majority in both the House and Senate, was able to pass a number of his priority measures—including the Family and Medical Leave Act, his Crime Bill, the Brady Bill on handgun control, the so-called "motor-voter" voting registration act, and the North American Free Trade Agreement (NAFTA), other high-priority measures, such as Clinton's health care measures and campaign finance reform, either failed to pass the Congress or were so disfigured once passed, as were his economic reforms with the Senate having gutted the main BTU taxing source substituting a less controversial gasoline tax, that they became almost unrecognizable.[104]

Since divided government seems to be more the norm than it was in the 1930s and 1940s, presidents need to develop bipartisan or nonpartisan strategies to get on with both parties in Congress. This requirement poses many difficulties for a president, and very few presidents have been able to succeed in getting their programs through Congress undamaged. Clinton found it particularly difficult in 1994 once he lost the Democratic majority in both the House and Senate. With Republicans numbering 231 to 203 Democrats in the House and Senate Republicans numbering 53 to 47 Democrats, in the beginning days of the 104th Congress Republican leaders Newt Gingrich (R–Ga.) and Dick Armey (R–Texas), could structure the agenda as they saw fit,—a situation that clearly put Clinton on the defensive.[105]

Most presidents have thus enjoyed rather modest records of legislative achievement in social policy. To succeed in this role, the president must appreciate the myriad political conditions that increase or decrease his ability to influence the legislative process and then must go well beyond the formal legal relationship between the presidency and the Congress.

The Opinion/Party Leader and Social Policy

This last combined role blends the efforts of a president that other scholars have noted under the roles of *chief of state*, *chief of party*, and *voice of the people*. We choose to combine the two roles for purposes of analysis because they both depict a president's responses to the people. A president in this joint role attempts to generate public support for his own program, for his administration, and for his party. Contact with the public provides the president with the opportunity to draw attention to issues that he considers important and that will play a part in his national agenda.

Of all the roles, this is perhaps the president's weakest since there are few resources available to call upon. A successful president in this role will, of necessity, rely on personal skills and influence rather than established authority since there is little of that associated with the role. Success with the mass media can help, as can a well-organized party. The media have a great influence on agenda setting in ignoring or overemphasizing certain issues over others. The media also influences public perceptions of elected officials, as exemplified by Dan Quayle, who from the beginning of his term of office as George Bush's vice president was depicted in the press as stupidly out of control in most situations.

Fred Greenstein maintains that a president serves several important psychological functions for the people in this role.[106] He suggests that the president, as the most visible elected official, simplifies our understanding of what government is and does; symbolizes for the citizen that someone is in charge of events; acts as a way for citizens to identify with his life in a personal way; and represents a national unity and a social stability.

Crisis can affect the public in several ways and can affect the president in this role. If illness or accident strikes down a president, the people will rally to the president; when scandal affects the president, however, it is uncertain how the public will react. While Bill Clinton's popularity maintained itself in the upper 50's and mid-60's percentile, not all presidents would be guaranteed this figure. Popularity can be affected negatively because of all of the forces affecting public information that are out of a president's control.

While presidents who have been able to strengthen themselves in the opinion/party leader role are rare, Franklin Roosevelt, John Kennedy, and Ronald Reagan were all impressive in using it as a leadership position in effectively communicating their wishes and policy stances to the public as well as to other elected policymakers. Much of a president's strength in this role rests on an ability to persuade citizens through public appearances and speeches. The president may take an issue and "go public" with it,[107] making the issue visible and enhancing the administration's identification with it. To do this, a president would probably want to rely on one or more major speeches—the Inaugural address, the State of the Union message, and special addresses to the Congress and the nation—that highlight issues which should be included in the legislative agenda. One study indicated, however, that social policies have not played a major role in any of these important addresses, comprising no more than 20 percent of any of them.[108]

A president as opinion/party leader is, thus, in a rather weak position because of a lack of formal authority and fragmented resources associated with this role. By communicating with Congress and the public, the president can make a modest difference by identifying and making visible those social issues he considers most important for placement on the public agenda, and he may also suggest measures for implementing them. In this way a president can express the values and principles of the administration, help set the legislative agenda, and highlight the presidential role as party leader.

CONCLUSION

The last six decades or so have been characterized by an increase in the frequency of national debates over social policies. These debates have routinely divided the rulers from the ruled and from each other. They have put the president, as the most prominent and, in many ways, the most dominant elected official, in positions where the public expects that the president will play a key role in resolving these policy dilemmas. Yet as Lyn Ragsdale perceived, "Presidents often seem uncomfortable as leaders on social rights issues. They implicitly recognize the fallout they may experience because the policies, by definition, redistribute benefits from one group to another."[109]

Social policies have become an important part of the public agenda, and it is difficult for presidents to ignore them because it is difficult for the polity to ignore them. Although these policies have not necessarily been a defining factor in all presidential electoral politics, presidents' involvement with the more controversial ones have helped to mobilize segments of the electorate to action—through polarizing politics, encouraging the involvement of political activists, and creating an issue-oriented politics. This selection of issues and the presidents who have helped shape them will serve as the focus of this book.

ENDNOTES

1. T. Alexander Smith, *The Comparative Policy Process* (Santa Barbara, CA: CLIO Press, 1975).
2. See Raymond Tatalovich and Byron W. Daynes, *Social Regulatory Policy: Moral Controversies in American Politics* (Boulder CO: Westview Press, 1988) and the updated ver-

sion of this book, *Moral Controversies in American Politics: Cases in Social Regulatory Policy* (Armonk, NY: M. E. Sharpe, 1998).

3. Christopher Z. Mooney and Mei-Hsien Lee, "Legislative Morality in the American States: The Case of Pre-*Roe* Abortion Regulation Reform, *American Journal of Political Science* 39 (1995): 599–627.

4. As cited in our preface, George McKenna lists the environment as a social issue because the political dynamics are very similar to those of other social issues, invoking both "moral questions" and "social concerns." We accept this categorization and treat environmental policy as a social issue in this book. See George McKenna, *The Drama of Democracy: American Government and Politics* (Guildford, CT: Dushkin, 1994) 435. In his assessment of American public opinion, pollster Louis Harris also includes the environment in the same category as other social issues included in this study (e.g., with abortion, gun control, and pornography). See Louis Harris, *Inside America* (New York: Vintage Books, 1987) 135–273.

5. George Gallup, Jr., maintains that moral values today are more important now than at any other time in sixty years of public opinion polling. See Patricia Edmunds and Ann Oldenburg, "Morality Issues Matter More," *USA Today* 6, Aug. 1996; moreover, according to a July 18–22, 1996 *USA Today*/CNN/Gallup poll, nine of ten voters who were questioned before the 1996 presidential election indicated that a candidate's "stand on moral values" would be important to winning their vote. Ann Oldenburg and Patricia Edmunds, "Morals and Mixed Signals," *USA Today* 7, Aug. 1996: 4A.

    —A Peter Hart Research Associates poll issued for Shell Oil Company found results that would back up this conclusion. They found that 56 percent of citizens identified "moral values" as the most serious problem in the nation, whereas those who answered the survey selected "standards set by public officials," as the fifth most important reason for the cause of moral decline in the nation. Reasons considered more important included families not teaching values; increased drug use; parental examples; and portrayal of life in movies and on TV. Compiled by Robert Kilborn and Lance Carden, "Parents Are Key to Raising Moral Values, Survey Finds," *Free-Mail Subscription* <freemail-support@csmonitor.com>, 18, May 1999. Accessed 18 May 1999.

6. Ben J. Wattenberg, "Social Issues Will Elect Our Next President—And Clinton Knows It," *American Enterprise*, Jan./Feb. 1996, 3.

7. See Ronald Inglehart, *Culture Shift in Advanced Industrial Society* (Princeton, NJ: Princeton University Press, 1990).

8. See Carey Goldberg, "On Adultery Issue, Many Aren't Ready to Cast First Stone," *New York Times*, 9 June 1997, A1, A12.

9. Raymond Tatalovich and Byron W. Daynes, *The Politics of Abortion: A Study of Community Conflict in Public Policymaking* (New York: Praeger, 1981), v.

10. Because all presidents up to the present have been men, the masculine pronoun is used throughout this book. Moreover, references to the presidency and presidents in general also use the masculine pronoun. This usage in no way excludes the possibility or anticipation that in the future women will surely occupy this office.

11. In July 1996, a *USA Today*/CNN/Gallup poll indicated that nine out of every ten persons who were questioned before the 1996 presidential election indicated that Clinton's and Dole's positions, on "moral values" would be important in determining their votes for the presidency. See Edmonds and Oldenburg, "Morality Issues Matter More": 4a.

12. Both the Democratic and Republican candidates for the presidency in the year 2000 were talking more freely to potential voters about their religious beliefs as this book went to press. Those candidates include Vice President Al Gore, George W. Bush, and Elizabeth Dole as well as Gary Bauer. Moreover, the public seems more accepting of candidates doing so than in years past. See Linda Feldmann, "Campaigning for President . . . Or for Preacher?" *Christian Science Monitor*, 8, June 1999, 1, 9; also see A. N. Wilson, "God as a Running Mate," *New York Times*, 8, June 1999, A31. For the references to the "V-words," see Jill Lawrence, "In Iowa, Republicans Come Out of the 'Values' Closet," *USA Today*, 15, June 1998, 14A.

13. Mark Wattier, Byron W. Daynes, and Raymond Tatalovich, "Abortion Attitudes, Gender, and Candidate Choice in Presidential Elections: 1972 to 1992," *Women and Politics* 17 (1997): 69.

14. U.S. President, "The President's News Conference—June 27, 1962," in *Public Papers of the Presidents of the United States*, (Washington, DC: Government Printing Office, 1963), 511.

15. Lowi, "Forward," in Tatalovich and Daynes, *Social Regulatory Policy*, 216–17.
16. See Theodore J. Lowi's pioneering effort at policy arena divisions in "American Business, Public Policy, Case Studies, and Political Theory," *World Politics* (July 1964): 677–715; also see Randall B. Ripley and Grace A. Franklin, *Congress, the Bureaucracy, and Public Policy*, rev. ed. (Homewood, IL: Dorsey, 1980), 22–23.
17. See Tatalovich and Daynes, *Social Regulatory Policy*, 216.
18. It was Tatalovich and Daynes who argued, in fact, that "Republicans exploit social regulatory policy to mobilize conservative voters whereas Democrats are constrained not to abandon liberalism." See *Social Regulatory Policy*, 216.
19. See Barbara Hinckley, *Problems of the Presidency* (Glenview, IL: Scott, Foresman, 1985), 230.
20. See Fred I. Greenstein, *The Hidden-Hand Presidency* (New York: Basic Books, 1982).
21. See David K. Nichols, *The Myth of the Modern Presidency* (University Park, PA: Pennsylvania State University Press, 1994).
22. See Sidney M. Milkis and Michael Nelson, *The American Presidency: Origins and Development, 1776–1998*, 3rd ed. (Washington, DC: Congressional Quarterly Press, 1999).
23. See Tatalovich and Daynes, *Moral Controversies in American Politics*.
24. The discussion of the theoretical framework has been taken from Raymond Tatalovich and Byron W. Daynes, *Presidential Power in the United States* (Monterey, CA.: Brooks/Cole, 1984).
25. Byron W. Daynes, Raymond Tatalovich, and Dennis L. Soden, *To Govern a Nation: Presidential Power and Politics* (New York: St. Martin's Press, 1998), 2.
26. See Clinton Rossiter, *The American Presidency*, 2nd ed. (New York: Harcourt, Brace and World, 1960); Edward S. Corwin, *The President: Office and Powers*, 4th ed. (New York: New York University Press, 1957) and Louis W. Koenig, *The Chief Executive*, 4th ed. (New York: Harcourt Brace Jovanovich, 1981). Also see Thomas A. Bailey, *Presidential Greatness: The Image and the Man from George Washington to the Present* (New York: Appleton-Century-Crofts, 1966).
27. As indicated in note 10, use of the masculine pronoun does not exclude the possibility of a female U.S. president. In fact, popular candidate Elizabeth Dole had as good a chance as anyone of securing the Republican Party nomination for president in the year 2000.
28. This role distribution first appeared in Tatalovich and Daynes, *Presidential Power in the United States*, 16. We also included this continuum in Daynes, Tatalovich, and Soden, *To Govern a Nation*, 2.
29. See Cyril C. Means, Jr., "The Phoenix of Abortional Freedom: Is a Penumbral or Ninth Amendment Right about to Arise from the Nineteenth-Century Legislative Ashes of a Fourteenth-Century Common Law Liberty?" *New York Law Forum* 17 (1971): 335–410.
30. See James C. Mohr, *Abortion in America: The Origins and Evolution of National Policy, 1800–1900* (New York: Oxford University Press, 1978).
31. Raymond Tatalovich, "Abortion: Prochoice versus Prolife," in Tatalovich and Daynes, *Social Regulatory Policy*, 177.
32. In a recent *Gallup poll*, Americans remained consistent in answering the question: "Now, on the issue of abortion—do you think abortions should be legal under any circumstances, legal only under certain circumstances, or illegal in all circumstances?" To this question, 23 percent answered, "Legal under any circumstances"; 59 percent answered, "Legal only under certain circumstances; and 17 percent answered, "Illegal in all circumstances"; and 1 percent expressed no opinion. "Gallup Short Subjects," *Gallup Poll Monthly* 388 (January 1998): 34.
33. This 1972 commission was established under Lyndon Johnson but reported its results during the Nixon Administration.
34. "Text of 1976 Republican Platform," *Congressional Quarterly Almanac 1976* (Washington, DC: Congressional Quarterly, 1977); 907, 909.
35. Barbara Hinkson Craig and David M. O'Brien, *Abortion and American Politics* (Chatham, NJ: Chatham House, 1993), 159–60.
36. See Tatalovich and Daynes, *Social Regulatory Policy*, 198.
37. Garland A. Haas, *Jimmy Carter and the Politics of Frustration* (Jefferson, NC: McFarland, 1992), 44.
38. Karen O'Connor, *No Neutral Ground? Abortion Politics in an Age of Absolutes* (Boulder, CO: Westview Press, 1996), 151.
39. U.S. President, "Remarks to Participants in the March for Life Rally–January 23, 1989," *Public Papers of the Presidents of the United States: George Bush* (Washington, DC: Government Printing Office, 1990), 12.

40. O'Connor, *No Neutral Ground?*, 9.

41. O'Connor, *No Neutral Ground?*, 90.

42. The commission that reported on September 1970 was known as the Obscenity and Pornography Commission.

43. See Richard C. Morais, "Porn Goes Public," *Forbes*, 14, June 1999: 214–20.

44. See *Jacobellis v. Ohio*, 378 U.S. 476 (1964).

45. U.S. President, "The President's News Conference—June 17, 1953," *Public Papers of the Presidents of the United States* (Washington, DC: Government Printing Office, 1954), 431.

46. In a 1995 Gallup poll, there did seem to be a reluctance on the part of the public to accept government restriction of pornography. To the question, "Do you think the federal government should become involved in restricting sex and violence in the entertainment industry, or should the industry be left alone to make these decisions on its own?" 35 percent wanted federal government involvement, but 63 percent wanted the industry left alone, with 2 percent having no opinion. See "Gallup Short Subjects," *Gallup Poll Monthly* 357 (June 1995): 31–32.

47. To the question, "Which of these statements comes closest to your feelings about pornography laws?" some 59 percent of the respondents to a National Opinion Research Center poll in 1994 answered, "There should be laws against the distribution of pornography to persons under 18." In the same sample, 37 percent answered that "there should be laws against the distribution of pornography whatever the age." See Survey Research Consultants International, *Index to International Public Opinion* (Westport, CT: Greenwood Press, 1996) 276.

48. See for example, the following: Lucilius A. Emery, "The Constitutional Right to Keep and Bear Arms," *Harvard Law Review* 28 (1914–1915): 473–77; Eric S. Freibrun, "Banning Handguns: *Quilici v. Village of Morton Grove* and the Second Amendment," *Washington University Law Quarterly* 60 (Fall 1982): 1087–118; Roy G. Weatherup, "Standing Armies and Armed Citizens," *Hastings Constitutional Law Quarterly* 2 (1975): 961–1001; and Howard I. Bass, "*Quilici v. Village of Morton Grove*: Ammunition for a National Handgun Ban," *DePaul Law Review* 32 (Winter 1983): 371–98.

49. See Merrill Jensen, *The New Nation* (New York: Random House, 1962), 29.

50. See, for example, the following: Lucilius A. Emery, "The Constitutional Right to Keep and Bear Arms," *Harvard Law Review* 28 (1914–1915): 473–77; Eric S. Freibrun, "Banning Handguns: *Quilici v. Village of Morton Grove* and the Second Amendment," *Washington University Law Quarterly* 60 (Fall 1982): 1087–118; Roy G. Weatherup, "Standing Armies and Armed Citizens," *Hastings Constitutional Law Quarterly* 2 (1975): 961–1001; and Howard I. Bass, "*Quilici v. Village of Morton Grove*: Ammunition for a National Handgun Ban," *DePaul Law Review* 32 (Winter 1983): 371–98.

51. See, for example, David I. Caplan, "Restoring the Balance: The Second Amendment Revisited," *Fordham Urban Law Journal* 5 (Fall 1976): 31–53; and David T. Hardy and John Stompoly, "Of Arms and the Law," *Chicago Kent Law Review* 51 (Summer 1974): 62–114.

52. 307 U.S. 174 (1939)

53. 859 F. 2d. 1318 (1988).

54. Robert J. Spitzer, *The Politics of Gun Control* (Chatham, NJ: Chatham House, 1995) 152–153.

55. Bill Clinton and Al Gore, *Putting People First* (New York: Times Books, 1992) 105–7.

56. Robert J. Spitzer, "Gun Control: Constitutional Mandate or Myth?" in Tatalovich and Daynes, *Social Regulatory Policy*, 126.

57. See James Brooke, "Terror in Littleton: The Overview; 2 Students in Colorado School Said to Gun Down as Many as 23 and Kill Themselves in a Siege," *New York Times*, 21 April, 1999 <http://web.lexis-nexis.com/univers . . . 5 = 8e8b87437ac08fde2e265db82057b 947> Accessed 14 May 1999, and "Terror in Littleton: Clinton Plans Meeting," *New York Times*, 30 April, 1999 <http://web.lexis-nexis.com/univers . . . 5 = 673ff4ce63210c8a81b 1095095797a61> Accessed 14 May 1999.

58. Katherine Q. Seelye, "Clinton Holds Youth Violence `Summit,'" *New York Times*, 11 May, 1999 <http://web.lexis-nexis.com/univers . . . 5 = f17fcba5a272c5011441449c5d5a250b> Accessed 14 May 1999.

59. See, for example, "H. R. 2122—Bill to Require Background Checks at Gun Shows, and for Other Purposes" (106th Congress, 1st Session; Introduced 10 June 1999; last action 18 June 1999). Text from: *Bill Tracking Report*. Available from: *Congressional Universe* (Online Service). Bethesda, MD: Congressional Information Service. Accessed 30 June 1999. This

bill was defeated in the House by a vote of 147 in favor to 280 opposed. Also see "S. 254—Violent and Repeat Juvenile Offender Accountability and Rehabilitation Act" (106th Congress, 1st Session; Introduced: 1/20/99; Last Action: 5/20/99). Text from: *Bill Tracking Report.* Available from: *Congressional Universe* (Online Service). Bethesda, MD: Congressional Information Service. Accessed 30 June 1999. This bill passed the Senate and was sent to the House on 26 May 1999, but has received no action yet.

60. See, for example, Michael Nava and Robert Dawidoff, *Created Equal: Why Gay Rights Matter to America* (New York: St. Martin's Press, 1984).

61. See Margaret Ellis, "Gay Rights: Lifestyle or Immorality?" in Tatalovich and Daynes, *Moral Controversies in American Politics*, 105.

62. See, for example, John M. Finnis, "Law, Morality and Sexual Orientation," *Notre Dame Law Review* (1994): 11–40 and Samuel A. Marcosson, "The 'Special Rights' Canard in the Debate over Lesbian and Gay Civil Rights," *Notre Dame Journal of Law, Ethics and Public Policy* 9 (1995): 137–83.

63. See Randy Shilts, *Conduct Unbecoming: Gays and Lesbians in the U.S. Military* (New York: St. Martin's Press, 1993).

64. See Ellis, "Gay Rights: Lifestyle or Immorality?" 106.

65. David Lauter, "Clinton Compromises, Partially Lifts Gay Ban," *Los Angeles Times* 30 Jan. 1993: A1, A18.

66. See Ellis, "Gay Rights: Lifestyle or Immorality?" 107.

67. See Senate Armed Services Committee, Congressional Research Service, as it appeared in the *Los Angeles Times*, 31 January 1993, A28.

68. See David W. Moore, "Public Split on Clinton's Compromise Plan," *Gallup Poll Monthly* (July 1993): 30–31.

69. Melissa Healy, "74% of Military Enlistees Oppose Lifting Gay Ban," *Los Angeles Times*, 28 February 1993, A1, A23.

70. See Kevin Phillips, "Getting America's Priorities All Wrong," *Washington Post*, 8–14 February 1993 National weekly edition, 23.

71. U.S. Congress, House Committee on the Judiciary, Subcommittee on the Constitution, *Group Preferences and the Law: Hearing before the Subcommittee on the Constitution.* 104th Cong., 1st sess., 3 April 1995: 2.

72. In responding to the Depression's severely high unemployment rate, Roosevelt barred defense contractors from discriminating in their hiring practices in a series of executive orders; in addition, the Federal Employment Practices Committee (FEPC) was created by executive order on September 8, 1939, to implement these orders. See Executive Order 8242, 8 September 1939, in *Public Papers and Addresses of Franklin D. Roosevelt* (New York: Russell and Russell, 1941), 490–509.

73. Gary Bryner, "Affirmative Action: Minority Rights or Reverse Discrimination?" in Tatalovich and Daynes, *Social Regulatory Policy*, 157–58.

74. Bryner, "Affirmative Action," 158–159; Theodore C. Sorenson, *Kennedy* (New York: Bantam Books, 1965) 474.

75. Joan Hoff, *Nixon Reconsidered* (New York: Basic Books, 1994), 93.

76. Melvin Small, *The Presidency of Richard Nixon* (Lawrence, KS: University Press of Kansas, 1999), 176.

77. Bryner, "Affirmative Action," 159.

78. Bryner, "Affirmative Action," 160.

79. See *Firefighters v. City of Cleveland*, 478 U.S. 501 (1986); and *Bazemore v. Friday*, 478 U.S. 385 (1986).

80. Bryner, "Affirmative Action," 57.

81. Office of the Press Secretary, The White House, "Increasing Participation of Asian Americans and Pacific Islanders in Federal Programs," 1999-06-07 Executive Order on Asian Americans in Federal Programs, 7 June 1999, <www.pub.whitehouse.gov> Accessed 8 June 1999.

82. Paul J. Quirk, "Domestic Policy: Divided Government and Cooperative Presidential Leadership," in Colin Campbell and Bert A. Rockman, eds. *The Bush Presidency: First Appraisals* (Chatham, NJ: Chatham House Publishers, 1991), 75.

83. Michael Satchell, "Clinton's 'Mother of all Land-Grabs,'" *U.S. News and World Report*, 20 January 1997, 42.

84. See Richard Lowitt, "Conservation, Policy On," in Leonard W. Levy and Louis Fisher, eds., *Encyclopedia of the American Presidency*, vol. 1 (New York: Simon and Schuster, 1994), 289.
85. See Michael E. Kraft, *Environmental Policy and Politics* (New York: HarperCollins, 1996), 71.
86. Kraft, *Environmental Policy and Politics*, 79.
87. See John Holusha, "Bush Pledges Aid for Environment," *New York Times*, 1 September, 1988, 9.
88. Kraft, *Environmental Policy and Politics*, 81.
89. Paul Rauber, "Elephant Graveyard," *Sierra* 81, no. 3 (May/June 1996): 24.
90. See Warren W. Hassler, Jr., *The President as Commander in Chief* (Menlo Park, CA: Addison-Wesley, 1971), 11.
91. See Maureen Dowd, "President Seems to Blunt Calls for Gulf Session," *New York Times* 15 November 1990, A1, A8.
92. See Richard Rose, *The Postmodern President: George Bush Meets the World*, 2nd ed. (Chatham, NJ: Chatham House, 1991).
93. Justice Sutherland, quoting John Marshall, *U.S. v. Curtiss-Wright Export Corp.*, 299 U.S. 304 (1936).
94. Sutherland quoting Marshall, *U.S. v. Curtiss-Wright*.
95. Edmund L. Andrews, "Germany's Efforts to Police Web Are Upsetting Business," *New York Times*, 6 June 1997, A7, C2.
96. See James MacGregor Burns, "Our Super-Government—Can We Control It?" *New York Times*, 24 April 1949, 30.
97. Before he found Janet Reno to serve as attorney general, for example, Clinton had asked Zoe Baird and Kimba Wood, both of whom were rejected by the Senate. Controversial appointees like his first surgeon general, Joycelyn Elders, and those ill equipped to handle their assignment, like Thomas F. "Mack" McLarty III, chief of staff, also taxed his presidency.
98. Frank Kessler, "Walter Mondale," in L. Edward Purcell, *The Vice Presidents: A Biographical Dictionary* (New York: Facts on File, 1998), 373.
99. Two early studies that support this idea are Lawrence H. Chamberlain, *The President, Congress and Legislation* (New York: Columbia University Press, 1946) and Ronald C. Moe and Steven C. Teal, "Congress as Policy-Maker: A Necessary Reappraisal," *Political Science Quarterly* (September 1970), 443–70.
100. Lawrence H. Chamberlain, *The President, Congress and Legislation* (New York: Columbia University Press, 1946).
101. Moe and Teal, "Congress as Policy-Maker."
102. Aaron Wildavsky, "The Two Presidencies," *Trans-Action* (December 1966): 7–14. See also the later study of Lance T. LeLoup and Steven A. Shull, "Congress versus the Executive: The Two Presidencies Reconsidered," *Social Science Quarterly* (March 1979), 704–19.
103. See Daynes, Tatalovich, and Soden, *To Govern a Nation*, 164.
104. Michael Foley, "Clinton and Congress," in Paul S. Herrnson and Dilys M. Hill, eds., *The Clinton Presidency: The First Term, 1992–1996* (New York: St. Martin's, 1999), 33.
105. Foley, "Clinton and Congress," 33.
106. See Fred I. Greenstein, "The Psychological Functions of the Presidency for Citizens," in Elmer E. Cornwell, *The American Presidency: Vital Center* (Glenview, IL: Scott, Foresman, 1966); and Fred I. Greenstein, "What the President Means to Americans," in James David Barber, ed., *Choosing the President* (Englewood Cliffs, NJ: Prentice-Hall, 1974), 146–47.
107. Samuel Kernell, *Going Public* 2nd ed. (Washington, DC: Congressional Quarterly Press, 1993).
108. Jeffrey E. Cohen, "Presidents, Public Opinion, and Civil Rights," in James W. Riddlesberger, Jr., and Donald W. Jackson, eds., *Presidential Leadership and Civil Rights Policy* (Westport, CT: Greenwood Press, 1995), 3–13.
109. Lyn Ragsdale, *Presidential Politics* (Boston: Houghton-Mifflin, 1993), 363.

THE OPINION/PARTY LEADER
AND THE SOCIAL AGENDA

INTRODUCTION

The president as *opinion/party leader* attempts to mobilize public support for the policies and programs of the administration and party on one hand and respond to constituent interests on the other. According to Paul Light, it is the president who sets the agenda and who presents "a vision of the past and the future."[1] At the same time, the president must decide which issues to address and then present a case for them to the public. Richard Neustadt has argued that presidents have choices that define the prospects for effectiveness and influence; at the same time, presidents appear weakened, facing multiple constraints.[2] Further, when presidents become involved with policy issues, they inevitably are viewed as partisan to the exclusion of the societal good. In other words, what does a president have to gain (or lose) as opinion/party leader with respect to the social agenda?

Public attitudes toward specific policy issues and electoral considerations are fundamental concerns for the president. Given the politics of "high exposure"[3] (politicians are always in the public eye) and the potential constraints or risks confronting the president, the occupant of the White House must carefully consider the type of response to give to social issues. After all, the president must behave in such a way that he enhances his prospects for re-election. Once these issues become politicized by whatever means, however, a president finds it difficult to avoid them. Yet the potential inability of political institutions, including the presidency, to resolve conflict arising over social issues threatens the polity.

During the last several decades, the frequency of public controversies over social issues has increased resulting in a series of conflictual national debates that have divided American society and public officials alike. Recent commentary about the role of social issues in American electoral politics has emphasized that "values matter most" so much that the social agenda has become a defining aspect of the public presidency when involved in both the electoral process and presidential politics.[4] Given the divisiveness of these types of issues, what role does the president as opinion/party leader play?

Basis of Authority

Compared to the other presidential roles, the opinion/party leader is substantially weaker, lacking a formal constitutional authoritative base. As Tatalovich and Daynes point out, "That a relationship between presidential leadership and public opinion exists cannot be denied, but this linkage cannot be traced to the Founding Fathers."[5] Nonetheless, presidents do employ a variety of techniques in an effort to influence the public or at least establish a symbolic link with specific constituency groups. For example, "presidents frequently attempt to influence public opinion with speeches over television or radio or to large groups."[6] Moreover, presidents also engage in news conferences, minor policy speeches, and appearances before partisan groups.

The Framers of our Constitution were also wary of "direct" democracy and political parties, which is why the Constitution does not mention the role of opinion/party leader. Eight decades ago, Woodrow Wilson observed that the president "must be the leader of his party. He is the party's choice and is responsible for carrying out the party platform."[7] James Davis holds that "among the many hats that the president wears, none is more important to his long-term success than that of party leader.[8] Despite what he refers to as the "office's vague specifications for the role of party leader," Louis Koenig argues that "parties are the best political invention yet struck by the human mind to stabilize political influence and to transpose promises into policy."[9] However, Richard Pious points out that "presidents have always had trouble leading their parties."[10] Overall, then, partisanship is important to the president; however, the president must rely on personal influence and political skills in order to be successful as opinion/party leader.

Public Opinion and Leadership

As opinion/party leader, the president can respond to public demands by reaching out to citizens over the heads of Congress in an effort to mobilize support for the administration's agenda. If we use the environment as an example, the State of the Union message was used by Presidents Truman,

Eisenhower, and Nixon when speaking about the "wise" use and conservation of the nation's natural resources. During Nixon's first term in office, more than half (53%) of the American public indicated that environmental quality was the most important problem facing the nation—only crime ranked higher than the environment in the national poll.[11] Consequently, in his 1970 State of the Union message, Nixon devoted considerable time to the environment and stated in particular: "The program I shall propose to Congress will be the most comprehensive and costly program in this field in America's history."[12]

Ronald Reagan entered the White House with a decidedly anti-environmental philosophy. Reagan was more concerned about economic growth and development, but he faced public opinion and opposition in both houses of the Congress where there was bipartisan consensus for environmental protection. After Reagan, George Bush used campaign events to identify himself as the "environmental president," and Bill Clinton used Earth Day speeches to render support for the environment. In his 1994 Earth Day speech, for instance, Clinton articulated his public and party commitment to environmental protection by citing the stirring words of President John Kennedy: "It is our task in our time and in our generation to hand down undiminished to those who come after us, as was handed down to us by those who came before, the natural wealth and beauty which is ours."[13] During his first term in office, Clinton was confronted with a divisive value conflict involving habitat and employment. In an effort to achieve a compromise among the major players involved in the Pacific Northwest dispute over the endangered spotted owl, its habitat, and jobs in the timber industry, Clinton organized a "timber summit" between environmentalists and the logging community.[14]

The president has many roles, including that of moral leader as well as defender of free expression, which confronts the president with a political dilemma. For example, John Kennedy exhibited a free expression position when he publicly supported enforcement of existing laws and the Supreme Court decision in 1962, which prohibited the postal service from curtailing use of the mail for distribution of pornographic material.[15] In contrast, Richard Nixon spoke strongly in favor of an antipornography agenda when he stated in 1970:

> So long as I am in the White House, there will be no relaxation of the national effort to control and eliminate smut from our national life. . . . The warped and brutal portrayal of sex in books, plays, magazines, and movies, if not halted and reversed, could poison the wellsprings of American and Western culture and civilization.[16]

Partisanship and Leadership

As opinion/party leader, the president assumes a dual role— the voice of the party and the voice of the people in setting the public agenda. Koenig observes: "If there is an aspect of the presidency that is hobbled by uncertainty and frailty, it is the office's vague specifications for the role of party leader" he also argues that "through his party, the president can mobilize majorities to transform his promises into legislated policies."[17] The separation of powers and decentralization of the Congress have also constrained presidential power, but despite these limitations, if a president's party maintains majority control in both houses of the Congress, the president is better able to push forward the administration's policy priorities. As James Davis states: "While the president faces numerous constraints in the Madisonian system of checks and balances, he nevertheless can, if he has the inclination and leadership drive, use his party ties to lead the nation to new heights."[18]

Partisanship has played an important role in the complex relationship among presidents, public policy, and the social agenda. Alan Monroe has demonstrated that political parties tie public policy to the preferences of the electorate.[19] Moreover, Budge and Hofferbert's study of presidential campaigns from Truman through Reagan found a positive relationship between party promises and government performance.[20] All in all, presidents have supported the national party agenda most of the time.[21] For example, presidents' positions on affirmative action/equal opportunity have been influenced by partisanship. Lyndon Johnson, Jimmy Carter, and Bill Clinton all have spoken out in support of affirmative action. Carter emphasized the numbers of women and minorities he had appointed to positions in his administration, while Clinton argued that he had worked hard in an effort to achieve a government that reflected America's diverse society. Moreover, notwithstanding delays in the appointment-making process, Clinton's top-level appointments in the executive branch as well as his judicial appointments reflected his earlier campaign commitment to emphasize gender and ethnic diversity over other concerns.[22] Likewise, Republicans Reagan and Bush echoed the position of their party in their vocal opposition to timetables and quotas. According to Lucius Barker and Mack Jones, Reagan in 1989 went even further, accusing civil rights leaders of "exaggerating America's discrimination towards blacks in order to further their own political careers."[23] In the case where a presidential candidate holds a position contrary to the party, the candidate is often constrained in engaging in public discourse about an issue or might even ignore it.

First we will examine the Democratic and Republican party platforms in order to assess the salience of the social agenda during the campaign period from 1932 to 1992. Next, we will evaluate public opinion in the context of the president and the social agenda.

Party Platforms, Presidential Performance, and the Social Agenda

One way presidents are linked to the partisan faithful and to the electorate is through the party platform.[24] Party platforms are important because they provide the goals and objectives of the party and enumerate the issues that are

Table 2.1 Party Platforms and the Social Agenda

	Abortion	Affirmative Action Equal Opportunity	Environ- ment	Gay Rights	Gun Control	Pornog- raphy
1932						
Democrat	−	+	+	−	−	−
Republican	−	+	+	−	−	−
1936						
Democrat	−	+	−	−	−	−
Republican	−	+	+	−	−	−
1940						
Democrat	−	+	+	−	−	−
Republican	−	+	+	−	−	−
1944						
Democrat	−	+	−	−	−	−
Republican	−	+	+	−	−	−
1948						
Democrat	−	+	+	−	−	−
Republican	−	+	+	−	−	−
1952						
Democrat	−	+	+	−	−	−
Republican	−	+	+	−	−	−
1956						
Democrat	−	+	+	−	−	−
Republican	−	+	+	−	−	−
1960						
Democrat	−	+	+	−	−	−
Republican	−	+	+	−	−	−

important to the party and the presidential candidate. Moreover, Gerald Pomper and Susan Lederman as well as Michael Krukones have shown that there is a close correlation between party platforms and presidential action.[25] Before the presidential candidate assumes power, party platforms provide a guide to prominent issues during successive historical eras and help identify issues with specific presidents across American presidential history.

An examination of party platforms and the social agenda over the last sixty years encompassing eleven administrations shows both similarities and differences in the salience of social issues over time (Table 2.1). During the period from Franklin Roosevelt through Kennedy, affirmative action/equal opportunity and the environment predominated in both the Democratic and Republican platforms, showing the importance of these social issues for that period. During these decades, both parties referred to their commitment to "equal opportunity" for all Americans and to the conservation of the nation's resources. Although pornography appeared in the 1964 Republican platform,

	Abortion	Affirmative Action Equal Opportunity	Environ- ment	Gay Rights	Gun Control	Pornog- raphy
1964						
Democrat	−	+	+	−	−	−
Republican	−	+	−	−	−	+
1968						
Democrat	−	+	+	−	−	−
Republican	−	−	+	−	−	−
1972						
Democrat[1]	−	+	+	−	+	−
Republican	−	−	+	−	+	−
1976						
Democrat	+	+	+	−	+	−
Republican	+	+	+	−	+	+
1980						
Democrat	+	+	+	−	+	−
Republican	+	+	+	−	+	−
1984						
Democrat	+	+	+	−	+	−
Republican	+	+	+	−	+	+
1988						
Democrat	+	+	+	+	+	−
Republican	+	+	+	−	+	+
1992						
Democrat	+	+	+	+	+	−
Republican	+	+	+	+	+	+

[1]Although the platform committee rejected "equal rights for homosexuals" and "repeal of all restrictions on abortion," these issues were presented as minority reports on the convention floor.

Note:
(+)Denotes that the social issue was included in the party platform.
(−)Denotes that the social issue was not included in the party platform.

it was not until the 1976 presidential campaign that social issues were clearly present in the platforms of both parties. After the turning point in 1976, the social agenda had clearly become institutionalized every four years in both the Democratic and Republican party platforms.

Although the social agenda has become an integral part of the platforms upon which presidents run the electoral campaign, differences in party orientation on the issues are evident. Partisan differences have separated Democrats from Republicans on abortion and gun control, with Democrats supporting abortion rights (and Republicans in opposition) and favoring restrictions on handguns (and Republicans in favor of the right to bear arms). As far as affirmative action/equal opportunity is concerned, both parties have indicated their commitment to "equal opportunity" for all citizens. Yet Democratic presidents have taken a distinctly liberal approach in fulfilling party commitments to affirmative action/equal opportunity, while Republicans have been divided on the issue.[26] For example, where Eisenhower took a more liberal orientation, Reagan and Bush reflected a conservative position. In recent years, Democrats have also been more supportive of efforts to promote diversity and remedies for past discrimination. On the other hand, Republicans have argued in favor of equal treatment but have strongly opposed quotas and timetables. All in all, presidents have fulfilled a majority of their party platform pledges. [27] Presidents have also fulfilled a majority of their party platform commitments to the social agenda while also exhibiting ideological differences.[28]

Over the last sixty years, the social agenda has increasingly become a conspicuous part of party platforms. Although they were less noticeable during the earlier presidential era, social issues have now assumed an important place in contemporary party politics. As party leader, the president must respond to these issues in the electoral arena every four years. To what extent do presidents articulate their positions on these issues once they assume the role of opinion/party leader? Before we address this question, we first turn briefly to the interrelation among public opinion, the presidency, and social issues.

PUBLIC OPINION, PARTY, AND THE SOCIAL AGENDA

We will begin our discussion of modern presidents as they have interacted with public opinion and political parties with the issue of abortion.

Abortion. American sentiment about abortion has been also reflected in numerous surveys that have been conducted over the years. Public opinion polls have shown that American citizens reflect a "complex set of opinions about the morality and legality" of abortion and are evenly split on the issue as the "pro-choice position is maintained by about 48% of Americans while 42% consider themselves pro-life."[29] At the same time, a majority of the American public supports a woman's right to choose, under certain circumstances. This was the case even prior to *Roe v. Wade.* In 1965, for example, a majority of Americans supported a woman's right to choose to have an abortion when the health of the mother was threatened (77%) as well as when chances were high that the child might be born deformed (54%).[30] Since 1973, a majority (about 55% of the public) has favored abortion as an option under "certain circumstances" while three out of ten Americans felt that abortions should be legal under "any circumstances."[31]

Partisanship has also divided Americans on the abortion issue since the pro-choice position has become more associated with the Democrats and

Independents while the pro-life orientation has become the position of most Republicans.[32] When the party's official position conflicts with the officeholder's personal views on social policy, it is the party that is likely to win the argument, one way or another. For example, where the Republican party has articulated a pro-life position on abortion in the party platform, or where party professionals have made it clear that Republicans should be pro-lifers, a Republican president or candidate who might hold a conflicting pro-choice view will either refrain from publicly expressing that view or, if possible, ignore the abortion issue altogether. Either way, the party's official position remains intact.

This has been the case with Republican presidents Nixon, Ford, Reagan, and Bush, all of whom sided, to varying degrees, against a woman's right to choose.[33] Gerald Ford's position was perhaps the clearest as he advocated that the abortion issue could best be handled by each state. This was a pre- *Roe v. Wade* position.[34]

On the Democratic side, presidents Jimmy Carter and Bill Clinton reflected a pro-choice political position although Carter, in particular, equivocated when explaining the difference between his personal political philosophy in relation to public positions taken as a presidential candidate and later as president.

Affirmative Action. Because American citizens had been denied equal access to employment as well as the enjoyment of other benefits of American society, government policies to ensure affirmative action/equal opportunity became the focal point of public debate. How has the American public responded to this issue? Poll data indicates that a majority of citizens oppose affirmative action practices. For instance, during the mid-1940s, about half (52%) of the American public felt that "whites should have the first chance at jobs."[35] From 1977 to 1991, over 80 percent of American citizens felt that individuals should be evaluated in terms of "test scores only" and not be given "preferential treatment."[36]

Compared to their Democratic counterparts, Republican presidents have been less inclined to use the *bully pulpit* on their public position of prominence to promote and advocate equal opportunity. Nonetheless differences did exist among Nixon, Ford, Reagan, and Bush. The political agenda of presidents Ford, Reagan, and Bush did not include active campaigning for equal opportunity. While they offered symbolic public support for equal opportunity practices, they also opposed quotas and implemented budget cuts in various social policy areas. In effect, the actions of these presidents demonstrated either an attempt to reverse existing policies or slow the progress that had occurred over the previous several decades.

The Environment. For years, environmentalists have argued in favor of public policy initiatives to conserve natural resources and implementation procedures to deal with air and water pollution among other issues. Despite the generally pro-environment orientation of the American public, however, when the environment is included on a list of "most important problems," it falls behind the economy, jobs, health care, and crime as salient national issues.[37] Nonetheless, in 1990, when asked about the role of environmental laws and regulations, more than half (54%) of the American public indicated that they have not gone "far enough" up from 34% in 1973.[38] In 1990, 71 percent of those questioned in a national poll stated that the U.S. government was spending "too little" to improve the environment, up from 61 percent in 1973.[39] By 1994, 83 percent of Americans believed that more work was needed to protect the environment.[40] Moreover, by the late 1990s, a majority of Americans (55%) believed that "only some progress" had been made in protecting the environment.[41] It is also interesting to note that Americans tend to trust the federal government over private business on environmental issues.[42]

The president as opinion/party leader attempts to attract public support for the institution of the presidency, for the individual incumbent president and the Administration's policies, and for the party of the president. During Richard Nixon's first term of office, public opinion indicated that 53 percent of the public felt that environmental quality was one of the most important problems facing the nation at the time, with crime being the only other issue that placed higher in the national poll.[43] Though he was no natural environmentalist, having suggested to his close adviser, John Ehrlichman, that the environment was an issue for the "privileged," that the entire movement was "overrated," and that the issue just "crap,"[44] Nixon was a consummate enough politician to see that leadership on this issue would attract votes and might bolster his presidency by distinguishing the Republican Party from the Democratic Party. It was the opinion/party role that he used to mobilize support for the administration's agenda.

Despite some fluctuations in public opinion about the environment suggested by Downs'[45] five-stage cycle of social problems, the American public has generally been supportive of environmental initiatives. In fact, almost seven out of ten Americans have supported environmental protection at the risk of threatening economic growth.[46] Most presidents probably would have shared in Bill Clinton's attitude toward the environment as well. In his first term Clinton introduced what he referred to as "environmental justice," a concept assuring all citizens rich or poor, regardless of living conditions, that all were deserving of a healthy and secure environment. As the President stated in a February 18, 1994, Executive Order: "All Americans have a right to be protected from pollution— not just those who can afford to live in the cleanest, safest communities. Today we direct Federal agencies to make environmental justice a part of all that they do."[47]

Homosexuality.   Like other minorities in the country, homosexuals have been victims of discrimination and violence over the years. About half of the American public thinks that homosexual relations between consenting adults should be legal.[48] Moreover, over 80 percent of Americans now believe that homosexuals should have "equal rights" in job opportunities.[49] At the same time, over the last few years the proportion of American citizens who are opposed to the legalization of marriage between homosexuals has increased from four out of ten citizens to six out of ten.[50] Notwithstanding the general uneasiness among American citizens about homosexuality, most Americans are opposed to government sanctioned discriminatory practices leveled against citizens due to their sexual orientation. Moreover, only one out of five Americans oppose protecting homosexuals under state "hate crime" legislation.[51]

Although the Uniform Code of Military Justice made sodomy a felony, it was not until the 1980s that the issue of homosexuals serving in the military assumed increasing importance. Homosexuals faced dismissal from military service due to new Department of Defense regulations implemented in 1981, during the Reagan administration.[52] A decade later, "gays in the military" became a major public issue when Democratic presidential candidate Bill Clinton actively courted the electoral support of the gay and lesbian communities. In doing so, he embraced the position that it was time to end the restrictions on military service faced by any citizen in American society. Reagan and Clinton represent a clear distinction in partisanship in their approach to the issue.

Gay rights/homosexuality and military service captured national attention during the presidential campaign of 1992 as contending forces worked to influence policymakers on the issue. When asked whether the ban on homosexuals serving in the military should be ended, 43 percent of Americans agreed and 50 percent disagreed.[53.] After rancorous public debate involving the president and Congress, the policy of "Don't ask, don't tell" emerged as a means by which individuals could serve their country as long as they did not openly engage in homosexual behavior.[54] Almost six in ten Americans (58%) supported the approach taken on this issue.[55]

Gun Control. As one political observer has argued, "Involvement of the presidency with the issue of gun control has occurred primarily on a symbolic level; that is, presidents periodically have expressed their views on the subject but rarely have played an active role in gun-related policymaking."[56] The notion that some form of "gun control" be enacted first surfaced in a 1938 Gallup poll when over 80 percent of Americans supported the registration of handguns.[57] Support for a gun "permit" emerged twenty years later in a 1959 survey of the American public.[58] Generally, when asked about restrictions on the sale of handguns, 70 percent of the American public has preferred that the laws be more rather than less strict).[59] American public opinion on this question has been fairly consistent over the last twenty years. Moreover, distinct demographic differences (gender, age, education, region) are evident between those who support and oppose stricter gun laws. Those who support more restrictions are likely to be female, younger rather than older, college educated and reside in eastern states and metropolitan areas.[60]

Pornography.   Two issues involving pornography that have elicited presidential public positions are using the postal service to distribute "obscene materials" and, more recently, child pornography. Public opinion has been somewhat inconsistent on the issue. For instance, at the time of the Supreme Court decision in *Miller v. California* in 1973, almost six out of ten (58%) Americans preferred that each community set its own "obscenity" standards.[61] Yet only four years later, a plurality (45%) of American citizens supported a "nation-wide" standard rather than "community standards."[62] During the period 1973–1988, about 41 percent of the American public agreed that "there should be laws against the distribution of pornography whatever the age," while some 50 percent of their fellow citizens preferred that "there should be laws against the distribution of pornography to persons under 18."[63] In recent years, the public has reflected somewhat inconsistent views— almost two-thirds oppose strict government regulation of the entertainment industry, yet almost six out of ten citizens support laws that prohibit the dissemination of pornography to minors.[64] It is not surprising, therefore, that in the public arena the president has remained relatively quite on the issue of pornography. Nonetheless, the issue did elicit symbolic action from some presidents either in the electoral arena or during their respective term in office.

PRESIDENTIAL SPEECHES AND THE SOCIAL AGENDA

According to Mary Stuckey, "The president has become the primary focus of national political attention, and the president's talk has become the primary focus of the presidency."[65] Is there a "cycle of attention" that can be applied to presidential talk about the social agenda?

Public communication provides the president with the means by which to focus on issues considered to be important for the president's administration and party[66] as well as highlighting specific issues in an effort to set the national agenda.[67] Presidential attention to social issues can assume several forms. It can be *substantive*, in that presidents "go public"[68] in an attempt to give greater visibility to the social agenda and enhance their administration's identification with specific issues either in a *supportive* or *opposing* role. Presidents can also play a *symbolic* role by showing support but making limited public gestures toward social issues. Presidents also reserve the right to remain relatively silent on issues by practicing *avoidance*. Moreover, several issues on the social agenda have an exceedingly divisive impact on presidential politics, including but not limited to abortion, gay rights/homosexuality, and gun control, as reflected in recent presidential elections. Consequently, some social issues have greater salience or risks for the president than do others, a factor that might influence presidential attention to the issue.

Methods to Assess Presidential Speeches
and the Social Agenda

To assess presidential discourse on social agenda issues, we examined the public papers of the Presidents of the United States. Public statements (e.g., speeches, press releases, town meetings) by Presidents Franklin Roosevelt, Truman, Eisenhower, Kennedy, Johnson, Nixon, Ford, Carter, Reagan, Bush, and Clinton were analyzed to determine the amount of presidential attention given to social issues. We measured presidential attention to the social agenda by the number and content of public speeches in which the president mentioned a specific social issue.[69] Presidential statements were divided into *major* and *minor* speeches. While presidents make major and minor speeches about numerous public policy issues, social issues might be considered "discretionary"[70] and can be included or ignored in the president's public statements. *Major public speeches* include the Inaugural Address, the State of the Union messages, and addresses to the Congress and the nation. Major speeches are important because they contain the values and principles of the administration, set the legislative agenda, highlight the president as party leader, and provide a linkage between the president and the people.[71] *Minor public speeches* include news conferences, interviews with reporters, press releases, presidential speeches to interest/partisan groups, and town meetings. These types of outlets are important because they provide the president with a diversity of formats in which to engage in public discourse and establish a link with the citizenry. Presidents have used a variety of outlets when making public statements about social agenda issues. Consequently, as opinion/party leaders they are not limited in the means by which they communicate with citizens.[72]

To ascertain the number of speeches that included a reference to social agenda issues made by each president, we examined the index at the end of each of the annual volumes of the president's public papers. The following categories were used in each volume's index as follows; abortion (abortion); affirmative action/equal opportunity (affirmative action, equal employment opportunity, equal opportunity); environment (environment, environmental protection, pollution, conservation); gay rights/homosexuality (gays, homosexuality, lesbians); gun control (gun control, law enforcement); pornography (obscenity, pornography). We counted the number of speeches in which the president mentioned the issue using a "three line rule"—the president's reference to the social issue had to be at least three sentences in length.

Presidents make many major and minor speeches about public policy issues during their years in office. Whether and to what extent a president gives attention to or avoids references to the social agenda is an important consideration for presidential politics, the social agenda, and American society. The discussion that follows is an empirical examination of the extent to which presidents from Franklin Roosevelt through Clinton have included social agenda issues in their public discourse.

Major Addresses

In his study of the major speeches made by the presidents, Jeffrey Cohen found that two-thirds of presidential State of the Union addresses are concerned with the economy and foreign policy and therefore all other policy areas receive less attention.[73] Yet if the variety of social agenda issues plays, to some degree, a significant role in presidential politics, it is important to assess the extent to which these issues show prominence during the presidential administrations from Roosevelt through Clinton in their public discourse.

In the speeches examined, social issues were mentioned infrequently over the last sixty years or so (Table 2.2). In fact, in most cases references to social issues comprise less than 20 percent of all speeches made by the opinion/party leader.[74] Social issues range from a high of 28.6 percent during the Clinton administration to a low of 8.3 percent during the administration of Franklin Roosevelt. The average proportion of speeches is 13.8 percent per presidential term and 22.7 percent per administration.

At the same time, in considering the social agenda and the president's reference to it in public discourse, we find that the environment and affirmative action/equal opportunity constitute the issues most frequently cited by the eleven presidents (Table 2.3). However, presidential attention to those issues among others is not uniform: Some presidents give the issue greater attention while other presidents make no mention of it in their speeches.

Affirmative action/equal opportunity is present in the major speeches of almost every president, while the environment is present in the speeches of a majority of the presidents. For instance, on several occasions Presidents Truman and Eisenhower used the State of the Union message to emphasize their concern about natural resources and the environment. While Truman stressed the twin goals of conservation and economic development, Eisenhower supported conservation but favored political control at the state and local level over that of the federal government. Jimmy Carter made four major speeches to the nation about the energy crisis, and he finally deferred on his forthcoming fifth speech when informed by his pollster that "he would be wasting his time."[75]

Abortion, gun control, and pornography were cited by at least one president in at least one speech. Gun control became a salient issue beginning with the Johnson administration, while pornography gained prominence during Nixon's term in office. Abortion was a voluminous issue in Reagan's major speeches.

As Table 2.2 shows, a large proportion of the total speeches made by Presidents Kennedy, Carter, and Clinton contained references to social issues. All three Democrats emphasized affirmative action/equal opportunity and the environment. For example, in a radio and television address to the American people in June 1963, President Kennedy stated that the American people were "confronted primarily with a moral issue" regarding whether all Americans

Table 2.2   Major Speeches and the Social Agenda

President	Total Number of Speeches	Proportion of Speeches Including a Reference to Social Issues (% of total)
Roosevelt		
First term	12	8.3
Second term	13	0.0
Third term	19	0.0
Fourth term	1	0.0
Truman		
First term	17	11.8
		(14.6)[1]
Second term	15	26.7
Eisenhower		
First term	21	19.1
		(10.3)
Second term	20	10.0
Kennedy	15	20.0
Johnson	23	17.4
Nixon		
First term	23	17.4
		(13.8)
Second term	13	8.0
Ford	12	16.7
Carter	17	23.5
Reagan		
First term	20	15.0
		(14.9)
Second term	27	14.8
Bush	17	11.8
Clinton	14	28.6

[1]Average for entire term in office.

Source: Adapted and complied from *Public Papers of the Presidents of the United States* (Washington, DC: Government Printing, 1932–1996) and Lyn Ragsdale *Vital Statistics on the Presidency* (Washington, DC: Congressional Quarterly Press, 1996), 156–66.

would be treated the same in terms of equal opportunity.[76] Presidents Clinton, Carter, and Truman (in his second term) made the most references to social agenda issues, while Franklin Roosevelt, and Eisenhower, and Nixon in their second terms, in effect downplayed these issues in their major speeches. President Johnson made reference to affirmative action/equal employment opportunity in two speeches and also highlighted the importance of gun control in three speeches. In January 1964, for example, Johnson stated that his administration was committed to increased opportunities in employment which he viewed as a "moral" as well as a political issue.[77]

Table 2.3 Distribution of References to the Social
Agenda by Issue (Major Speeches)

Social Issue	Percent of Total
Abortion	6.9
Affirmative action/ equal opportunity	31.0
Environment	46.6
Gay rights/Homosexuality	0.0
Gun control	10.3
Pornography	5.2
	100.0
	(N = 58)

Ronald Reagan made references to a wider variety of social agenda issues compared to the other presidents. Yet as a proportion of his overall major speeches, social agenda issues remained less important than economic and foreign policy issues. When he spoke about social issues, he made references to abortion, affirmative action/equal opportunity, the environment, and pornography. Nonetheless, Reagan believed that abortion in particular was the salient issue to be addressed in a national forum by the president. He cited abortion in three State of the Union messages and in his 1988 message publicly supported the "Human Life Amendment," arguing that the medical evidence confirms that the "unborn child" is a living human being entitled to life, liberty and the pursuit of happiness.[78]

Minor Speeches

While social issues have received greater or lesser attention by some presidents compared to others, the president can communicate with the public in many ways. In addition to major speeches to the Congress and the nation, presidents have used a variety of outlets when making public statements about the social agenda. The president can participate in a news conference, make a speech to an organized interest or partisan group, meet with citizens in a town meeting or community forum, or speak to a national audience via a radio address. For example, when the Supreme Court ruled that pornographic material could not be restricted by the post office, John Kennedy stated his support for the Court's decision in a public news conference, indicating that it was the responsibility of the post office to carry out the law rather than consider the content of the mail.[79] Richard Nixon publicly opposed pornography in numerous speeches to organized interests and partisan groups. In 1969, he argued his case to a National Governor's Conference that his fight against pornography was one of his top priorities, and in the same year he encouraged the National Federation of Republican Women to ask the Congress to support his anti-pornography legislation.[80] President Clinton addressed the nation by radio in response to the congressional opposition to the ban on assault weapons.[81] Clinton demanded that the Congress not "repeal the efforts" to protect citizens and the police.

A second way, therefore, to determine empirically the salience of social issues is to assess the extent to which the presidents have given attention to social agenda issues in minor speeches during their respective terms in office (Table 2.4). Truman, Eisenhower, and Kennedy spoke frequently about the environment and affirmative action/equal opportunity with little or no attention given to other social issues. Kennedy's successor, Lyndon Johnson, spoke frequently about these same two issues and also gave considerable attention to gun control.

During his years as president, Richard Nixon made more references in his minor speeches to affirmative action/equal opportunity, environmentalism, and pornography than he did to abortion, gun control and homosexuality. What is interesting about Nixon's public statements about the social agenda generally is that most of them were made during his first term in office. During his second term, Nixon emphasized his foreign policy priorities (Vietnam, relations with the Soviet Union and the People's Republic of China). Nixon's domestic agenda did not place social issues in a prominent place during his second term, as reflected by the considerable decline in the number of references made by him during this period in his administration (after all, Nixon's second term was increasingly being consumed by the Watergate scandal). Nixon's successor Gerald Ford highlighted abortion, environment, affirmative action/equal opportunity, and gun control in his speeches while neglecting the other two issues. The majority of President Carter's references to the social agenda were focused on the environment, abortion, and affirmative action/equal opportunity.

Ronald Reagan stands as the anomaly among the eleven presidents in the amount of attention he gave in his public statements to social agenda issues. Unlike his Democratic and Republican presidential predecessors, President Reagan referred to the *entire* social agenda in his minor speeches. Among these issues, Reagan emphasized abortion more often than any other issue. What is notable, however, is the drop in the amount of attention to social agenda items when he moved on to his second term in office. By this time, Reagan's public references to the social agenda had clearly declined. Although he continued to vocalize his position on these issues from time to time to reaffirm his link to favored constituency groups, his energy was clearly spent as little substantive change occurred, a resurgent Congress emerged in 1986, and his attention became increasingly directed toward the Iran-Contra scandals.

George Bush followed Reagan's pattern by making references to the broad range of social issues, although he emphasized in his minor speeches his concern about the environment. Bush also reaffirmed his opposition to abortion rights and argued against broad gun control measures. During his first term in office, Bill Clinton's pattern of public discourse in minor speeches regarding

Table 2.4 Minor Speeches and the Social Agenda by Presidential Administration (percent)

President	Abortion	Affirmative Action/Equal Opportunity	Environment	Gay Rights	Gun Control	Pornography	Total	N
Roosevelt	0%	17%	83%	0%	0%	0%	100%	25
Truman	0	23	77	0	0	0	100	47
Eisenhower	0	35	62	0	4	0	101	26
Kennedy	0	49	49	0	0	2	100	45
Johnson	0	30	55	0	15	0	100	107
Nixon	2	12	69	0	2	16	101	126
Ford	17	14	54	0	15	0	100	52
Carter	19	15	65	0	1	0	100	75
Reagan	42	12	29	2	10	6	101	136
Bush	24	10	50	1	15	1	101	166
Clinton	17	10	22	16	35	0	100	119

(N = 924)

Note: Percentages may not add up to 100 due to rounding.

the social agenda differed from other presidents as he focused his attention primarily on gun control. He also spoke about the environment, affirmative action/equal opportunity, abortion, and gay rights/homosexuality. Clinton was quite vocal in his support for gun control legislation and abortion rights and he argued his case to Congress and the public about gays serving in the military.

COMPARING PRESIDENTIAL ADMINISTRATIONS AND THEIR SOCIAL AGENDAS

Besides examining the amount of attention given to social agenda issues by *each* presidential administration, it is also important to assess presidential references to social issues in minor speeches *across* administrations to compare and empirically track fluctuations over the last six decades (Figures 2.1–2.6). In conducting this assessment, we find that while *abortion* was included in the minor speeches of Nixon, Ford, and Carter, the issue gained prominence during the Reagan and Bush administrations, although there was a sharp decline in Reagan's attention to the issue as he moved from his first to second term.

Although affirmative action/equal opportunity received attention from all presidential administrations, the level of attention fluctuated over the years. Among the eleven presidents, Kennedy and Johnson gave most attention to the issue, and thereafter it assumed a less prominent place on the social agenda through Clinton's first term.

Compared to the other social agenda issues—with the one exception of affirmative action/equal opportunity—the environment has received public attention from all of the presidents. Environmental issues, including conservation of natural resources and air and water pollution, in particular, have transcended presidential partisanship and administrations. Nixon and Bush included the environment in more minor speeches than any of their Democratic or Republican counterparts, followed by Democrats Johnson and Carter. In contrast, inclusion of the environment in minor speeches by the other presidents fell below 10 percent of all minor speeches to a low of 3 percent during the Eisenhower administration. In contrast to their predecessors, recent presidents have begun to address new "third-generation" issues.[82] For example, Bush and Clinton have spoken in public forums about global warming, biodiversity, and depletion of the ozone layer. Gay rights /homosexuality was primarily a nonissue until the Reagan era and then captured a considerable amount of attention from candidate and then President Clinton. In Clinton's case, the issue was relatively narrowly defined, focusing on homosexuals and service in the nation's military.

Gun control remained a relative nonissue until President Johnson responded to it in his support for gun control legislation following a period of tragic political assassinations. It then declined in prominence until the 1980s,

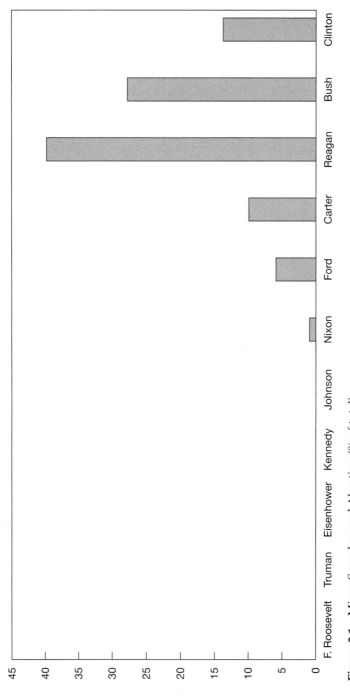

Figure 2.1 Minor Speeches and Abortion (% of total).

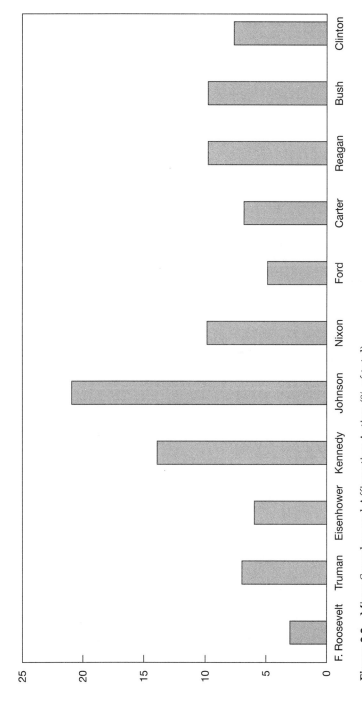

Figure 2.2 Minor Speeches and Affirmative Action (% of total).

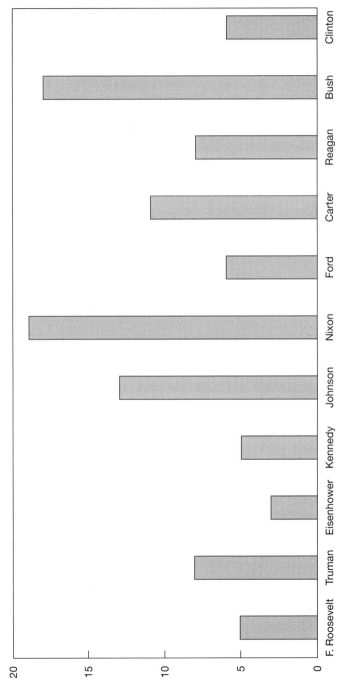

Figure 2.3 Minor Speeches and the Environment (% of total).

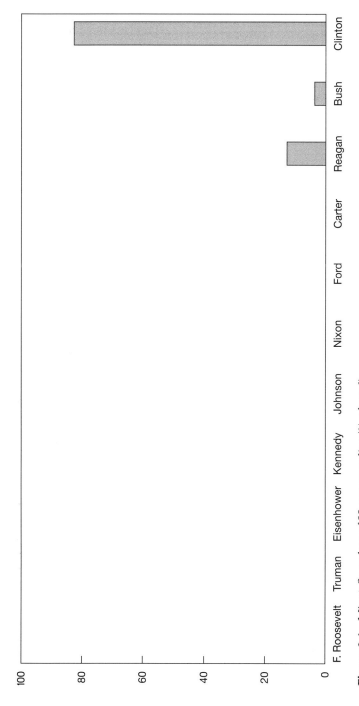

Figure 2.4 Minor Speeches of Homosexuality (% of total).

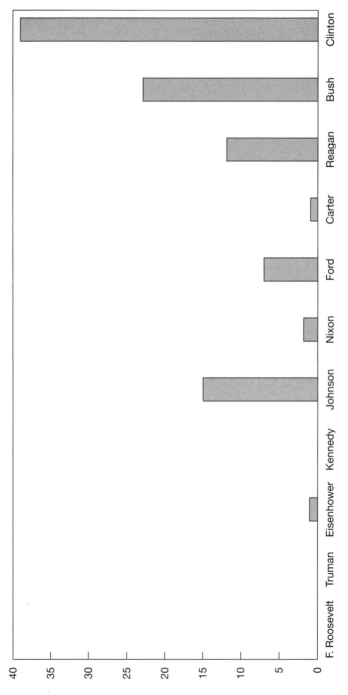

Figure 2.5 Minor Speeches and Gun Control (% of total).

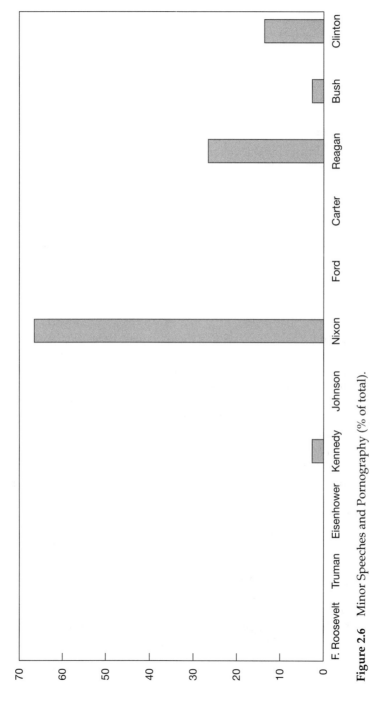

Figure 2.6 Minor Speeches and Pornography (% of total).

when Reagan, Bush, and Clinton addressed the issue. Clinton and Johnson before him, in particular, were responding to heightened public interest in the issue. For Johnson, the assassination of President Kennedy and later, Martin Luther King, Jr., and Senator Robert Kennedy, heightened public attention and concern over the easy availability of handguns. In Clinton's case, public perception of crime and the apparent easy accessibility of semiautomatic assault weapons played a role, in part, in his public emphasis on gun control measures. In contrast, Reagan and Bush maintained the "right to bear arms" philosophy and spoke in opposition to increasing the restrictions on firearms. Ironically, as noted earlier, Reagan used the public forum to support the Brady bill *after* he was out of office.

Pornography has been a concern at all levels of government and the focal point of State and local cases. However, among the presidents since Franklin Roosevelt, only Richard Nixon, and to a lesser extent Ronald Reagan, made frequent mention of the issue in their minor speeches. Nixon, however, drew attention to the issue primarily during his first term in office. Although directing less attention than other presidents to the issue in general, Nixon did oppose child pornography, as did Reagan and Bush.

Partisan Differences

We have seen that presidential talk about the social agenda has several outlets, including major speeches (e.g., The State of the Union address) and a variety of opportunities for minor speeches (e.g., talks to interest groups, town meetings). Since the opinion/party leader lacks formal constitutional authority, presidents must choose which issues to emphasize in a public forum since they must rely on their personal skills and resources. As we have seen, although the environment received considerable public attention from modern presidents, different presidents have emphasized different issues. To what extent does *partisanship* influence the presidents' public discourse on the social agenda?

As Table 2.5 indicates, partisanship strongly divides the presidents with respect to their attention to social issues. Democrats made references more frequently to affirmative action/equal opportunity, gay rights/homosexuality, and gun control than did their Republican colleagues. Republican presidents also gave more attention in their public speeches to abortion and pornography, and slightly more emphasis to the environment compared to the Democratic presidents. Overall, Democrats generally support affirmative action/equal opportunity issues and gun control, while Republicans have been most vocal in their opposition to any effort that includes affirmative action quotas or restrictions on gun ownership.

The abortion issue, in particular, has created a schism *between* the parties and to a lesser extent *within* the two major parties. The abortion issue has also played a role in electoral as well as presidential party politics.[83] There have been significant differences in terms of the emphasis placed on the issue by the

Table 2.5 Partisanship and the Social Agenda (All Speeches)

Social Issue	Democrats	Republicans	Percentage Difference Index
Abortion	23%	77%	− 54
	(34)[1]	(112)	
Affirmative action/			
Equal opportunity	60	40	+ 20
	(103)	(70)	
Environment	46	54	− 8
	(227)	(266)	
Gay rights/			
Homosexuality	83	17	+ 66
	(19)	(4)	
Gun control	56	44	+ 12
	(64)	(50)	
Pornography	3	97	− 94
	(1)	(32)	
	(N = 448)	(N = 534)	

(+)Denotes Democratic advantage.
(−) Denotes Republican advantage.
[1]Number of speeches.

political parties as reflected by national party platforms as well as the attention presidents have paid to the debate over abortion over the years. Moreover, Republican presidents have generally taken a pro-life position, whereas Democratic presidents have failed to take a unified stand. For instance, Jimmy Carter pursued a cautious and perhaps ambiguous approach to the issue in contrast to Bill Clinton, who assumed a decidedly pro-choice orientation reflected in his speeches and social policy.

Among those presidents who addressed the issue of pornography, the value of free expression was supported by Democratic President Kennedy in contrast to Republican President Nixon (and to a lesser extent, Reagan and Bush), who used the presidential office to campaign against pornography.

As far as the environment is concerned, both Democratic and Republican presidents tended to argue, at least publicly, in support of conserving natural resources and protecting the air and water. Eisenhower spoke in favor of state and local control over the environment instead of supporting federal authority. Fellow Republican Richard Nixon declared the 1970s as the decade of the environment and was much more supportive of federal control over the environment. Democrat Lyndon Johnson argued in favor of a program to "beautify" the nation, while Ronald Reagan publicly proclaimed his support for environmental protection but at the same time also supported development and regulatory relief for business in contrast to preservation. In fact, Reagan's "administrative presidency" worked toward reversing years of bipartisan support for the environment in the Congress.[84] George Bush entered the White House as the self-proclaimed "environmental president" only to be rebuffed by environmentalists who believed that he reversed his position too often on environmental issues during his administration. Bill Clinton, whom environmentalists saw as their great "green hope," actually emphasized the environment in fewer speeches than any of his Democratic and Republican counterparts.

Over a decade ago, Tatalovich and Daynes pointed out that partisanship has divided presidents on social issues when they became involved in the social agenda.[85] Clearly, for Democratic presidents, social justice has been a key consideration, as reflected in the attention they have paid to affirmative action/equal opportunity and more recently, gay rights/homosexuality. In contrast, Republicans have been more concerned about issues related to regulating personal behavior, demonstrated by the amount of attention they have given, in particular to abortion and pornography.

CONCLUSION

Although presidents have given comparatively less attention to the social agenda than to the economy and foreign and national security policy, over the last six decades or so, the eleven presidents from Franklin Roosevelt to Clinton have had the opportunity as opinion/party leader to take a *public* position on the six social agenda issues. As we have seen, the environment and affirmative action/equal opportunity received the most attention by these presidents. What is noteworthy, however, is the variation in the amount of references given to specific issues by different presidents. Although Tatalovich, Daynes, and Soden remind us that the opinion/party leader is the weakest role of the presidency, our discussion of this role raises an interesting paradox — that in some ways it is the strongest role when applied to social policies and the president's use of the bully pulpit.

As we have mentioned elsewhere in this book, some presidential roles have formal constitutional authority, customs, traditions, and statutory legislation that provide a basis for power. As opinion/party leader, the president lacks these types of resources and must rely on personal skills. This does not mean, however, that the role does not play a part in a president's attempt to support or oppose, for example, social agenda issues. To the contrary, the fact that the president takes the time to speak about an issue in a major address or to highlight it in a talk to constituency groups, as did Lyndon Johnson about equal opportunity, demonstrates the importance the president assigns to the issue. At the same time, presidents might use the bully pulpit in support of an issue knowing full well that it is for purely electoral or political reasons. Although Ronald Reagan included a pro-life position in numerous speeches to maintain his connection with anti-abortion constituents, congressional action was not forthcoming. Moreover, the president who fails to understand the political landscape faces the prospect of strong opposition to his public position. Although Bill Clinton was confronted with massive opposition to his position on gays serving in the military and ended up compromising in the process, by "going public" he set the stage for a future president to raise the issue yet again. Finally, let us not forget that the president as party leader has the opportunity to respond to party platform pledges. As we have discussed earlier, presidents have been moderately successful in fulfilling the party promises about social policy.

While some presidents have given considerable attention to particular social issues, other presidents have been silent or avoided these same issues. We might be inclined to categorize some presidents, in this role as opinion/party leader, as advocates in emphasizing publicly some social issues (e.g., Johnson and affirmative action/equal opportunity; Reagan and abortion; Clinton and gun control). At the same time, we could argue that other presidents should be characterized as opponents of social issues (e.g., Reagan and affirmative action/equal opportunity; Bush and abortion rights).

The opinion/party role is important but weak. It is important because the president can place issues on his public agenda and try to mobilize public sentiment. It is weak because the opinion/party leader faces several constraints, including a fragmented political system and lack of authority and resources.[86] In this role, the president can make only a *modest* difference by proposing or opposing action or acting as party leader where he has the opportunity to fulfill party platform promises. Nonetheless, in the hands of an *activist* president, the opinion/party role can be very effective in promoting the social agenda.

ENDNOTES

1. Paul Light, *The President's Agenda* (Baltimore, MD: Johns Hopkins University Press, 1982), 233.
2. Richard Neustadt, *Presidential Power* (New York: Free Press, 1990).
3. Anthony King and Giles Alston, "Good Government and the Politics of High Exposure," in Colin Campbell and Bert Rockman, eds., *The Bush Presidency: First Appraisals* (Chatham, NJ: Chatham House, 1991), 249–85.
4. Ben J. Wattenberg, "Social Issues Will Elect Our Next President—And Clinton Knows It," *"The American Enterprise* (January/February 1996): 50; Ben J. Wattenberg, *Values Matter Most* (New York: The Free Press, 1995).
5. Raymond Tatalovich and Byron W. Daynes, *Presidential Power in the United States* (Monterey, CA: Brooks/Cole, 1984), 82.
6. George C. Edwards III, *The Public Presidency* (New York: St. Martin's Press, 1983), 39.
7. James W. Davis, *The American Presidency* (Westport, CT: Praeger, 1995), 120.
8. James W. Davis, *The President as Party Leader* (New York: Greenwood Press, 1992), 1.
9. Louis W. Koenig, *The Chief Executive*, 6th ed. (New York: Harcourt Brace, 1996), 117.
10. Richard Pious, *The Presidency* (Boston: Allyn and Bacon, 1996), 162.

11. Mary Etta Cook and Roger H. Davidson, "Deferral Politics: Congressional Decision Making on Environmental Issues in the 1980s," in Helen M. Ingram and R. Kenneth Godwin, eds., *Public Policy and the Natural Environment* (Greenwich, CT: JAI Press, 1985), 48.

12. U.S. President, "Annual Message to the Congress on the State of the Union—January 22, 1970,"*Public Papers of the Presidents of the United States: Richard Nixon* (Washington, DC: Government Printing Office, 1971).

13. U.S. President, "Remarks on the Observance of Earth Day, April 21, 1994,"*Public Papers of the Presidents of the United States: William J. Clinton* (Washington, DC: Government Printing Office, 1995).

14. Lettie McSpadden, "The Courts and Environmental Policy," in James P. Lester, ed., *Environmental Politics and Policy*, 2nd ed. (Durham, NC: Duke University Press, 1995), 248.

15. Byron W. Daynes, "Pornography: Freedom of Expression or Societal Degradation?" in Raymond Tatalovich and Byron W. Daynes, eds., *Social Regulatory Policy: Moral Controversies in American Politics* (Boulder, CO: Westview Press, 1988), 230.

16. U.S. President, "Statement about the Report of the Commission on Obscenity and Pornography—October 24, 1970, "*Public Papers of the Presidents of the United States: Richard Nixon* (Washington, DC: Government Printing Office, 1971), 940.

17. Koenig, *The Chief Executive*, 117.

18. Davis, *The President as Party Leader*, 14.

19. Alan Monroe, "American Party Platforms and Public Opinion," *American Journal of Political Science* 27 (1983): 27–42.

20. Ian Budge and Richard I. Hofferbert, "Mandates and Policy Outputs: U.S. Party Platforms and Federal Expenditures," *American Political Science Review* 84 (1990): 111–31.

21. Jeff Fishel, *Presidents and Promises* (Washington, DC: Congressional Quarterly Press, 1985).

22. David M. O'Brien, "Clinton's Legal Policy and the Courts: Rising from Disarray or Turning Around and Around," in Colin Campbell and Bert A. Rockman, eds., *The Clinton Presidency: First Appraisals* (Chatham, NJ: Chatham House, 1996) and Joel D. Aberbach, "The Federal Executive under Clinton," in Colin Campbell and Bert A. Rockman, eds., *The Clinton Presidency: First Appraisals* (Chatham, NJ: Chatham House, 1996).

23. Lucius J. Barker and Mack H. Jones, *African-Americans and the American Political System*, 3rd ed. (Englewood Cliffs, NJ: Prentice-Hall, 1994), 290–91.

24. Donald Bruce Johnson and Kirk H. Porter, *National Party Platforms: 1840–1972* (Chicago: University of Illinois Press, 1973).

25. Gerald M. Pomper and Susan S. Lederman, *Elections in America*, 2nd ed. (New York: Longman, 1980) and Michael G. Krukones, *Promises and Performance* (Lanham, MD: University Press of America, 1984).

26. Glen Sussman and Byron W. Daynes, "Party Platforms and Presidential Performance: Social Policies of the Modern Presidents, FDR–, Clinton," *Southeastern Political Review* 28, no. 1 (March 2000): 111–30.

27. Fishel, *Promises and Performance*; Pomper and Lederman, *Elections in America*.

28. Sussman and Daynes, "Party Platforms and Presidential Performance."

29. Lydia Saad, "Poll Releases, May 18, 1999: Americans Divided over Abortion Debate" <http://www.gallup.com/poll/releases/pr990518.asp> Accessed 7 June 1999.

30. George Gallup, *The Gallup Poll: Public Opinion 1935–1971*, vol. 3 (New York: Random House, 1972), 1985.

31. Saad, "Poll Releases, May 18, 1999."

32. Saad, "Poll Releases, May 18, 1999."

33. Raymond Tatalovich, "Abortion: Prochoice versus Prolife," in Tatalovich and Daynes, *Social Regulatory Policy*, 197.

34. Barbara Hinkson Craig and David M. O'Brien, *Abortion and American Politics* (Chatham, NJ: Chatham House, 1993), 159–60.

35. Elaine B. Sharp, *The Sometime Connection: Public Opinion and Social Policy* (Albany, NY: State University of New York Press, 1999), 74.

36. George Gallup, Jr., and Frank Newport, "Blacks and Whites Differ on Civil Rights Progress," *The Gallup Poll Monthly* 311 (August 1991), 56.

37. George Gallup, Jr., *The Gallup Poll: Public Opinion 1993* (Wilmington, DE: Scholarly Resources, 1994), 168.

38. Riley E. Dunlap and Angela G. Mertig, *American Environmentalism* (Washington, DC: Taylor & Francis, 1992), 104.

39. Dunlap and Mertig, *American Environmentalism*, 104.
40. Christopher J. Bosso, "Seizing Back the Day: The Challenge to Environmental Activism in the 1990s," in Norman J. Vig and Michael E. Kraft, eds., *Environmental Policy in the 1990s*, 3rd ed. (Washington, DC: CQ Press, 1997), 55.
41. Saad, "Poll Releases, April 22, 1999."
42. George Gallup, Jr., *The Gallup Poll: Public Opinion 1995* (Wilmington, DE: Scholarly Resources, 1996), 66.
43. Mary Etta Cook and Roger H. Davidson, "Deferral Politics: Congressional Decision Making on Environmental Issues in the 1980s," in Ingram and Godwin, *Public Policy and the Natural Environment*, 48.
44. See Stanley I. Kutler, *The Wars of Watergate: The Last Crisis of Richard Nixon* (New York: Knopf, 1990), 78.
45. Anthony Downs, "Up and Down with Ecology—The 'Issue-Attention Cycle,'" *Public Interest* 28 (1972): 38–50.
46. Saad, "Poll Releases, April 22, 1999," George Gallup, Jr. *The Gallup Poll: Public Opinion 1991* (Wilmington, DE: Scholarly Resources, 1992), 189.
47. "Statement on the Executive Order on Environmental Justice," *Weekly Compilation of Presidential Documents*, 30, no. 7 (11 February 1994): 283; and "Executive Order 12898—Federal Actions to Address Environmental Justice in Mining Populations and Low-Income Populations," *Weekly Compilation of Presidential Documents* 30, no. 6 (11 February 1994), 276.
48. "Gallup Social and Economic Indicators: Homosexual Relations," <http://www.gallup.com/poll/indicators/indhomosexual.asp> Accessed 7 July 1999; *Gallup Report Monthly* 38 (July 1992).
49. Lydia Saad, "Americans Growing More Tolerant of Gays," *Gallup Poll Monthly* 375 (December 1996): 12–13.
50. Gallup Social and Economic Indicators: Homosexual Relations; Margaret Ellis, "Gay Rights: Lifestyle or Immorality?" in Raymond Tatalovich and Byron W. Daynes, eds., *Moral Controversies in American Politics* (Armonk, NY: M. D. Sharpe, 1998), 29.
51. Mark Gillespie, "Poll Releases, April 4, 1999: Americans Support Hate Crimes Legislation That Protects Gays." <http://www.gallup.com/poll/ releases /pr990447.asp> Accessed 7 July 1999.
52. Denise Bostdorff, "Clinton's Characteristic Issue Management Style: Caution, Conciliation, and Conflict Avoidance in the Case of Gays in the Military," in Robert E. Denton, Jr., and Rachel L. Holloway, eds., *The Clinton Presidency* (Westport, CT: Praeger, 1996), 196.
53. Lydia Saad and Leslie McAnery, "Americans Deeply Split over Ban on Gays in Military," *The Gallup Poll Monthly* 328 (January 1993): 6.
54. Denise Bostdorff, "Clinton's Characteristic Issue Management Style" 198.
55. George Gallup, Jr., *The Gallup Poll: Public Opinion 1993* (Wilmington, DE: Scholarly Resources Inc., 1993), 131.
56. Robert J. Spitzer, "Gun Control: Constitutional Mandate or Myth?" in Tatalovich and Daynes, *Social Regulatory Policy*, 126.
57. Frank Newport, "Poll Releases, June 16, 1999: Americans Support Wide Variety of Gun Control Measures," <http://www.gallup.com/poll/ releases /pr990616.asp> Accessed 7 July 1999.
58. Spitzer, "Gun Control," *Moral Controversies in American Politics*, 172.
59. Leslie McAnery, "Americans Tell Congress: Pass Brady Bill, Other Tough Gun Laws," *Gallup Poll Monthly* 330 (March 1993): 2.
60. Robert J. Spitzer, "Gun Control," *Moral Controversies in American Politics*, 172.
61. George Gallup, *Gallup Poll: Public Opinion 1972–1977*, vol. 1 (Wilmington, DE: Scholarly Resources, 1978), 142.
62. Gallup, *Gallup Poll: Public Opinion 1972–1977*, vol. 2 (Wilmington, DE: Scholarly Resources, 1978), 1026.
63. Richard Niemi, John Mueller, and Tom W. Smith, *Trends in Public Opinion* (New York: Greenwood Press, 1989), 200.
64. "Gallup Short Subjects," *Gallup Poll Monthly* 357 (June 1995): 31–32; Survey Research Consultants International, *Index to International Public Opinion* (Westport, CT: Greenwood Press, 1996), 276.
65. Mary E. Stuckey, *The President as Interpreter-in-Chief* (Chatham, NJ: Chatham House, 1991), 134.
66. Light, *The President's Agenda*.

67. John Kingdon, *Agendas, Alternatives and Public Policies*, 2nd ed. (New York: HarperCollins, 1995).
68. Samuel Kernell, *Going Public*, 2nd ed. (Washington, DC: Congressional Quarterly Press, 1993).
69. See Steven A. Shull and Albert C. Ringelstein, "Presidential Rhetoric in Civil Rights Policy-making, 1953–1992," in James W. Riddlesperger, Jr., and Donald W. Jackson, eds., *Presidential Leadership and Civil Rights Policy* (Westport, CT: Greenwood Press, 1995) and Steven A. Shull, *The President and Civil Rights Policy: Leadership and Change* (Westport, CT: Greenwood Press, 1989).
70. Steven A. Shull. *A Kinder, Gentler Racism: The Reagan-Bush Civil Rights Legacy* (Armonk, NY: M.E. Sharpe, 1993).
71. Karlyn Kohrs Campbell and Kathleen Hall Jamieson, *Deeds Done in Words: Presidential Rhetoric and the Genres of Governance.* (Chicago: University of Chicago Press, 1990).
72. James W. Davis, *The President as Party Leader* and William W. Lammers, "Presidential Attention-Focusing Activities," in Doris A. Graber, ed., *The President and the Public* (Philadelphia: Institute for the Study of Human Issues, 1982).
73. Jeffrey E. Cohen, "Presidents, Public Opinion, and Civil Rights," in Riddlesperger and Jackson, *Presidential Leadership and Civil Rights Policy.*
74. Cohen, "President, Public Opinion, and Civil Rights."
75. Kernell, *Going Public*, 1.
76. U.S. President, "Radio and Television Report to the American People on Civil Rights—June 11, 1963," *Public Papers of the Presidents of the United States* (Washington, DC: Government Printing Office, 1964), 469.
77. U.S. President, "Annual Message to the Congress on the State of the Union, January 8, 1964," *Public Papers of the Presidents of the United States* (Washington, DC: Government Printing Office, 1965), 116.
78. U.S. President, "Address Before a Joint Session of the Congress on the State of the Union—January 25, 1988," *Public Papers of the Presidents of the United States* (Washington, DC: Government Printing Office, 1989), 88.
79. U.S. President, "The President's News Conference—August 29, 1962," *Public Papers of the Presidents of the United States* (Washington, DC: Government Printing Office, 1963).
80. Byron W. Daynes, "Pornography: Freedom of Expression or Societal Degradation?" in Tatalovich and Daynes, *Social Regulatory Policy*, 50.
81. U.S. President, "The President's Radio Address—15 April 1995," *Public Papers of the Presidents of the United States* (Washington, DC: Government Printing Office, 1996), 537–38.
82. First-generation issues include air and water pollution and second-generation issues include toxic waste, whereas third-generation issues focus on somewhat more controversial and abstract problems, including global warming, stratospheric ozone depletion, and biodiversity. Michael E. Kraft, *Environmental Policy and Politics: Toward the Twenty-First Century* (New York: HarperCollins, 1996), 14.
83. Louis Bolce, "Abortion and Presidential Elections: The Impact of Public Perceptions of Party and Candidate Positions," *Presidential Studies Quarterly* 18 (1988): 815–29.
84. Richard Nathan, *The Administrative Presidency* (New York: Wiley, 1983).
85. Tatalovich and Daynes, *Social Regulatory Policy*, 216.
86. Tatalovich and Daynes, *Social Regulatory Policy*, 122.

THE LEGISLATIVE LEADER
AND THE SOCIAL AGENDA

INTRODUCTION

A president as *legislative leader* can easily become involved in political con-
tentiousness and competitiveness with Congress. While this role is one of the
president's weaker roles, lacking in both authority and resources, it is, nevertheless, a role of lasting consequence to most presidents—and a role that can
build a president's social agenda. So significant is this role that presidency
scholars Edward Corwin and Louis Koenig once suggested that "virtually all
presidents who have made a major impact on American history have done
so in great degree as legislative leaders."[1]

Illustrating the potential combativeness of this role, Arthur Schlesinger,
Jr., compared it to "guerrilla war," with Congress ever watchful for its chance
to attack the forces of the executive branch.[2] There are many manifestations
of this conflictual behavior, of course: The President may veto important acts
of Congress, refuse to appoint persons having legislative support to administrative positions, or neglect to consult with representatives or senators on policy issues. Congress can override presidential vetoes, refuse to act on
presidential nominees for the courts and executive agencies, ignore presidential suggestions for legislation, or be reluctant to advise and consent to
the president's foreign policy overtures. Discord can also come from stag-
gered elections, in which the president and members of Congress are elected
at different times, from constituencies of various sizes, to offices of varying

term lengths. Differences can also come from "divided government," in which one party controls the Congress or one of its chambers and the other party controls the executive branch.

THE LEGISLATIVE LEADER AND THE VETO

Although as legislative leader the president occupies an acknowledged weakened role, the *veto* can be either a president's most effective instrument for enforcing his will or it can prove to be a decided sign of weakness as the president confronts the Congress. Since only about 7 percent of all regular vetoes (between the years 1789 and 1996) have ever been overridden by a two-thirds vote in both houses of the Congress, it appears as if the veto should work to the advantage of the president in building a social agenda.[3]

Yet early presidents seldom used the veto, and, in those rare instances when they did, they only vetoed legislation they thought to be unconstitutional. Although George Washington vetoed two bills, John Adams and Thomas Jefferson never cast a veto. This tradition of infrequent use of the veto, however, came to an abrupt end with President Andrew Jackson, whose twelve vetoes set a record unbroken until the presidency of Andrew Johnson. More important was Jackson's justification for those vetoes. He established a new precedent by using the veto power to *shape* public policy as well as reject it. Since Jackson, presidents have followed this precedent and have used the veto as a bargaining instrument with the Congress.

The veto has been used most frequently by liberal Democrats to secure social policy and protect the First Amendment. John Kennedy's concern for the First Amendment led to his pocket veto of a District of Columbia bill that would have required the Post Office to put up public notices to warn citizens of potentially obscene material in the U.S. mails while at the same time allowing citizens to return the questionable material to the Post Office. Kennedy felt that the bill as written was too broad and would threaten access to information. In justification of his veto, he stated: "Such a brief delay in the enactment of this legislation seems a small price to pay in order to obtain an enforceable law which will achieve the worthy objectives which prompted the bill before me."[4]

George Bush used the veto to prevent public money from being used to fund abortions, much as Ronald Reagan had done before him. In 1989, Bush vetoed an appropriations measure as well as a measure that would send money to the United Nations because both of these bills would fund abortions both in the United States as well as countries abroad.[5] Consistently supportive of the pro-life position, Bush also vetoed the 1992 amendments to the National Institutes of Health that lifted the moratorium on using fetal tissue obtained from induced abortions in tissue transfers.[6]

A more recent example was Bill Clinton's October 10, 1997, veto of a bill to ban a particular late-term abortion procedure. According to the bill, anyone who was convicted of performing such an abortion was subject to a financial penalty as well as a two-year prison term. Clinton's veto of this measure held; the Senate, on September 18, 1998, failed to achieve a two-thirds majority of 67 votes to override the veto.[7]

Dwight Eisenhower used the veto both to advance his political perspective and to add to his own social agendas. Through his veto of an amendment to the Federal Water Pollution Control Act in 1960, Eisenhower was able both to protect clean water and to ensure that the federal government did not accumulate excessive power at the expense of the states.[8]

In 1995, Bill Clinton used the veto as a defensive strategy to ward off unwanted Republican attacks against what he considered the environmental advances his administration had made during his first term. Although Clinton cast no vetoes during his first two years in office, two of his thirty vetoes cast between 1995 and 1999 were directly related to the environment. His 1995 environmental veto dealt with a fiscal year (FY) 1996 Department of the Interior appropriations bill, whereas his 1996 veto was on a land acquisition bill dealing with wildlife refuges.[9] Despite the limited number of vetoes cast by Clinton, congressional Republicans referred to him disparagingly as "Veto Bill."[10]

On close examination of those presidents who have used the veto, it is unclear whether the veto should be an index of presidential strength or one of presidential weakness for a legislative leader. For those who have relied on it but had their action overturned, the veto could be said to be a sign of weakness, as it was when Richard Nixon, concerned about the $24 billion it would cost, vetoed the Federal Pollution Control Act Amendments of 1972 on October 17, 1972. Congress clearly felt otherwise and overrode his veto the next day by a vote of 247–23 in the House and 52–12 in the Senate.[11]

The Veto Alert

For some presidents, the threat of a veto rather than the actual veto itself has been their device for notifying Congress of their wishes on the legislation at hand. In 1996, for example, Clinton left little doubt where he stood on the National Defense Authorization Act for fiscal year 1996. Opposed both to the section that would remove those affected with HIV from military service and to the section that would prevent women from obtaining abortions in military hospitals, Clinton indicated that he might veto the measure if Congress excluded these sections but also made it clear that he was very willing to work with Congress to change those sections so that he would be able to sign the measure.[12]

Clinton did not always succeed in his efforts, though. On February 28, 1996, he sent Congressman John Conyers, Jr., a message on abortion legislation indicating that he would veto any legislation that would not allow for late-term abortions when a mother's health was in question. Congress did not listen to his advice, forcing Clinton to veto the legislation two months later.[13] In his veto message on April 10, 1996, Clinton indicated that he had tried to convince Congress not to pass this bill, but he was unable to change congressional minds.[14]

George Bush did not always have his veto threats heard, either, as he responded to social policy. Bush warned members of the Senate Appropriations Committee on Federal Funding of Abortions on October 17, 1989, that he would have to veto the bill they were intending to pass because it would provide federal funding for abortions, something he and his party were opposed to.[15] Few listened to the threat, and Bush ended up having to cast yet another veto, this time against the Departments of Labor, Health and Human Services, and Education, and Related Agencies Appropriation Act of 1990.[16] Two years later, President Bush threatened again to veto an affirmative action bill with built in-quotas—something Bush and his fellow Republicans had long opposed. This time, congressional leaders realized that Bush was serious and wrote a different version of the bill that excluded quotas.[17]

THE PARTY AND THE CONGRESSIONAL PROCESS

George Edwards was right when he suggested that regardless of how much shall in legislative relations a president possesses, this skill operates at the margins of legislative leadership.[18] Even with the president in control of the veto, Congress has the decided advantage, if not the dominant influence.[19] Perhaps this is the reason Franklin Roosevelt met every Monday with congressional leaders to keep abreast of their activity on his programs.[20] Ronald Reagan and Bill Clinton also recognized the importance of working through their own party leadership to facilitate passage of legislation. Of Bill Clinton's efforts to stay in close contact with congressional leaders, Richard Berke observed that "at times it can be hard to figure out who is working for whom."[21]

While presidents clearly have advantages in dealing with Congress when they have substantial party support, it can be on occasion a double-edged sword. Conventional wisdom suggests that where a president's party has a majority of the seats in the House and the Senate, that president has a better chance of getting his program enacted. Since World War II, any presumed benefits from "unified government" have flowed to Democratic presidents because, until Bill Clinton, it was more likely that Republican presidents had to deal with divided government at some time during their tenure. Since 1933, Democratic presidents had Democratic Congresses for all but six of these years—1946–48 under Truman, and 1995–96 and 1997–98 under Clinton—while Republican presidents were able to work with Republican Congresses for only two years—1953–55 under Eisenhower—and a Republican Senate for another six years—1981–86 under Reagan. Nixon, Ford, and Bush confronted Democratic majorities in both House and Senate during their entire time in office.

The advantage of unified government can be seen in the avalanche of New Deal and Great Society legislation under Franklin Roosevelt and Lyndon

Johnson. Clearly, without this advantage, gridlock or stalemate might have resulted, posing some additional difficulties for these two presidents. Yet David Mayhew and Charles Jones indicate that legislative deadlock has been relatively rare and has *not* frequently characterized the political system. Studying the major legislation that has come from Congress as well as congressional investigations of the executive branch affairs over five decades, Mayhew concluded that Congress was equally productive during eras of divided or unified rule.[22] Jones examined the role played by both houses of Congress and their various committees and concluded that it was rare for any president, Republican or Democrat, to have his way with Congress in shaping legislation.[23] In their 1999 study of Congress, David Epstein and Sharyn O'Halloran indicate that divided government was not significant as far as the volume of important legislation passed by Congress, but it was probably more important as to the content of that legislation. As an example, they point to the Civil Rights Acts of 1957 and 1960 under divided government as more limited in scope than the Civil Rights Acts of 1964 and 1965, passed during unified government.[24]

Jimmy Carter, according to one analyst, became a "trusteeship" president who naively wanted to do what was right, not what was politically expedient. He was forced to tackle "new"issues that were not amenable to solutions based on Democratic liberalism.[25] Environmental issues and the energy crisis, for example, could not be resolved by debating left-right principles. This explanation does not absolve Carter's lack of legislative skills nor his inexperience but accounts partly for his unwillingness to be ideologically joined with many of the Democratic leaders of Congress.

Confrontation between the president and Congress became the regular pattern of interaction as Bill Clinton tried to deal with the Republican-dominated 104th Congress, which had a negative effect on social policy. Clinton could not tame this Congress, which had in mind his defeat in 1996. Once Republicans became the majority party in Congress after the 1994 midterm election, the partisan strategy based on Newt Gingrich's and Dick Armey's "Contract with America" policy undercut many of the social policies supported by the president and focused Republican energies. The greatest threat in the Contract to the administration's social agenda was its stand against environmental legislation. As Carol Browner, Environmental Protection Agency head, saw it, this Congress would "undermine virtually every public-health and environmental protection that Americans have come to depend on."[26] To do this, congressional Republicans complicated the legislative process with funding as a primary tool, using risk-assessment, cost-benefit analysis and doing away with unfounded mandates.[27] Moreover, Republican efforts to reduce both health protections and public safety and environmental regulations were also frequent. House Republicans reduced Fish and Wildlife programs by $2 billion, making it impossible to list additional endangered animals to the protected category, as well as taking $1.3 billion from a fund set aside to ensure safe drinking water.[28] A final action of the 104th Congressional Republicans was to reduce budgeting for the national park system, insisting that spending should be decreased by 36 percent and risking closure of more than 200 national parks.[29] In reflecting on the Republican control of the new Congress, environmentalist Michael W. Robbins, editor of *Audubon*, stated in the March-April 1995 issue: "What's alarming is the ignorance and radical anti-government view . . . held by some congressmen now chairing key House committees. In their 'hurl-out-the-baby-with-the-bath water' zeal to reduce the federal government, these ideologues assault the very idea of the commonwealth."[30]

STRATEGIES OF THE LEGISLATIVE LEADER

In this sort of uncertain milieu, what separates the successful legislative leader from the mediocre one as far as building a strong social agenda? For one thing, the successful legislative leader must rely on *individual skills* of the negotiator and persuader as well as *external resources* and *creativity* to compensate for the fact that a president has little real authority to exert over Congress in this role.

Budget Strategies

A legislative leader who succeeds in encouraging the passage of social policy recognizes the benefits of having sufficient funds to build a social agenda. Franklin Roosevelt and Bill Clinton both indicated that environmental policy was important to them. This could be seen in the budgetary allotments for the environment they insisted on. Roosevelt devoted as much as 20.8 percent of his budget in 1935 to environmental concerns, whereas the lowest percentage of the budget devoted to environmental and conservation policy in that first term came in 1936, with 11.2 percent devoted to environmental pursuits. While Clinton's percentages were much lower, Clinton's overall budget, of course, was much higher. Clinton devoted 1.3 percent of the budget to the environment, in 1994 and 1.4 percent in 1995.[31]

Aware that he needed additional money to build a strong social agenda, Clinton was particularly bothered by what he perceived as monetary constraints that were threatening his plan to restore the Florida Everglades in the Water Resources Development Act of 1996. While the federal government was set to pay 35 percent of the total, Clinton wanted the federal government to pay at least 50 percent, since he was concerned that state money would run out before the total restoration project was completed.[32]

Other presidents have also shown how crucial money is to the support of a social agenda, as Richard Nixon did when he asked congressional leaders in his Annual Budget message for fiscal year 1972 for $2.4 billion more than Congress was willing to provide for the environment.[33] The next year, Nixon changed his strategy, asking Congress for $5 billion for the environment but as an allotment to the states to assist them in their environmental programs.[34]

Ronald Reagan found he could starve environmental legislation by reducing funds allotted to environmental programs, as he did in 1985, when he cut a Soil and Water Conservation Bill in order to "avoid the specter of higher interest rates, choked-off investment, renewed recession, and rising unemployment."[35]

Strategies in Speeches

Presidents who have been effective as legislative leaders have put their case before the Congress in formal speeches as well as informal ones both to give greater visibility to the issue and to indicate how important social policy is to the president's agenda.

Franklin Roosevelt and Bill Clinton were both careful to focus on environmental policy priorities in their State of the Union addresses. Roosevelt chose a special message, explaining a veto, to present to Congress his comprehensive national plan for conservation and water resources.[36]

Ronald Reagan also used communication with Congress to attempt to change its orientation on environmental issues, encouraging Congress to cut back on federal funding of environmental programs in an effort to shift more responsibility to the states. In his July 14, 1984 radio address, he asked Congress for additional money for the environment so that the federal government could purchase lands for additional national parkland and let the states take more responsibility for environmental issues.[37]

Ronald Reagan was consistent in his demands of the Congress on environmental policy, requesting that private enterprise become more involved with environmental concerns. In 1986, it appeared as if the president and environmentalists shared something in common. At that time, in his Annual Report of the Council on Environmental Quality for 1986, Reagan asked Congress for more money to supplement the Superfund program to clean up the environment more effectively. This was where environmentalists and Reagan differed, since Reagan, in order not to spend governmental resources to manage the environment, would support the additional funds for clean-up only if market practices were used.[38]

Like Roosevelt, Eisenhower used a special message to the Congress to stress the need to pass new laws that would make the desegregation of schools a federal crime as well as to request financial aid from the federal government to assist states in the desegregation process.[39]

Lyndon Johnson took civil rights and affirmative action most seriously and used every technique possible to encourage passage of his measures. On March 15, 1965, he delivered a special message to Congress on the progress and state of civil rights and affirmative action and then delivered a second special message concerning how many African Americans were denied the right to vote. As part of his civil rights campaign, Johnson challenged Congress in a special message on April 28, 1966, pleading for prompt action and stronger civil rights legislation.[40]

Richard Nixon devoted his greatest energies to obscenity and pornography issues in 1970, using his State of the Union message on January 22 of that year to set the theme that he would echo in each congressional district where he campaigned for Republicans during the midterm elections—namely, that government was to have a special responsibility to bring a halt to pornography. Legislation, however, was not forthcoming, which prompted Nixon to send Congress another special message in September. The next month, while he was on the campaign trail, Nixon rebuked the Congress for doing so little on his antipornography legislation. He pledged that despite Congress's reluctance, he would do all in his power to eliminate "smut," declaring: "So long as I am in the White House, there will be no relaxation of the national effort to control and eliminate smut from our national life."[41] Some eighteen months passed before Congress responded to Nixon's pressure to pass his antipornography legislation. As one might have expected, of course, this was just before the election.[42] In 1971, President Nixon made his last strong appeal to convince Congress to enact antipornography legislation by resubmitting two pieces of legislation designed to enforce strong penalties and use the federal government's power through interstate commerce to limit pornography.[43] Nixon made it quite clear to Congress that it was essential to act immediately since he saw that "the tide of offensive materials seems yet to be rising."[44]

While Congress did not respond to Nixon's repeated messages about the need to eliminate pornography, his messages were heard by the people. In a Harris poll taken in January 1971, the public was asked who among the candidates for office—Nixon, Muskie, or George Wallace—could best control pornography. While not winning by an overpowering margin, Nixon did win the support of 32 percent of the public, with Muskie attracting 25 percent support and Wallace 11 percent.[45] After 1971, Nixon made no more official speeches on the subject, nor did he take any further action against pornography during his second term except for mentioning his past successes, boasting in 1973 how he had used the federal government to protect the citizenry from the evils of pornography.[46]

While Ronald Reagan exhibited little interest as legislative leader in antipornography legislation during his first term, he became active during his second term, sponsoring ten pieces of antipornography legislation. On January 25, 1984, he told a Joint Session of Congress in his State of the Union message that "parents need to know their children will not be victims of child pornography and abduction. This year we will intensify our drive against these and other horrible crimes like sexual abuse and family violence."[47] By May 1984, Reagan had signed the Child Protection Act of 1984 (PL 98-292), expressing his disgust for those who abuse children. In strong language, he charged that "there's no one lower or more vicious than a person who would profit from the abuse of children, whether by using them in pornographic material or by encouraging their sexual abuse by distributing this material."[48] He added that pornography was "ugly and dangerous" and that he did not believe the findings and conclusion drawn by the 1967 Presidential Commission on Obscenity and Pornography that there was no connection between explicit sexual materials and delinquent or criminal behavior. Reagan maintained that there was such a link "between child molesting and pornography" and one between "pornography and sexual violence." He stressed that if no action was taken to protect the children of the nation, "then we, as a society, just aren't worth much."[49] The next year Reagan emphasized again the need for stronger child pornography laws to ban its production for private and commercial use, as well as halting its advertising.[50] The president felt sure he could achieve his objectives by adapting the 1962 Racketeer Influenced and Corrupt Organizations Act (RICO) laws originally written to restrict racketeering and control corrupt industries, for use against the pornography industry.[51]

In that same year, President Reagan made it clear to Congress what the most important issue in his social agenda was in his Message to the Congress on the Agenda for the Future. His address had plenty of references to his social agenda, affirming that he was willing to exert time, energy and funding in his fight against abortion.[52] By 1988, he also alerted the Congress to two other aspects of his social agenda when he noted his goals to both eliminate discrimination and to decrease the spread of child pornography, in his Legislature and Administrative Message: A Union of Individuals address.[53]

Bill Clinton often used the State of the Union message to encourage the passage of social policy. In 1995, this message reflected his opposition to any repeal of the assault weapons ban. As he stated: "A lot of people have laid down their seats in Congress so that police officers and kids wouldn't have to lay down their lives under the hail of assault weapon attack, and I will not let that be repealed. I will not let it be repealed."[54]

The Bully Pulpit.   Presidents have also used the bully pulpit to offer additional support for social legislation and to bring added pressures on the Congress to pass legislation. Franklin Roosevelt used his overwhelming success in the legislature during his first hundred days in office to his advantage in his campaign addresses for his second term to put additional pressures on the Congress to respond even more favorably to the president. During his first term, Roosevelt managed to send fourteen major pieces of legislation to Congress, including the important acts that authorized the Tennessee Valley Authority (TVA) and the Civilian Conservation Corps (CCC).

Richard Nixon recognized it was the power of the bully pulpit that would actually determine whether his social legislation passed or not. Nixon proposed making it a federal crime to mail unsolicited pornographic materials to youths under the age of eighteen, but he also appealed to the public to become involved in a grassroots movement against pornography, recognizing that statutory laws are one thing but that the people's wishes and desires were clearly most important in ridding the nation of pornography. He maintained that "when indecent books no longer find a market, when pornographic films can no longer draw an audience, when obscene plays open to empty houses, then the tide will turn. Government can maintain the dikes against obscenity, but only people can turn back the tide."[55] In a September 1969 speech to the National Governors' Conference, in fact, President Nixon again announced that antipornography legislation was one of his twenty-four high priority issues for congressional action.

In his message to Congress transmitting the proposed legislation (the Child Protection and Obscenity Enforcement Act of 1987), Ronald Reagan acknowledged how critical public support was to the success of his legislation. "The Federal Government alone just does not have the resources to do the whole job. We will need all the help we can get from decent-minded citizens across the country who know when it is time to stand up and be counted."[56] To further assist in the passage of this bill, at a 1987 White House briefing Reagan put the power of interstate commerce behind the effort to bring to a halt trafficking in pornography when he supported an amendment that would "prohibit the use of Federal roads, interstate railroads, motor vehicles, boats, airplanes, or other methods for obscenity trafficking across State lines." This meant, he explained, that "an interstate phone call from a retailer to a distributor regarding an interstate shipment of obscenity would itself be a criminal offense, as would be the use of the mails to pay for such a shipment."[57]

In 1993, a year after he came into office, Bill Clinton used the bully pulpit to reinvigorate interest among the public in social policy. On September 24, 1993, he talked to reporters supporting gun control legislation and opposing assault weapons. He not only supported the Brady bill,[58] but announced through the Office of Press Secretary exactly what he was going to ask of Congress in the near future. On December 6, 1998, in a radio address, Clinton told listeners first that there should be a permanent waiting period of at least three days to check the records of those purchasing handguns; second, that checks for "violent juveniles" should be expanded; and third, that gun show checks for those purchasing weapons should be instituted.[59] Clinton also used question-and-answer sessions with small groups of people to put forth his position on social legislation, as he did on October 2, 1995, when he justified his support of the assault weapons ban, despite its unpopularity, by suggesting that it was the right thing to do.[60]

Bill-Signing Ceremonies.   The more successful legislative leaders have also enhanced the visibility of their social policies through bill-signing ceremonies in an effort to win added support for their legislation.

One of the more interesting signing ceremonies took place in 1968, when Lyndon Johnson authorized a gun control measure and then promptly wrote a letter to *Washington Post* editorial writer Alan Barth thanking him for the many pieces he had written that had laid a groundwork for the federal gun control legislation that he signed.[61]

Richard Nixon also maximized the use of the bill-signing ceremony to focus attention on the environment. When he signed the Clean Air Amendments of 1970, he took the opportunity to lay before the public his environmental vision for that year, labeling the new year the "Year of the Environment." Later he suggested that he had been influenced by Theodore Roosevelt in making this designation.[62]

George Bush stated a number of times that clean air, particularly improving the air in polluted urban areas, was a high priority of his. In signing the Clean Air Act of 1990, he indicated that passing this law had been the culmination of his administration's year-long crusade. "It is my mission to guarantee it for this generation and for the generations to come," Bush stated. "Mission defined, mission accomplished."[63]

When Bush decided he wanted to convince Americans that he was an "environmental president," he used a bill-signing ceremony at the Grand Canyon to sign an environmental agreement to emphasize the point. On September 18, 1991, he praised this Grand Canyon agreement as a major landmark because it had been passed as a result of a heterogeneous group of supporters.[64] Despite this signing, not everyone believed that Bush was really a committed environmentalist. He therefore found it necessary to repeat his commitment to the environment as he signed the Los Padres Condor Range and River Protection Act in June 1992, but this time he did not return to the park area for the bill signing.[65]

On occasion presidents have also used these signing opportunities to criticize Congress for not responding as they felt it should. When he signed the Safe Drinking Water Act Amendments of 1996, Bill Clinton accused Congress of forfeiting the use of some funds that might have been available because of its slow pace in passing the measure.[66]

In reflecting on his years in office, Ronald Reagan maintained that antipornography had been one of his highest-priority concerns. While signing the Anti-Drug Abuse Act of 1988, he excoriated those who sold and distributed pornographic materials, reminding all that in addition to this new anti-drug bill there were also "harsh new laws to deter the greedy and heartless who sell or distribute obscene material or child pornography. With fines up to $100,000 and prison terms of 20 years, we hope to put these people out of business for good."[67] In recognizing the enormity of his task, Reagan admitted: "Our battles aren't fought by any single person nor can they be won by a single bill, but with the measures we have taken over the past 8 years and the significant additions made today, we are one step closer to an America free of the degrading and dehumanizing effect of obscene material and child pornography."[68]

As far as pornography was concerned, George Bush's primary focus was also the elimination of child pornography. Here he praised his own administration's successful "Project Postporn" for its near elimination of mail-order pornography. As a legislative leader, he gladly signed the Crime Control Act of 1990, a bill that had a section devoted to protecting children from child abuse and child pornography.[69]

Bill Clinton, wanting to convince Congress that he was serious about his opposition to child pornography, selected December 1995 as a time to sign legislation to increase the penalties for all those convicted of encouraging children to engage in sexual offenses and for those who distributed pictures of those events. For those convicted of causing a child to engage in sexually explicit offenses before a camera, the penalty would become seventy to eighty-seven months in prison. For those convicted of distributing visual pictures of such activities, penalties increased to twenty-four to thirty months in prison.[70]

Related to this, Clinton also encouraged the passage of the Telecommunications Act of 1996, which had, as a part of the statute, the Communications Decency Act, which dealt with obscenity, harassment, and the misuse of telecommunications facilities. Opponents of the bill pointed to failure to define crucial terms like *decency, obscenity, lewdness,* or *sexually explicitness,* leaving the interpretation of these disputable terms in the hands of those who would implement the law and, ultimately, in the hands of lower court judges. On this matter, the president lost out to the Supreme Court, which declared this portion of the act unconstitutional.[71]

George Bush used the occasion of bill signing to present an elaborate exposition of his political and social philosophy. As he signed the Civil Rights Act of 1991, for example, he made sure that everyone knew that he was delighted that this bill did not encourage the establishment of quotas, which was one thing he clearly rejected. Bush also took the opportunity to spell out his vision of what America could be — where all could have a job if they wished; where all could receive a first-rate education; where all could have a right to equal protection under the law; where all could be assured of a climate free from despair.[72] In the same speech he stated: "I believe in the ideals we all share, ideals that made America great: decency, fairness, faith, hard work, generosity, vigor."[73]

Lobbying Congress

Lobbying incorporates actions and activities designed to influence public officials. This is precisely what the president does in approaching Congress and attempting to persuade members of Congress to his way of thinking. Such contact can take various forms, depending on the particular president and or the situation presented. A president like Lyndon Johnson often used strong-arm tactics with Congressional members but could also appeal intellectually or emotionally to members of Congress and their families to persuade them to his way of thinking. Johnson did his best to pressure Congress into passing effective affirmative action and civil rights legislation. In a statement following the Senate's passage of the Civil Rights Bill of 1964, Johnson indicated that the passage of this act was a beginning that would help "educate" people, help them be "civil" to one another, and help renew commitments to equal rights.[74] In a news conference in 1966, Johnson announced and outlined his intentions for Congress, stating that he had already requested more than 90 bills that should be passed and expected that the House would act on at least 70 of them during this particular session.[75]

In addition to these techniques, Johnson wrote letters to congressional leaders to encourage and instruct them on how and when to pass civil rights legislation. In 1965, he wrote such a letter to the President of the Senate proposing ways to eliminate barriers to the right to vote;[76] in 1968, he wrote two letters to the Speakers of the House asking the House to pass his Civil Rights bill and his Fair Housing Bill.[77]

Richard Nixon used a news conference to lobby Congress when he advocated a gun control position to handle the sale of "Saturday night specials"—the weapons then most commonly *used* in street crime. He announced in his news Conference that he had asked the Senate Judiciary Committee to generate a consensus and compromise on gun control so that the bill that came out of committee would not offend hunters.[78]

Clinton also exerted some psychological pressure on Congress in selecting the name for a legislation he introduced in 1995 designed to limit the availability of handgun armor-piercing ammunition. The name he came up with was "Saving Law Enforcement Officers' Lives Act of 1995." What Congressperson would dare oppose a bill with a name like that?[79] Clinton could also get very specific in his instructions and criticisms of Congress. During an exchange with reporters on November 19, 1993, he began, to congratulate the Senate for passing his crime bill. Then he criticized the Senate and House for not coming to an agreement on their mutual differences and strongly repeated his distress over the Senate's filibuster of the Brady Bill.[80]

Clinton also felt he should lobby Congress on gun control during a flight from Paris to a meeting in Cologne on June 17, 1999. While in flight he was busily telephoning Republican and Democratic members, asking them to support Rep. Carolyn McCarthy's (D–NY) gun control measure that would require a gun show background check within three business days; gun records would then be destroyed within ninety days after the sale. Unfortunately for the president, these efforts were not enough and could not overpower lobbying by the National Rifle Association (NRA) and its supporters. The measure lost by a vote of 235–193.[81]

Richard Nixon perhaps best exhibited his lobbying style during the campaign years 1968–69. He was most persistent with his demands on Congress to pass his antipornography legislation. In late December 1968, even before he took office, Nixon made it clear that legislation was necessary in order to make the mailing of pornographic material to children a criminal offense. The following year, in a special message to Congress, Nixon announced his intention to propose legislation that would stop the "peddlers of obscenity."[82] He did not know what could best be done to counteract obscenity, he stated, but he was willing to experiment with what had not been tried. Consequently, he announced to Congress in 1969 that he would ask the attorney general and postmaster general to submit three proposals that would protect children from receiving pornographic materials in the mails as well as restrict advertising of pornographic materials.[83] When Congress did not act immediately on the Nixon proposals, the president used this delay to blame congressional Democrats for the lack of response.

Ronald Reagan, looking for every opportunity to convince policymakers of his pro-life position on abortion, went so far as to encourage select members of the Senate to support an Anti-Abortion Amendment to a Federal Debt Ceiling Bill in 1982.[84] To the public he recommended that individual citizens encourage their representatives to pass his Human Life Amendment. He also urged Congress to write legislation to prevent women from getting abortions to satisfy their "psychiatric" needs. Reagan's solution to the increases in the number of abortions was to encourage an increase in adoptions.[85]

Bill Clinton would often use his weekly radio addresses to lobby Congress for legislation he saw as necessary. He would often disagree with Congress on the radio, as he did on June 24, 1995, when he expressed his opposition to legislation before Congress that would restrict abortion to mothers on welfare and women serving in the military.[86] Clinton also used personal messages sent to congressional leaders to express his opposition to that same legislation to express his disagreement with the action taken by Congress because the legislation would deny poor women abortions even in cases of rape or incest. On that score, he stated: "I will not allow our people to be sacrificed for the sake of political ideology."[87]

Clinton could also be direct in his criticism of legislation. Considering water pollution on May 30, 1995, he indicated that if Congress should pass the legislation that was being considered, the water would end up dirtier than before; that if the current legislation should pass, the water would get progressively worse. He then blamed the particular form of the bill on the lawyers and lobbyists.[88]

Social legislation was extremely important to Bill Clinton. He even lobbied the Congress while acting in his chief diplomat role, engaged in foreign policy concerns. The first such example was in a 1996 news conference with Chancellor Helmut Kohl of Germany, when he directed the concerns of the news conference to domestic homosexuality concerns indicating that he was quite willing to allow states to deny recognition of homosexual marriages that occurred in other states.[89]

Presidential Style

At times, Congress has submitted to the force of a president's personality and the support he has had from his own party members.

The Johnson Style. Lyndon Johnson had a forceful style, sophisticated political instincts, and a keen knowledge of how Congress worked. Yet pushing civil rights through Congress taxed even his abilities. As a southerner, however, and using some of the same techniques he used as the prototype majority leader in the Senate, Johnson was able to do the impossible in working with southern congresspersons in passing effective affirmative action legislation as well as gun control measures.

In addition to style, of course, Johnson had political support outside the Congress during his early years as president. In the election of 1964, Lyndon Johnson's margin of victory over Barry Goldwater was of landslide proportions, so his coattails carried many new liberal Democrats into the Congress.[90] Democrats in the 89th Congress also had the largest majorities in the House (295–140) and the Senate (68–32) since 1937. Moreover, President Johnson was popular with the American people, enjoying an approval rating of 66 percent in 1965.[91] His success in passing so many of the Great Society domestic programs was due chiefly to the size of these Democratic majorities in Congress.

Because Johnson assumed office in 1963 following President Kennedy's assassination, he began his tenure with extraordinary national unity. The early 1960s was also a time of economic prosperity (the most prosperous decade since World War II), which provided rising federal revenues and a positive mood for Johnson's Great Society proposals. Congress was responsive to Johnson because he was a product of the Senate, having spent twenty-three years there including his eight years as Senate majority leader. Unlike Kennedy, Johnson was a Texan and as such had good rapport with the senior Southern Democrats in both chambers. That meant that Johnson, as president, could work with relatively few congressional leaders, including those in the so-called "inner club" of Southern Democrats who effectively controlled the Senate, and be assured of the votes needed from the rank and file for his programs. Whenever Southern Democrats refused support for a Johnson program, specifically on civil rights legislation, Johnson was able through his long experience in the Senate, to reach out to those in the other party, working closely with minority party leader Senator Everett McKinley Dirksen (R–IL).

Johnson was an activist legislative leader who personally courted congresspersons. He delighted in shepherding a bill through the legislative process, confronting committee chairs when necessary, and appealing to the rank and file. LBJ's success in the 89th Congress (1965–1966) was better than any president during the entire 1953–1995 period.

Johnson used all of his strengths in pushing through social legislation. In considering Johnson's and Clinton's successes on gun control, for example, Joseph A. Califano, Jr., a former aide to Johnson, said, "If Clinton gets to sign some sort of gun control legislation, he might take the opportunity to acknowledge that another president [namely, Lyndon Johnson] 'took on' the NRA and got Congress to act."[92] Califano went on to suggest that even though Bill Clinton saw himself as the first president to take on the National Rifle

Association on gun control, it was Lyndon Johnson who demanded national registration of all guns and licensing of gun owners, encouraged Congress to limit access of minors to guns, and pushed for prohibition of mail order guns and the importation of the "Saturday night special."[93]

The Carter Style.   Jimmy Carter, by contrast, represented quite a different sort of legislative leader. Carter was depicted by the press as indecisive and irresolute in his dealings with others. He did not always consult with members of Congress nor vigorously lobby them, which is why this president suffered some very close victories, too many narrow defeats, and much unnecessary criticism.

Not all of Carter's problems were the result of his personal style, of course; Congress in 1977 was quite a different institution than it had been during Johnson's term. Congressional scholars have characterized the post-1973 Congress as a "post-reformed" Congress[94] because it had democratized its internal procedures. In the aftermath of Vietnam and Watergate, Congress also reasserted its authority over war-making and the budgeting process. Moreover, congressional Democrats owed Jimmy Carter very little since Carter ran well behind most Democrats who sought reelection in 1976.

The Democratic leadership in Congress no longer could dictate terms to its rank-and-file members and had to contend with the newly reformed but fragmented decision-making process. Standing committees lost power to their subcommittees, and longstanding legislative caucuses like the liberal Democratic Study Group and the House Wednesday Group of moderate Republicans were joined by many groups such as the Black Caucus and Hispanic Caucus, which represented special interests.

Eventually Carter learned from his mistakes. His legislative liaison staff became more effective in building a working relationship with Democratic leaders in Congress by 1978, and the president began to lobby Congress in order to win some narrow victories. Carter also corrected one of his worst legislative mistakes by limiting his priority bills, thereby allowing his liaison staff to concentrate their limited resources on fewer bills. Commenting on the improved Carter liaison efforts, one observer noted that "what began as a comedy of errors has definitely matured . . . now people on the Hill are more willing to work with Frank Moore[assistant to the president for congressional liaison]."[95]

The Bush Style.   A completely different sets of problems gripped the legislative leadership of George Bush, who faced divided government and intense partisanship on Capitol Hill. At first, Bush's open and bipartisan approach was welcomed by Congress. But Bush's bipartisan overtures did not last long as he confronted the Democratic-controlled 102nd Congress. A *New York Times* columnist described it this way:

> A furious exchange over the presidential campaign was a typical punctuation mark for the end of a Congress that began with stately speeches about

the Gulf war but dissolved quickly into partisan wrangling over the economy. Then it descended into dismal reflection over the House bank scandal and the Senate Judiciary Committee's handling of the Clarence Thomas-Anita Hill confrontation over allegations of sexual harassment.[96]

George Bush did his utmost to protect a presidency under siege by the Congress. Secretary of Defense Dick Cheney described Bush's dilemma this way: "The president . . . genuinely respects the role of Congress, but he also has decided to stand up forthrightly to preserve the powers of his own office."[97] This attitude was bound to lead to frequent clashes between the branches, and it did. The veto became a primary weapon of the Bush presidency, and in terms of numbers Bush was successful. While he cast thirty five vetoes before any were overridden,[98] his reliance on the veto power bore out the ominous prediction from Professor Robert Spitzer that "as a substantive power, it is potent, but politically dangerous for presidents who use it too much."[99]

The consequence of George Bush's rancor against Congress was legislative disaster. Bush's presidential "support" score in Congress for 1992, indicating how often legislators voted on bills in conformity with the president's wishes, it was the second lowest since the 1950s and his 1990 score was the fourth worst in terms of getting legislators to support his policy positions. None of his major 1992 legislative requests from the State of the Union message—health care reform, education proposals, or economic recovery package—was acted upon.[100]

These *three presidents* as legislative leaders represent success and failure in the legislative process. Lyndon Johnson, as a successful legislative leader, was able to convince the Congress to pass his social legislation—even affirmative action and civil rights bills. Both Carter and Bush, while successful on selected issues, as Table 3.1 indicates—Carter on affirmative action and Bush on the environment—were less successful in building their overall social agendas, which suffered as a result of their weakened legislative leadership.

Issue Focus and Individual Style

Presidents have found it somewhat easier to commit their time and effort to those policies that they are most committed to.

Roosevelt and the Environment.   One of Franklin Roosevelt's favorite areas of focus was the environment—particularly forestry and the use of public lands. In his first term, Roosevelt's agenda included legislation bearing two of his environmental interests, forestry and national parks, as well as legislation dealing with crop rotation, dam construction, water pollution, and preserving natural resources. Roosevelt was able to use his legislative skills effectively to have his domestic and foreign program adopted.[101] While campaigning in Elkins, West Virginia, on October 1, 1936, he detailed the passage of three environmental bills that he was particularly pleased with—the Duck Stamp Bill, the

Table 3.1 Presidents as Legislative Leaders and the Social Issues on Which They Focused Most Attention[1]

President	Issues
F. ROOSEVELT	• ENVIRONMENT[1] • [affirmative action]
TRUMAN	• environment, especially conservation • affirmative action • guns
EISENHOWER	• environment, especially conservation • affirmative action
KENNEDY	• [environment] • affirmative action
JOHNSON	• AFFIRMATIVE ACTION (active) • guns • pornography
NIXON	• guns—Saturday night specials • PORNOGRAPHY • abortion • ENVIRONMENT • affirmative action, equal access to housing
FORD	• environment • guns
CARTER	• AFFIRMATIVE ACTION (active) • environment
REAGAN	• ABORTION • [environment] • guns (even after being shot) • pornography, child pornography
BUSH	• ENVIRONMENT • guns • pornography, child pornography • affirmative action
CLINTON	• HOMOSEXUALITY • environment • GUNS • pornography • ABORTION • AFFIRMATIVE ACTION

[1]Capital letters designate issues on which presidents focused *most* of their attention. Lower case letters indicate other areas in which they were active. Issues suggest that a president paid some attention to these issues but not much when compared with other presidents.

Coordination Bill, and the Robinson Bill—to alert those in the Congress and other policymakers that he was supportive of the environment.[102]

Reagan and Abortion.   Anti-abortion legislation was probably the social policy that Ronald Reagan fought hardest for. Reagan felt comfortable in speak-

ing about abortion while defending his pro-life stance a
passage of pro-life legislation and a pro-life constitutional
abortion.[103] He used every possible means to convince Co
pro-life protections and thwart pro-choice legislation. In
Union message, Reagan claimed that the unborn needed !
achieve legal protections.[104] In his 1985 State of the Union message,
discourage the use of abortion by encouraging protection of the unborn.[105]

Other social policies Reagan supported were spelled out by Reagan in
a special January 27, 1987 Message to Congress titled. "A Quest for Excellence." In this address Reagan identified his social agenda, including the need
to prohibit federal funds from being used to fund abortions, the need to curb
child pornography, the need to pass a constitutional amendment to allow students to pray in school, the need to enforce civil rights legislation, and the
need to clean up the environment.[106] A year later, Reagan returned to a focus
on abortion, since he felt that Congress was not doing enough to curb it; this
led him thereafter to attach anti-abortion amendments to most of the legislation he submitted to Congress.[107] He became even bolder when he transmitted to Congress the Pro-Life Act of 1988, which would ban abortions and do
away with the basic guaranteed right to abortion that had been established in
Roe v. Wade.[108] In his 1988 legislative and administrative message, titled "A
Union of Individuals," Reagan asked Congress again to pass the Human Life
Bill and the Human Life Amendment.[109]

Crisis and Guns

Crisis may strengthen a president's leadership in Congress, but it is an
unreliable adjunct to legislative leadership in day-to-day lawmaking. Crisis
can serve as a reason for introducing social legislation to Congress, if not
always assuring its passage. After the Kennedy assassination in 1963, gun
control measures were introduced in 1965 to limit the sale of mail-order handguns to minors. As Robert Spitzer argues, however, even a successful legislative leader like Lyndon Johnson could not assure passage of any gun control
measure until after the shock of the two 1968 assassinations of Martin Luther
King, Jr., and Senator Robert F. Kennedy.[110]

Presidents Ford and Reagan were also the targets of attempted assassinations, but they remained defenders of gun access. And while George Bush
made an impressive statement against guns by renouncing his membership
in the National Rifle Association (NRA), it was not until the massacre of twelve
innocent high school students at Littleton, Colorado, in 1999 that such a crisis
offered the president some leverage to encourage the passage of gun
restrictions. Yet even this crisis could not assure Bill Clinton that the sort of
strong restrictions he wanted would result in legislation passed by a Congress
still so responsive to the NRA pro-gun perspective.

To encourage the passage of stronger gun control restrictions, a group of
eighty high school students from the Littleton-Denver area came to Washington

ly 15, 1999, and met with President Clinton. In 1999 Clinton became more involved with gun control than any other president since Lyndon Johnson when he decided both to console the friends and family of those victims who had been shot and to lobby Congress to ban assault weapons. On July 15, 1999, he also demanded that congressional leaders should listen to what 80 high school students from Littleton, Colorado and the Denver area had to say and then should immediately send gun control measures to the White House for his signature. Specifically, Clinton asked Congress to pass measures that would prevent weapons from being sold at gun shows without background checks on purchasers, that would insist that child safety locks to be installed on every handgun sold, that would restrict "violent juveniles" from owning guns, and that would ban the importation of high-capacity ammunition clips.[111]

Again, while crisis conditions have helped presidents like Lyndon Johnson to pass the Kennedy-Johnson social welfare programs, after the Kennedy assassination, and to take a more aggressive stance in support of gun control, it has not always helped other presidents in the same way. In 1995, for example, Clinton had to introduce legislation to counteract the Supreme Court's decision in *U.S. v. Lopez* (1995),[112] when the Court ruled that guns were not part of interstate commerce and could not be controlled by school systems—and that thus no "gun-free" zones could be created around schools. Clinton transmitted the Gun-Free School Zones Amendments Act of 1995, to circumvent this decision, stating: "I am committed to doing everything in my power to make school places where young people can be secure, where they can learn and where parents can be confident that discipline is enforced."[113]

CONCLUSION

For many reasons, presidential power in the role of legislative leader is problematic. A president lacks the authority to force Congress to enact his programs and instead must rely on resources and political skills or strategies unrelated to the role to prevent total dominance by Congress. In other words, for a president to succeed in this role—and we have had a number of presidents who were successful legislative leaders—a president must appreciate the myriad of political conditions that increase or decrease his ability to influence the legislative process and then must go well beyond the formal legal relationship he has with Congress to achieve his goals.

As a result of the difficult situation, most presidents enjoy rather modest records as legislative leaders, following more the Carter or Bush model than that of Lyndon Johnson. Those presidents who have been most effective in strengthening their social agendas in this role have approached Congress with clear priorities and persuasive messages, enhancing their chances of success for their social agendas. Table 3.1 indicates the differences that we have observed in those legislative leaders who have succeeded in passing legislation on the various social issues. Bill Clinton and Richard Nixon appear to have the best records as legislative leaders.

In terms of style, those presidents who seemed most assertive in pushing their social policies—Ronald Reagan, George Bush, Jimmy Carter, Lyndon Johnson, and Franklin Roosevelt—would join Clinton and Nixon in that category, as Table 3.2 shows. Truman, Kennedy, Eisenhower, and Ford could be described more as *reactors* when it came to encouraging the passage of social policy. Often the reactors wanted little to do with any of these issues.

Many of the presidents before Richard Nixon were only involved with a limited number of social issues. This did not mean, of course, that they were not successful in generating legislation on these selected issues; it may have meant, however, that many of these issues were not politicized at the time these presidents served, and thus they were unavailable to the earlier presidents. It may also have meant that these presidents chose to focus their attention on a fewer number of issues than more recent presidents because of public demands. The untouched issues may not have proven to be politically enticing enough to risk a president's time and energy in adding them to a social agenda. We know, for example, that Lyndon Johnson had monumental success with affirmative action and that Franklin Roosevelt made major gains in the environment, but that neither was as broadly focused as more recent presidents. We also know that no president in the 1990s, nor any in the next century, can afford to stand aside once these issues are politicized, from the many social policy demands made of them today. All these factors make comparisons of presidents over the years in some ways difficult.

Although Richard Nixon continually complained about Congress's slow response to social policies, the data in the appendix indicate his success. One of the most successful legislative leaders of all the presidents, Nixon was instrumental in the passage of thirteen pieces of legislation dealing with varying aspects of pornography alone. Thus there are reasons for considering the social and political milieu of each of the legislative leaders before a firm judgment of their success can be made.

Table 3.2   Assertive Reactive Legislative Leaders and Social Issues, by Party

	Assertive	*Reactive*
Democrats	F. Roosevelt	Truman
	Johnson	Kennedy
	Carter	
	Clinton	
Republicans	Nixon	Eisenhower
	Reagan	Ford
	Bush	

ENDNOTES

1. Edward C. Corwin and Louis W. Koenig, *The Presidency Today* (New York: New York University Press, 1956), 83.
2. Arthur Schlesinger, Jr., and Alfred deGrazia, *Congress and the Presidency: Their Role in Modern Times* (Washington, DC: American Enterprise Institute for Public Policy Research, 1967), 4–5.
3. See *Congressional Quarterly's Guide to the Presidency* (Washington, DC: Congressional Quarterly, 1989), 451 and *Congressional Quarterly Weekly Report*, 19 December, 1992: 3925–26.
4. "Obscenity Bill Pocket Veto," *Congressional Quarterly Weekly Report*, 26 October, 1962: 2061.
5. See U.S. President, "Message to the House of Representatives Returning without Approval the Departments of Labor, Health and Human Services, and Education, and Related Agencies Appropriations Act, 1990—October 21, 1989," *Public Papers of the Presidents of the United States* (Washington, DC: Office of the Federal Register, National Archives and Records Service, 1990), 1373–374.
6. See U.S. President, "Message to the House of Representatives Returning without Approval the National Institutes of Health Revitalization Amendments of 1992—June 23, 1992," *Public Papers of the Presidents of the United States* (1992), 1005–6.
7. See "1998 Congressional Voting Record: Partisanship at the Expense of Achievement," *ADA Today* 54. 1 (January 1999): 13.
8. U.S. President, "Veto of Bill to Amend the Federal Water Pollution Control Act—February 23, 1960," *Public Papers of the Presidents of the United States* (1961), 208–10.
9. Clinton's veto record looked like this:

1995	11 vetoes
1996	6 vetoes
1997	3 vetoes
1998	5 vetoes
1999	5 vetoes

   Although Clinton's veto numbers in 1997 were reduced to three, he used his newly acquired line-item veto to take specific items from eleven other bills. The source for the veto information is the *Congressional Quarterly Almanacs* for the appropriate years; the information on the 1999 vetoes comes from the *Congressional Quarterly Weekly Reports* for the indicated months.
10. "Election Watch," *Salt Lake Tribune*, 31 March 1996, A21.
11. U.S. President, *Public Papers of the Presidents of the United States* (1975), 990–93.
12. U.S. President, "Statement of Signing the National Defense Authorization Act for Fiscal Year 1996—February 10, 1996," *Public Papers of the Presidents of the United States* (1998), 226–27.
13. See U.S. President, "Letter to John Conyers, Jr., on Abortion Legislation—February 28, 1996," *Public Papers of the Presidents of the United States* (1998), 1263–64.
14. See U.S. President, "Message to the House of Representatives Returning without Approval Partial Birth Abortion Legislation—April 10, 1996,"*Public Papers of the Presidents of the United States* (1998), 567–68.
15. U.S. President, "Letter to Members of the Senate Appropriations Committee on Federal Funding for Abortion—October 17, 1989,"*Public Papers of the Presidents of the United States* (1990), 1348–49.
16. U.S. President, "Message to the House of Representatives Returning without Approval the Departments of Labor, Health and Human Services and Education, and Related Agencies Appropriations Act, 1990—October 21, 1989," *Public Papers of the Presidents of the United States* (1990), 1373–374.
17. U.S. President, "Remarks and a Question-and-Answer Session with the Industrial League of Orange County in Irvine, California—June 19, 1992," *Public Papers of the Presidents of the United States* (1992–93), 978–85.
18. George C. Edwards III, *At the Margins: Presidential Leadership of Congress* (New Haven, CT: Yale University Press, 1989).
19. See the early study by Lawrence H. Chamberlain, *The President, Congress, and Legislation* (New York: Columbia University Press, 1946) and the follow-up study by Ronald C. Moe and Steven C. Teal, "Congress as Policy-Maker: A Necessary Reappraisal," *Political Science Quarterly* (September 1970): 443–70.

20. William Doyle, *Inside the Oval Office: The White House Tapes from FDR to Clinton* (New York: Kodansha International, 1999), 26.
21. Richard L. Berke, "Courting Congress Nonstop, Clinton Looks for an Alliance," *New York Times*, 8 March, 1993, Al.
22. David R. Mayhew, *Divided We Govern* (New Haven, CT: Yale University Press, 1991).
23. Charles O. Jones, *The Presidency in a Separated System* (Washington, DC: Brookings Institution, 1994), 297.
24. David Epstein and Sharyn O'Halloran, *Delegating Powers: A Transaction Cost Politics Approach to Policy Making under Separate Powers* (Cambridge: University Press, 1999), 128. David Brady and Craig Volden in *Revolving Gridlock: Politics and Policy from Carter to Clinton* (Boulder, CO: Westview Press, 1998) blame gridlock and policy stalement not on the presence or absence of divided government but on budgetary politics—whether there is sufficient funding to make the hard choices of new funding or strengthening old programs. Finally, Keith Krehbiel in *Pivotal Politics* (Chicago: University of Chicago Press, 1998) suggests that success of a presidential program will depend on the size of the "gridlock region" or interval and where in this spectrum the president's program is located. Under divided government, he argues, one can expect the gridlock region to be somewhat larger than under unified government, but this effect can be modified depending on whether the legislature is polarized or not.
25. Charles O. Jones, *The Trusteeship Presidency: Jimmy Carter and the United States Congress* (Baton Rouge: Louisiana State University Press, 1988).
26. "Gingrich Flashes His 'Green' Card, but Is Color Faded?" *Salt Lake Tribune*, 17 February, 1995, A1.
27. See Ed Gillespie and Bob Schellhas, eds., *Contract with America* (Random House: Times Books, 1994), 125–41.
28. Bob Benenson, "Environmental Laws Take a Hit," *Congressional Quarterly Weekly Report* (18 March 1995): 797.
29. Public opposition to these cuts forced the House to cut its requests back to 10 percent. See "The President's Radio Address," *Weekly Compilation of Presidential Documents* 31, no. 35 (26 August 1995): 1457; see also "Clinton to Take a Swing at 'Anti-Green' GOP," *Salt Lake Tribune*, 18 August, 1995, A1.
30. Michael W. Robbins, "Earth Day and Clear Days," *Audubon* 97, no. 2 (March–April 1995): 6.
31. For Roosevelt, the first-term budget figures were based on funding for the Departments of Agriculture and Interior and the Federal Power Commission; the Clinton figures came from environmental funds granted to the Departments of Energy, Interior, and Agriculture.
32. U.S. President, "Statement on Signing the Water Resources Development Act of 1996— October 12, 1996," *Public Papers of the Presidents of the United States* (1998), 1830–31.
33. See U.S. President, "Annual Budget Message to the Congress, Fiscal Year 1972—January 29, 1971," *Public Papers of the Presidents of the United States* (1972), 46–68.
34. See U.S. President, "Annual Budget Message to the Congress, Fiscal Year 1974—January 29, 1993," *Public Papers of the Presidents of the United States* (1975), 32–48.
35. U.S. President, "Letter to the Speaker of the House of Representatives and the President of the Senate on Soil and Water Conservation—March 22, 1985," *Public Papers of the Presidents of the United States* (1986), 426.
36. U.S. President, "The President Presents a National Plan to the Congress for the Conservation and Development of Our Water Resources—March 10, 1938," *Public Papers of the Presidents of the United States: Franklin D. Roosevelt* (New York: Macmillan, 1941), 141–43.
37. See U.S. President, "Radio Address to the Nation on Environmental Issues—July 14, 1984," *Public Papers of the Presidents of the United States* (1986), 1045–46.
38. See U.S. President, "Message to the Congress Transmitting the Annual Report of the Council on Environmental Quality—February 19, 1986," *Public Papers of the Presidents of the United States* (1986), 225–27.
39. U.S. President, "Special Message to the Congress on Civil Rights—February 5, 1959," *Public Papers of the Presidents of the United States* (1960), 164–67.
40. See U.S. President, "Special Message to the Congress Proposing Legislation to Strengthen Civil Rights—April 28, 1966," *Public Papers of the Presidents of the United States* (1967), 461–69.
41. U.S. President, "Statement about the Report of the Commission on Obscenity and Pornography, October 24, 1970," *Public Papers of the Presidents of the United States* (1971), 940.

42. "Remarks in Mount Prospect, Illinois, October 29, 1970," *Presidential Papers Infobase*, CDex Information Group, Lindon, UT, <e-mail, cdex@autosim.com>.
43. U.S. President, "Special Message to the Congress Resubmitting Legislative Proposals—January 26, 1971," *Public Papers of the Presidents of the United States: Richard Nixon* (Washington, DC: Government Printing Office, 1972), 65.
44. U.S. President, "Special Message to the Congress—January 26, 1971."
45. The question asked by Louis Harris and Associates was this: "Let me hand you this card which has on it some problems people say they are concerned about these days. Who do you think could do the best job on this issue— control of pornography—as President—Richard Nixon, the Republican, Edmund Muskie, the Democrat, or George Wallace, Independent?" (Question ID: US HARRIS. 71 JAN R08J). The January 1971 survey included 1,600 adults nationwide using a personal interview method. 0065576/9 DIALOG (R) File 468: Public Opinion. © 1997 Roper Ctr for Public Opinion Res.
46. "State of the Union Message to Congress on Law Enforcement and Drug Abuse Prevention, March 14, 1973," *Presidential Papers Infobase*, CDex Information Group, Lindon, UT, <e-mail, cdex@autosim.com>.
47. "Address before a Joint Session of Congress on State of the Union, January 25, 1984," *Presidential Papers Infobase*, CDex Information Group, Lindon, UT, <e-mail, cdex@autosim.com>.
48. U.S. President, "Remarks on Signing the Child Protection Act of 1984—May 21, 1984," *Public Papers of the Presidents of the United States* (1985), 722.
49. "Child Protection Act of 1984: Remarks on Signing H.R. 3635 into Law, May 21, 1984," *Weekly Compilation of Presidential Documents* 20, no. 4 (1984): 743.
50. "Toughened Child Pornography Bill Signed by Reagan," *Los Angeles Times,* 8 November 1986, 3.
51. "Reagan Proposes RICO Law Based on Meese Porno Recommendations," *Publishers Weekly* (4 December 1987), 13.
52. U.S. President, "Message to Congress on America's Agenda for the Future—February 6, 1986," *Public Papers of the Presidents of the United States* (1986), 149–63.
53. U.S. President, "1988 Legislative and Administrative Message: A Union of Individuals—January 25, 1988," *Public Papers of the Presidents of the United States* (1990), 91–121.
54. U.S. President, "Address Before a Joint Session of Congress on the State of the Union—January 24, 1995," *Public Papers of the Presidents of the United States* (1996), 75–86.
55. "Text of President's Message on Obscenity," *Congressional Quarterly Weekly Report* (9 May 1969): 702.
56. "Message to the Congress Transmitting Proposed Legislation on Child Protection and Obscenity Enforcement—November 10, 1987," *Public Papers of the Presidents of the United States* (1988), 1313.
57. "Remarks at a White House Briefing for Supporters of Proposed Legislation on Child Protection and Obscenity Enforcement, November 10, 1987," *Public Papers of the Presidents of the United States: Ronald Reagan* (Washington, DC: Government Printing Office, 1988), 1317.
58. See U.S. President, "Remarks on NAFTA and an Exchange with Reporters—September 24, 1993, "*Public Papers of the Presidents of the United States* (Washington, DC: Office of the Federal Register, National Archives and Records Service, 1994), 1592–94.
59. 1998-12-50 Radio Address Paper on the Brady Law, "The Brady Law: Making a Bigger Difference Every Day," 5 December, 1998. The White House <www.pub.whitehouse.gov>. Accessed 7 December 1998.
60. See U.S. President, "Remarks in the Question and Answer Session in the Godfrey Sperling Luncheon—September 25, 1995," *Public Papers of the Presidents of the United States* (1996), 1473–86.
61. See Joseph A. Califano, Jr., "LBJ's Tough Stance on Gun Control," *Washington Post* 5 July. 1999, National Weekly Edition, 26.
62. See U.S. President, "Remarks on Signing the Clean Air Amendments of 1970—December 31, 1970," *Public Papers of the Presidents of the United States* (1971), 1166–68.
63. "Remarks on Signing the Bill Amending the Clean Air Act," 15 November 1990, *The Presidential Papers Infobase*, CDdex Information Group, Lindon, UT. <e-mail, cdex@autosim.com>.
64. U.S. President, "Remarks at an Environmental Agreement Signing Ceremony at the Grand Canyon—September 18, 1991," *Public Papers of the Presidents of the United States* (1992), 1173–76.
65. U.S. President, "Statement of Signing the Los Padres Condor Range and River Protection Act—June 19, 1992," *Public Papers of the Presidents of the United States* (1993), 985–86.

66. U.S. President, "Remarks on Signing the Safe Drinking Water Act Amendments of 1996—August 6, 1996," *Public Papers of the Presidents of the United States* (1998), 1262–63.

67. U.S. President, "Remarks on Signing the Anti-Drug Abuse Act of 1988—November 18, 1988," *Public Papers of the Presidents of the United States* (1989), 1531.

68. U.S. President, "Remark—November 18, 1988."

69. U.S. President, "Statement on Signing the Crime Control Act of 1990—November 29, 1990," *Public Papers of the Presidents of the United States* (1991), 1715.

70. David Elsner, "President Signs Measure to Fight Child Pornography," *Chicago Tribune*, 24 December 1995, 13.

71. See the recent case that declared the Communications Decency Act to be unconstitutional in a 7–2 decision. *Janet Reno, Attorney General of the United States, et al. Appellants v. American Civil Liberties Union et al.* (96-511).

72. See U.S. President, "Remarks on Signing the Civil Rights Act of 1991—November 21, 1991," *Public Papers of the Presidents of the United States* (1992), 1504–05.

73. U.S. President, "Remarks on Signing the Civil Rights Act of 1991—November 21, 1991."

74. U.S. President, "Statement by the President Following Senate Passage of the Civil Rights Bill—June 19, 1964," *Public Papers of the Presidents of the United States* (1965), 787–88.

75. U.S. President, "The President's News conference of June 18, 1966," *Public Papers of the Presidents of the United States* (1967), 625.

76. U.S. President, "Letter to the President of the Senate Proposing Legislation to Eliminate Barriers to the Right to Vote—March 17, 1965," *Public Papers of the Presidents of the United States* (1966), 292.

77. U.S. President, "Letter to the Speaker of the House Urging Prompt Action on the Civil Rights Bill—March 12, 1968," *Public Papers of the Presidents of the United States* (1970), and U.S. President, "Letter to the Speaker of the House Urging Enactment of the Fair Housing Bill—April 5, 1968," *Public Papers of the Presidents of the United States: Lyndon B. Johnson,* 496–97.

78. U.S. President, "The President's News Conference—January 31, 1973," *Public Papers of the Presidents of the United States* (1975), 53–61.

79. U.S. President, "Message to the Congress Transmitting Legislation to Limit the Availability of Certain Handgun Ammunition—June 30, 1995, " *Public Papers of the Presidents of the United States* (1996), 990–91.

80. U.S. President, "Remarks and an Exchange with Reporters Following Discussions with President Jiang Zemin of China, Seattle—November 19, 1993," *Public Papers of the Presidents of the United States* (1994), 2022–23.

81. Others who sponsored this Clinton-approved measure included Marge Roukema (R–NJ) and Rod Blagojevich (D–IL); See Kathy Kiely and Tom Squitieri, "Lobbying Frenzy Precedes Gun Vote," *USA Today*, 18 July, 1999, 3A.

82. U.S. President, "Special Message to Congress on Forthcoming Legislative Proposals Concerning Domestic Programs—April 14, 1969," *Public Papers of the Presidents of the United States* (1969), 284. Nixon's comments in late 1968 are found in "General Government," *Congressional Quarterly Weekly Report* (27 December, 1968): 3320.

83. U.S. President, "Special Message to the Congress on Obscene and Pornographic Materials—May 2, 1969," *Public Papers of the President of the United States* (1970), 345.

84. U.S. President,"Letter to Selected Members of the Senate on Antiabortion Amendment to a Federal Debt Ceiling Bill—September 8, 1982," *Public Papers of the Presidents of the United States* (1983), 1104–05.

85. U.S. President, "Address before a Joint Session of Congress on the State of the Union—January 26, 1988, "*Public Papers of the Presidents of the United States* (1990), 84–121.

86. U.S. President, "The President's Radio Address—June 24, 1995," *Public Papers of the Presidents of the United States* (1996), 938–940.

87. U.S. President, "Statement on House of Representatives Action on Appropriations Legislation—July 24, 1995," *Public Papers of the Presidents of the United States* (1996), 1139–40.

88. U.S. President, "Remarks on Clean Water Legislation,—May 30, 1995," *Public Papers of the Presidents of the United States* (1996), 762–65.

89. U.S. President, "The President's News Conference with Chancellor Helmut Kohl of Germany in Milwaukee, Wisconsin—May 23, 1996," *Public Papers of the Presidents of the United States* (Washington, DC: Office of the Federal Register, National Archives and Records Service, 1998), 805–12.

90. Milton Cummings, ed., *The National Election of 1964* (Washington, DC: Brookings Institution, 1966), 247–48.
91. Johnson's five-year average approval rating, however, was only 56 percent.
92. Joseph A. Califano, Jr., "LBJ's Tough Stance on Gun Control," *Washington Post* 5 July, 1999, national weekly edition, 26.
93. Califano, "LBJ's Tough Stance on Gun Control," 26.
94. Roger H. Davidson, *The Postreform Congress* (New York: St. Martin's Press, 1992).
95. Larry Light, "White House Lobby Gets Its Act Together," *Congressional Quarterly Weekly Report* (3 February, 1979): 200.
96. Adam Clymer, "Bills Sent to Bush as 102d Congress Wraps Up Its Work," *New York Times*, 9 October, 1992, A1.
97. See Chuck Alston, "Bush Crusades on Many Fronts to Retake President's Turf," *Congressional Quarterly Weekly Report*, (3 February, 1990): 291.
98. See "Veto Cloud Loomed Large over 1992 Floor Fights," *Congressional Quarterly Weekly Review* (19 December, 1992): 3854.
99. Robert J. Spitzer, *The Presidential Veto* (Albany, NY: SUNY Press, 1988), 145.
100. Phillip A. Davis, "Politics, Drop in Senate Support Put Bush's Ratings in Cellar," *Congressional Quarterly Weekly Report* (19 December, 1992): 3841.
101. FDR did, however, send aides and cabinet members to some conferences, including a 1934 trade conference in Rome, a 1935 World Power Conference, and a 1936 North American Wildlife Conference.
102. U.S. President, "Campaign Address at the Mountain State Forest Festival, Elkins West Virginia—October 1, 1936," *Public Papers and Addresses of Franklin D. Roosevelt* (New York: Macmillan, 1938), 396–400.
103. Reagan even wrote a book about abortion—*Abortion and the Conscience of the Nation* (Nashville: T. Nelson, 1984)—the only president to do so.
104. U.S. President, "Address before a Joint Session of the Congress on the State of the Union—February 25, 1984," *Public Papers of the Presidents of the United States* (Washington, DC: Office of the Federal Register, National Archives and Records Service, 1984), 87–94.
105. U.S. President, "Union—February 6, 1985," *Public Papers of the Presidents of the United States* (Washington, DC: Office of the Federal Register, National Archives and Records Service, 1988), 130–39.
106. U.S. President, "Message to Congress on 'A Quest for Excellence'—January 27, 1987," *Public Papers of the Presidents of the United States* (Washington, DC: Office of the Federal Register, National Archives and Records Service, 1988), 61–79.
107. U.S. President, "Letter to the Speaker of the House of Representatives and the President of the Senate Transmitting the District of Columbia Budget—April 29, 1988," *Public Papers of the Presidents of the United States* (1989), 534–35.
108. U.S. President, "Message to the Congress Transmitting the Pro-Life Act of 1988—June 8, 1988," *Public Papers of the Presidents of the United States* (1988), 744–45.
109. U.S. President, "1988 Legislative and Administrative Message: A Union of Individuals—January 25, 1988," *Public Papers of the Presidents of the United States* (1991), 91–121.
110. Robert J. Spitzer, *The Politics of Gun Control* (Chatham, NJ: Chatham House, 1995), 111.
111. The White House, Office of the Press Secretary, "1999-07-15 Fact Sheet on Protecting Children from Gun Violence: Protecting Children from Gun Violence—July 15, 1999." <www.pub.whitehousse.gov>. Accessed 15 July 1999.
112. See 514 U. S. 549 (1995).
113. U.S. President, "Message to the Congress Transmitting the 'Gun-Free School Zones Amendments Act of 1995—May 10, 1995," *Public Papers of the Presidents of the United States* (1996), 678.

THE CHIEF EXECUTIVE
AND THE SOCIAL AGENDA

INTRODUCTION

The role of *chief executive* appears on the surface to be a powerful one since no other elected official or board shares this power with the president. Yet often the president as chief executive is frustrated in establishing a social agenda because the Constitution fragments control over the bureaucracy, making it difficult for any president to control the executive branch and unify support for agenda programs. Powers of this role come directly from two clauses in Article II of the Constitution—the first at the beginning of the article stating that "the executive power shall be vested in a President of the United States of America" and the second indicating that the president has the responsibility to "take care that the laws be faithfully executed."

While the Framers chose to give Congress specific grants of power, the vague manner in which the president was granted these administrative powers makes it unclear exactly what a president is to do. The size of the federal government further complicates a president's efforts in exercising this role. Added to the more than three million civilian employees working for the federal government are an additional six to seven million employees in the private sector who are hired by the government. Furthermore, the complexity of the federal government is cause for concern, as evident in the thousands of statutes, regulations, and agency rules as well as the many administrative units and subunits into which the executive branch is organized.

While it may appear that the role of chief executive is filled with almost insurmountable barriers, there are presidents who have been able to exploit its strengths by using their constitutional mandate, their organizational skills, and whatever power accrues to them through statute, custom, and judicial precedent to secure their social agendas.

APPOINTMENTS AND THE SOCIAL AGENDA

One of the most important responsibilities a president has as chief executive is the power to make appointments. On coming into office, a president is first confronted with the responsibility to *staff* and *shape* an administration as well as the Supreme Court, a responsibility that never seems to end, particularly if the Senate Judiciary Committee is in the hands of one party and the president is a member of the opposition party.[1] This happened during the 106th Congress, when Republican Senator Orrin Hatch (R–UT), chair of the Senate Judiciary Committee, allowed few of President Bill Clinton's selected judicial nominees through the committee, and those that did make it through committee ran the risk of being voted down by the Republican majority in the Senate. One of the most controversial instances occurred when Clinton's efforts to strengthen affirmative action were frustrated on October 5, 1999, when Ronnie White, who had served as the first African American judge appointed to Missouri's supreme court and was nominated for a seat on the federal district court in Missouri, went unconfirmed by the Senate. Congressional Republicans had seen that blocking this nomination was a way to halt the successes of a Democratic president and vice president during an election year as well as a means to put additional pressures on the president to support nominees favorable to the Republican majority.[2]

There are many barriers that prevent a president from appointing those he would appoint. Civil service limits many of the major appointments, leaving only slightly more than 5,000 top-level policymaking positions open to presidential appointment,[3] but these positions are scattered among the 3 million–person bureaucracy. Such diverse spacing among appointees often makes it difficult for presidents to gather support for building their social agendas. Yet some conservatives like Ronald Reagan managed to develop *threshold* or *litmus tests* to screen applicants for certain positions so that they would be assured that those passing through the screening process likely shared the president's political orthodoxy and position on social issues. Liberals and some moderate-conservative presidents, on the other hand, while rejecting litmus tests, have frequently taken another tack in staffing their administration—namely, to recruit certain minorities to particular positions within the administration that gives it a distinctive appearance, reflecting the president's position on social policy.

Executive Branch Appointments

A position on affirmative action is one such policy that has received support from presidents of both parties and has influenced their appointments. Presidents Lyndon Johnson, Jimmy Carter, Ronald Reagan, and Bill Clinton all emphasized their support for affirmative action by recruiting African Americans as Secretaries of Housing and Urban Development (HUD). George Bush further showed his support when he selected African-American Louis Sullivan as Secretary of Health and Human Services.[4] Bill Clinton also broke precedent by appointing African American Ron Brown to be Secretary of Commerce; then, on June 12, 1997, Clinton looked to represent another minority group appointing the first Chinese American to the office of Assistant Attorney General for the Civil Rights Division in the Department of Justice[5] despite Republican opposition.[6]

The most controversial minority appointment Bill Clinton made to his administration was made in response to election support he had received from the gay community when he appointed Roberta Achtenberg as Assistant Secretary of Housing and Urban Development in 1995.[7] On June 29, 1999, the Senate confirmed another of Clinton's appointees from the gay community, James Hormel, as U.S. ambassador to Luxembourg, an appointment that had been held up for some two years because of Hormel's admitted sexual orientation. This appointment made Hormel the first openly gay U.S. ambassador in history.[8] Clinton, however, was not the first president to appoint an openly gay person to office. Ronald Reagan was the first president to do so when he appointed Dr. Frank Lilly, a geneticist at the Albert Einstein College of Medicine in the Bronx, to a thirteen-member Presidential Commission on the Human Immunodeficiency Virus Epidemic. This appointment, not surprisingly, angered conservatives, and Reagan never appointed another homosexual to office. Unlike Clinton, in not responding further to the gay community Reagan indicated that homosexuality was not to be a permanent part of his social agenda. In the one instance, however, Reagan opted for professional competence over controversy.[9]

Franklin Roosevelt combined both the creation of new offices with the appointment of activist environmentalists and conservationists to emphasize the importance of this focus of concern during his first term in office. Roosevelt's most important appointments included Secretary of Interior Harold Ickes and Secretary of Agriculture, Henry Wallace, both of whom were his close and, at times, impassioned advisers on conservation and the environment, and who often were in disagreement with each other. Other important FDR environmental appointments included Rexford Tugwell, staff aide; Hugh Bennett of the Soil Erosion Service; Arno Camerer of the National Park Service; Morris L. Cooke of the Rural Electrification Administration; F. S. Silcox of the Forest Service; Elwood Mead of the Bureau of Reclamation; and Frank T. Bell of the Bureau of Fisheries.[10] Many of those named served in Roosevelt's environmental "kitchen cabinet."

Finding the right appointee, a person who is both competent and loyal, has proven difficult for some presidents in the past. In his first term Bill Clinton had great difficulty in staffing his administration, as evidenced by the missteps and miscalculations he made in his early appointments.[11] Yet as far as emphasizing the importance of the environment through his appointments, Clinton was impressive. Mark Dowie estimated that Clinton hired about "two dozen environmentalists,"[12] placing them throughout the government agencies and departments, with some holding down newly created positions inside such unlikely departments and agencies as the State Department,[13] National Security Council, and the Office of Management and Budget.[14] The most important administrative pro-environmental appointments Clinton made, of course, were Vice President Al Gore and Secretary of the Interior Bruce Babbitt—both of whom had proven reputations among environmentalists prior to their appointments to the administration. Other environmental activists selected included Carol Browner, director of the Environmental Protection Agency (EPA); Mollie Beattie, head of the Fish and Wildlife Service; Jack Ward Thomas, head of the Forest Service; Kathy McGinty, manager of the newly created White House Office on Environmental Policy; and Roger Kennedy, superintendent of the National Park Service.[15]

Court Appointments

The Supreme Court as an institution has been particularly open to presidential appointments of persons representing individual presidents' positions on social issues.

Lyndon Johnson, for example, wanted judges who would enforce his civil rights policies and so broke the racial barrier that long had existed on the Supreme Court by appointing former civil rights activist NAACP counsel Thurgood Marshall as the first African American associate justice. Upon Thurgood Marshall's retirement, George Bush filled the vacancy with an African American conservative Republican, Justice Clarence Thomas. Jimmy Carter, although failing to appoint any Supreme Court justices during his term in office, nevertheless showed his sensitivity to minorities by appointing 202 district and 56 appellate court African-American personnel, increasing their representation on the federal judiciary from 4 percent to 9 percent.[16] Bill Clinton followed Carter's example in his initial appointment of 187 judges, 60 percent of whom were women or racial minorities.[17]

Ronald Reagan let his pro-life views on abortion politics significantly influence his staffing decisions on the court. As freely admitted in an address to the Knights of Columbus Convention in Chicago on August 5, 1986: "In many areas—abortion, crime, pornography, and others—progress will take place when the Federal judiciary is made up of judges who believe in law and order and strict interpretation of the Constitution. I'm pleased to be able to tell you that I've already appointed 284 Federal judges, men and women who share the fundamental values that you and I so cherish, and that by the time we leave office, our administration will have appointed some 45 percent of all Federal judges."[18] As a result of this approach to staffing, some critics accused Reagan of being a pro-life zealot.[19] Ignoring the critics, Reagan appointed over half of all federal lower court judges while relying on his "ideological litmus test " on abortion to guide his choices. [20] In this way Reagan helped embellish his social agenda, looking to the pro-life approach to abortion as a main focus. The greatest recruitment risk Reagan took, in fact, was in his selection of Sandra Day O'Connor, the first woman appointed to the Supreme Court, who had taken some stands on abortion while she was majority leader in the Arizona State Senate that gave great concern to conservatives. O'Connor had voted against Arizona's felony statutes for abortion, voted for providing family planning services to minors without parental consent, and voted against an Arizona House concurrent memorial that urged the U.S. Congress to pass a constitutional amendment against abortion.[21] These were not, however, important enough actions to keep Reagan from appointing the first woman to the high court.

REMOVALS AND THE SOCIAL AGENDA

The Constitution says nothing about a chief executive's removal power, and for this reason the president's power to remove administrators is more tenuous than his power to appoint. In fact, interpretations of the strength of a president's removal power have differed since the Constitutional Convention. In *Federalist Paper* no. 77, Alexander Hamilton argued that the removal power could be presumed from the president's power to appoint. In the first Congress, James Madison contended that a president's removal power is implied in the president's authority to "take care that the laws be faithfully executed." Other members of the first Congress supported the idea of allowing Congress to delegate removal authority to the president, if necessary, or giving the power to the judiciary or to the Congress. However, a majority of these early congressmen adhered more closely to Madison's view, granting removal power to the president.[22]

While there are few examples where social issues served as a reason for removing personnel from office, Ronald Reagan's secretary of defense, Frank C. Carlucci, did use the homosexuality of an unidentified cryptographic material control technician at the National Security Agency (NSA), referred to as "John Doe," as reason for removing the employee from his position. The "official reason" for refusing to grant this employee clearance for "sensitive compartmented information"—a classification above "top secret"—was that his behavior was "inconsistent with the national security" since it was alleged that the NSA operative had had sexual relationships with foreign nationals. The Supreme Court in the case of *Carlucci v. Doe* (1988) later reiterated that the

NSA was within its authority to remove the employee since "the power of removal from office is incident to the power of appointment, absent a specific provision to the contrary."[23]

ORDERS, PROCLAMATIONS, AND THE SOCIAL AGENDA

Executive orders have been extensively used by chief executives to establish their social agendas. Legal authority of an executive order, as it has been suggested, "derives either from existing statutes, or from the president's other constitutional responsibilities, not from any specific congressional approval."[24] *Proclamations*, on the other hand, do not carry the strength of executive orders but have frequently been used to shape social policy. Proclamations give the chief executive a way to recognize or approve of events or projects, setting aside a particular time or space to recognize it. Michael Nelson suggests further that "such proclamations promote national concern and awareness of worthy organizations and causes by indicating that the president thinks the object of the proclamation is important enough to recognize."[25]

Subject matter for executive orders and proclamations is as diverse as legislation itself. Lyn Ragsdale points out that Franklin Roosevelt's primary innovation with executive orders was to change them from being mere administrative devices to more important "policy-making devices."[26] Roosevelt frequently changed the focus of government through executive order.

To encourage integration in the national defense programs, for example, in 1935 Roosevelt barred all discrimination from the New Deal programs by executive order. This was perhaps his most important executive order, suggests William Doyle, since it helped to remake the Democratic Party when the following year African Americans "bolted from their traditional home in the Republican Party and joined the FDR coalition. By 1940, New Deal programs supported 1 million black families."[27] By 1943, Executive Order 8802 continued to support the African-American community, establishing the Fair Employment Practice Commission to further encourage integration and affirmative action and to process complaints about discrimination.[28]

Executive orders used by presidents since the election of FDR to reinforce affirmative action have in many ways been patterned after this Roosevelt executive order.[29] These orders included Harry Truman's directive to end segregation in military service in 1948 as well as Dwight Eisenhower's executive order of November 18, 1957 that helped to secure affirmative action by establishing an Equal Opportunity Day, which provided that on this day every American ought to join together to "abolish all artificial discrimination which hinders the right of each American to advance in accordance with his merits as a human being and his capacity for productive work."[30] In 1961, John Kennedy created the Equal Employment Opportunity Commission, which became an important structure to enforce integration, by executive order Lyndon Johnson, in all that he did in the area of civil rights, used an executive order to establish preferential hiring of minorities by government contractors.[31] Such examples of executive orders make it clear that presidents of both parties have been committed to the overall goals of affirmative action.

In addition, Franklin Roosevelt used executive orders to advance conservation and environmental concerns. So important to the environmental movement is Roosevelt that he has been called the president who introduced the "Golden Age of Conservation."[32] In 1934, Roosevelt strengthened his hold over the environment by withdrawing public lands for conservation purposes.[33]

Richard Nixon introduced several important environmental policies by executive order. One such order attempted to eliminate all air and water pollution in federal buildings.[34] Bill Clinton also introduced several new environmental programs by executive order that included his 1993 clean air program and his 1999 clean water policy.[35] Clinton's clean air policy mandated that the president's fleet of cars all convert their fuel system to cleaner fuel.[36] A potentially more controversial environmental program introduced in 1999 by the Clinton administration was the 1999 Clean Energy program, which focused attention on bio-based technologies. The administration argued that this program would both enhance the economy and help overcome global warming, and the executive order was designed to coordinate all federal efforts concerning biomass fuels and material to hasten their development during the twenty-first century.

A proclamation dealing with public lands that attracted more than its share of attention was the one that President Clinton used in setting aside 2 million acres in Utah that became the Grand Staircase–Escalante National Monument in 1996. This proclamation was issued without consultation with members of the Utah congressional delegation, and with full awareness that there was strong opposition from both Utah's governor and the state legislature.[37] Opponents accused Clinton of committing "federalization by fiat" and devising the "mother of all land grabs" with this action.[38]

Executive orders have also been used to enforce a president's views regarding abortion as occurred during the Administrations of both Ronald Reagan and Bill Clinton. So intent was Ronald Reagan on securing a pro-life administration that despite the Iran-Contra scandal, as Michael Kramer pointed out, Reagan was waging a war against abortion by executive order, which was, in his words, "a politically dangerous war."[39] Reagan indicated that he felt that the unborn had lost their right to speak for themselves and it fell to him to speak for them. Reagan also felt it necessary to set aside by proclamation a Sanctity for Human Life Day, again illustrating his particular pro-life preferences.[40] Reagan's anti-abortion preference also came through as he set aside two other special days by proclamation—one, to remember adoption as an alternative to abortion, called "Adoption Day;"[41] and the other, more subtle pro-lifers month, called Pregnancy and Infant Loss Awareness Month.[42] That same year, Ronald Reagan impounded congressional funds, imposing a moratorium on federal funding of fetal tissue research[43] as well as declaring a ban on abortion counseling for any group or agency receiving federal funding through executive orders. These last actions failed in the long run, when Bill Clinton, in one of his first official acts as chief executive and in fulfillment of a campaign promise, reversed both of these Reagan actions on January 22, 1993, using a series of five presidential orders to reverse the Reagan position.[44]

In addition to his focus on abortion, Reagan was also equally concerned about child pornography and used an executive proclamation to attempt to restrict pornography. In 1985, for example, a Reagan proclamation reiterated the president's concerns for child pornography: "Child pornography should be straightforwardly condemned as inconsistent with a society that truly loves its children and respects the integrity of the childhood years. By speaking up and making their voices heard, concerned Americans can make a big difference in the kind of society our children will grow up in and even more, in their ability to grow up with the love and security that should be every child's birthright."[45]

Bill Clinton showed that gun control was also an extremely important social issue in his agenda when he proclaimed October 21, 1999 as a "National Day of Concern about Young People and Gun Violence." The purpose of the day set aside by proclamation was for adults to assist youth in avoiding violence as well as ensuring that schools and neighborhoods would again be "safe havens for learning and recreation."[46]

ADMINISTRATIVE DECISION MAKING

Administrative decision making, of course, may include more than just the president. Typical actors that might be involved with the president in establishing a social agenda include the president's advisory system, the bureaucracy, and subnational political elites as well as Congress, the Supreme Court, and even clientele groups. What control a president has over the bureaucracy, for example, may well depend on how he uses his office and whether he comes to an agreement with these other actors.

Congress

Congress affects executive decision making in a variety of ways. Virtually the entire bureaucracy is and has been established by law and statute. Congress, in other words, controls the entire organization of the federal civil service affecting examinations, promotions, confirmation of appointments, salaries, hiring, firing and retirements, and Congress can also stipulate the qualifications, powers, and duration of those executive positions created.

Franklin Roosevelt had an unusually cooperative Congress in his first term, which facilitated his accomplishments; Bill Clinton, on the other hand, found the support he had received during the 103rd Congress faded in its last months and all but disappeared in the Republican-controlled 104th Congress. Clinton was also confronted with record-breaking threats to his legislative program in the House and uses of the filibuster in the Senate, limiting his legislative efforts.

During 1999, Clinton became more of an activist in his support of gun control measures and made an effort to work with Congress to shore up his effort against youth violence. Clinton appealed to Congress to pass what he referred to as "commonsense measures" to keep weapons out of the hands of the wrong people. These measures included a juvenile crime bill to close the gun show loophole allowing people to purchase weapons without a background check. In addition, he encouraged gun manufacturers to ensure that guns would come with safety locks and continued to work with Congress to pass legislation banning the importation of large-capacity ammunition clips.[47]

Reorganization

Structural reorganization has often proven an effective route to reinforce a president's social agenda. Franklin Roosevelt was in an unusual position his first two years in office. In 1933, Congress gave Roosevelt the sort of leniency it has not shown to any other president, allowing him a delegated power to reorganize the government for two years undisturbed by congressional oversight.[48]

Roosevelt took full advantage of this latitude, letting both his passion for the environment and his desire to put people back into the workforce prevail. He created the Civilian Conservation Corps (CCC), which must be considered his most important environment-oriented agency. The first New Deal agency approved in 1933 by the Congress, the CCC not only put people back to work during the Great Depression, but put them to work in the national parks and forests, resulting in the building of roads, visitor pathways, and other improvements benefiting the environment.[49] Roosevelt created a number of other offices focusing on the environment and conservation that helped to facilitate advances made in environmental policy. These included the Office for Social Erosion, the National Park Service, the Rural Electrification Administration, the Forest Service, the Bureau of Reclamation, and the Bureau of Fisheries.

On other occasions, however, Congress has proven uncooperative toward presidential plans of reorganization. In 1977, Jimmy Carter attempted to obtain support to create a Department of Energy. In order to do so, Carter had to submit to major modifications of his proposal, even to stripping the department of its authority to control energy prices.

The most ambitious reorganization plan of any president with some affect on social policy may have belonged to Richard Nixon, who weakened the clientele-related Departments of Agriculture, Commerce, Labor, and

Transportation and allocated their functions to four "super" departments—one of which, Natural Resources, was, among other things, focused on environmental affairs. In this reorganization, the "new" cabinet would include eight departments rather than the eleven that had existed under previous presidents. Congress refused to approve the plan, however, even though it was sympathetic to the need for overall government reorganization.

While this reorganization failed, Nixon's creation of the Environmental Protection Agency (EPA) did not fail and remains one of the most important environmental agencies of the federal government.[50] Two other environmental agencies of importance created under Nixon's authority, the Environmental Quality Council and a Citizens' Advisory Committee on the Environment,[51] suggest the emphasis Nixon put on the environment in his social agenda.

The Clinton-Gore "reinventing" of government allowed their administration to reorganize and reduce the size of federal government, making government less expensive and more efficient.[52] This reorganization could be seen as giving some support to the environment as a priority in Clinton's social agenda, since the objective of the reorganization was to "protect people, not bureaucracy; promote results, not rules; get action, not rhetoric."[53] Yet another result of this "reinvention," the National Performance Review (NPR), was to cut the workforce by 12 percent by 1999 through cutting red tape, simplifying federal rules, and coordinating federal management as well as streamlining purchasing mechanisms. Environmental agencies have complied quite well in carrying out this streamlining. In terms of reducing government workers, however, some of those very agencies that dealt directly with environmental policy were reduced in size, including the Department of Energy (reduced by 53 persons), the Environmental Protection Agency (38 persons), the Department of Interior (29 persons), and the Federal Emergency Management Agency (22 persons). In addition, these same departments and agencies saw their headquarters staff adjusted: The Department of Energy was reduced by 27 persons, the EPA by 10 persons, and the Department of Interior by 27 persons.[54]

Clinton did make a number of other structural changes in the executive branch that were designed to facilitate environmental policy, including the creation of the National Biological Service, the White House Office on Environmental Policy, and the Council on Sustainable Development. To introduce biobased technology, Clinton organized an Interagency Council on Biobased Products and Bioenergy. This organization was to be staffed by the Secretaries of Agriculture, Commerce, Energy, and Interior as well as the Administrator of the Environmental Protection Agency, the Director of the Office of Management and Budget, the Assistant to the President for Science and Technology, the Director of the National Science Foundation, the Federal Environmental Executive, and the heads of other relevant agencies as determined by the co-chairs of the Council on Sustainable Development.[55] The Council was to prepare strategic plans for the president outlining how the development of biobased products and bioenergy could come about. Biobased products would include commercial and industrial chemicals, pharmaceuticals, and products with large carbon sequestering capacity.[56]

Finally, Clinton attempted to put a greater emphasis on the environment by elevating the Environmental Protection Agency (EPA) to cabinet rank.[57] Unfortunately for environmental policy, this proposal ran into a great deal of opposition or, at the least, lack of interest among members of Congress, who either ignored the president's request for this change or reacted, as did Congressman Billy Tauzins (D–La.), by insisting that a congressional investigation look at the EPA for any "illegal" involvement in the environment.[58] Such a response to the president's reorganization request did nothing but increase hostility between the president and Congress during that session.

Quite possibly the most important reorganization of the Eisenhower administration, and one that showed Eisenhower's commitment to affirmative action, was the establishment of the Civil Rights Division of the Justice Department as well as the creation of the Civil Rights Commission.[59] Once John Kennedy was elected, he retained the Civil Rights Commission but changed its focus, making it an even more effective institution for civil rights by ensuring that it would become a national clearing house of information regarding acceptable civil rights practice.[60]

Jimmy Carter's main reorganization of the bureaucracy affected both civil rights and affirmative action. As Carter stated to Congress: "Fair employment is too vital for haphazard enforcement. My administration will aggressively enforce our civil rights laws. Although discrimination in any area has severe consequences, limiting economic opportunity affects access to education, housing and health care. I, therefore, ask you to join with me to reorganize the administration of the civil rights laws and to begin that effort by reorganizing the enforcement of those laws which ensure an equal opportunity to a job."[61] To show how serious he was about strengthening civil rights and affirmative action, Carter stressed to the heads of all the executive departments and agencies that "the government of all the people should not support programs which discriminate on the grounds of race, color or national origin. There are no exceptions to this rule; no matter how important a program, no matter how urgent the goals, they do not excuse violating any of our laws—including the laws against discrimination."[62]

In addition to his emphasis on the environment, Bill Clinton also was very concerned about affirmative action and gun control. As a result, Clinton created a Civil Rights Working Group[63] to "evaluate and improve the effectiveness of Federal civil rights enforcement missions and policies."[64]

Important to Ronald Reagan's social agenda was taking a firm stance against pornography. Reorganization was the tool used in 1987, when Reagan and Attorney General Ed Meese established a special pornography unit within the Criminal Division of the Justice Department—the National Obscenity Enforcement Unit—to aggressively put pressure on producers, distributors, and retailers of pornography. The unit included two sections: (1)the Obsceni-ty Law Center, which was to be a clearinghouse for information on pornogra-phy; and (2) the Task Force, which was to work with the FBI, the Postal Service, the IRS, U.S. Customs, U.S. attorneys, and the Organized Crime Strike Forces to prosecute those involved with pornography. Through the attorney general, Reagan staffed the unit with those who had a particular concern and interest in prosecuting pornographers, including several who had been selected from the Citizens for Decency through Law (CDL), an Arizona-based interest group that for years had been in conflict with pornographic interests.

To deal more effectively with youth violence, Bill Clinton also estab-lished a White House Council on Youth Violence, a group that would allow the White House to coordinate the many programs and agencies at the federal level that are working to reduce youth violence caused by weapons.[65]

The Advisory Staff

The so-called *institutionalized presidency* was intended to help the presi-dent govern, but as many scholars have recognized, a president's advisers may further complicate the decision-making process and undermine his effectiveness in this role.[66] Included in the advisory system are such groups as the cabinet, "kitchen cabinets"(informal groups of advisors to the president) the Executive Office of the President, and whatever ad hoc or permanent com-missions and advisory committees a president chooses to utilize.

The Cabinet.   The oldest institution to advise the president is the cab-inet. The first cabinet created in George Washington's administration had four officials: the secretary of state, the secretary of the treasury, the secre-tary of war, and the attorney general.

Of the six social issues we are examining, those departments directed to handling the environment include the Department of the Interior and the Department of Energy. The Department of the Interior is one of the oldest cabinet departments dealing with the environment. This department has had as direct an impact as any department or agency because it is responsible for land management and water and resource management. It is also responsible for plant and animal preservation and making sure that preservation and the environment do not conflict. The department of the interim averages more than 67,865 employees as of 1997.[67] The Department of Energy also looks out after the environment because it promotes energy use. Established in 1977 to analyze energy information as well as regulate energy production, it proba-bly is the most removed of the agencies in its impact over the environment.

Departments in the cabinet that deal with the other five social issues include: Housing and Urban Development, the Department of Justice and the Department of Labor (affirmative action); the Department of Justice, the Department of Commerce, and the Treasury Department (gun control); Health and Human Services (abortion); and the Department of Justice and the Department of Commerce (pornography).

Although the number of departments in the cabinet has increased in size and complexity over the years, there has been no corresponding increase in the power of the cabinet as a whole. Richard Pious, in fact, contends that the cabinet no longer is an important source of policy or advice for the president and that it has little use except to function for "public relations symbolism."[68]

Individual Secretaries. While it is true that the cabinet does not act as an advisory body to the president, individual cabinet secretaries have been influential in advising the president on issue strategy in the six areas we are considering. Quite often these key cabinet members come from the so-called "inner four" positions—the secretaries of state, defense, treasury, and the attorney general—that were also represented in George Washington's original cabinet. These four departments are particularly influential since they involve policy areas important to the entire nation.

Presidents in the past have turned to individual secretaries to assist them in enforcing affirmative action. Lyndon Johnson went to Congress to ask it to increase the attorney general's authority to desegregate schools and then asked Congress to eliminate discrimination in housing. He also asked for an additional hundred new FBI agents to help enforce the civil rights laws. Finally, he urged immediate action on his civil rights legislation.[69]

Ronald Reagan had his attorney general, Ed Meese, articulate the administration's attitude on affirmative action. In essence, this attorney general became the logical extension of Ronald Reagan when it came to racial quotas, strongly arguing against them.[70]

In Franklin Roosevelt's situation, two secretaries in the cabinet were particularly important as close advisers on the environment. These included Secretary of Agriculture (and later Vice President) Henry Wallace and Secretary of the Interior Harold Ickes. Both of these men worked closely with Roosevelt and were instrumental in helping to shape his environmental programs.

When it came to Ronald Reagan's attitude toward environmental issues, the president showed his negative attitude toward federal involvement with the environment when he appointed James Watt, his first Secretary of Interior, he encouraged Watt to limit funding and cut back on the enforcement of federal rules. Doing this was not difficult for Watt who, as head of a public interest firm, had previously challenged the Department of Interior in court on some of its public land policies.[71]

For Bill Clinton, it was Vice President Al Gore, an established environmentalist, and Secretary of Interior Bruce Babbitt another highly visible environmentalist, whose presence symbolized to many environmentalists that Bill Clinton was serious about staying close to their needs. Like some presidents before him, Bill Clinton also used the federal government as the model for the rest of society when it came to his social agenda. He instructed the

Department of Energy, for example, to take the lead in reducing energy consumption in federal facilities by 30 percent as well as implementing effective water conservation programs in 1994.[72]

Cabinet secretaries have also assisted the president when there have been conflicts with the Court. When the Supreme Court refused to support a gun-free zone surrounding public schools in the *Lopez* case,[73] Bill Clinton asked Attorney General Janet Reno to discover ways to obtain the same results without federal legislation by encouraging states to ban guns allowing federal funds to be linked to the enactment of any gun-free zones.[74] The Secretary of Housing and Urban Development also assisted in putting together a supportive program against guns. To attempt to remove weapons from the streets, Clinton called on HUD to manage a "Gun Buyback" program that allowed all citizens to return weapons for money. Although there was a $50 cap on each weapon brought back, the $50 was supplemented by gift certificates for goods and services.[75]

Ronald Reagan used his cabinet to reinforce his social agenda. It was James Q. Wilson who first described Reagan's candidacy for office in 1980 as part of a larger "moral regeneration"[76] based on a social agenda consisting of several of the issues we address in this study. One of those issues, pornography, was not addressed by Reagan until the last year of his first term. In 1984, he took several steps, including having the Justice Department establish a teaching seminar for some two hundred state and federal prosecutors and investigators to teach them how to curb pornography more effectively.[77]

During the Reagan-Bush years, government struck hard at pornography, and again the Justice Department was at the heart of the process. Certain changes in procedures were adopted and several techniques perfected at the Justice Department to increase the rate of prosecutions among the distributors of sexually explicit films, books, and magazines. Attorney General Meese, for example, had the instruction manual, that is given to all U.S. attorneys changed to state that a multiple indictment strategy — in which distributors are indicted in multiple jurisdictions in several states at the same time — should be "encouraged" rather than "discouraged," despite the fact that three federal courts had condemned the technique as "abusive and unconstitutional."[78] The strategy seemed to have worked despite those constitutional questions, however. One mail-order distributor in 1990, for example, faced indictments in two districts in North Carolina, two in Alabama, and one in Virginia, with four trials scheduled within a two-month period. By 1990, the Justice Department had seen seven distributors go out of business. The one distributor that the Justice Department had difficulty with, however, was P.H.E. (also known as Adam and Eve), a North Carolina mail-order company. The Justice Department had indicted P.H.E. in the states of Kentucky, Utah, and North Carolina, but the distributor eventually sued the Justice Department and won its case two years later in a U.S. district court, charging the Justice Department with harassment.[79]

Occasionally presidents have found it necessary to reign in a cabinet secretary. John Kennedy found he had to limit the postmaster general, who was then in the cabinet, since Kennedy felt the postmaster general was involved in inappropriate action. In a news conference on August 29, 1962, Kennedy responded to a question concerning a court decision that would prevent the postmaster general from restricting pornographic matter in the mails, by stating that existing laws already governed such distribution of pornography and that he believed the Post Office's main responsibility was not to make judgments about the nature of pornography but simply to carry out the law.[80]

Bill Clinton also had to reprimand his attorney general on a pornography issue. As chief executive, Clinton had intended, to limit his involvement with pornography to talking of the evils of child pornography—which in most instances should have been a politically safe and noncontroversial position for the president. Even this focus was not free of controversy, for Clinton, who became the first president in history to be charged—by a number of individual congresspersons as well as spokespersons for family groups—with being "soft" on child pornography. This incident also led to a serious confrontation between the president and the attorney general. Clinton's critics in Congress—125 Republicans, joined by some Democrats in the House—along with two family rights groups—the National Family Legal Foundation and the American Family Association—attacked him,[81] bitterly complaining to the attorney general that the Clinton administration had reversed directions on the Supreme Court decision in *U.S. v. Knox* (1994).[82]

This case involved Stephen A. Knox, then a graduate student of Pennsylvania State University, who had been arrested by U.S . Customs undercover agents for possessing three videotapes depicting fully clothed young girls in sexually promiscuous positions. Knox felt certain that the girls' behavior exhibited in the video could not be considered "sexually explicit conduct," since that had always been defined as "lascivious exhibition of the genitals or pubic area." Nevertheless, Knox was arrested in 1991 and, after many court appeals, was ordered to go to prison on March 9, 1995 to serve a five-year sentence. Clinton appointee Solicitor General Drew S. Days III had asked the Court to lay aside the Knox judgment because the administration felt that the federal appeals court had given too broad an interpretation of the law in upholding the Knox conviction, since in prior cases persons convicted of similar violations had to be in possession of pictures of nude persons.[83] Attorney General Janet Reno at first also urged that the conviction be overturned, but then, in light of the criticisms that the Clinton administration received, reversed direction and on January 17, 1995, supported the conviction. The American Family Association added to the pressure by mounting a nationwide lobbying campaign charging that the administration's original position had "seriously weakened the government's efforts to prosecute the commercial exploitation of children."[84] Twenty-two senators and eighty-two members of the House—in addition to voting on a resolution condemning the Clinton Justice Department for its broadened interpretation of the child pornography law—went even further, requesting permission to argue their case in the U.S. Court of Appeals.[85] The high court let the conviction stand.

Feeling the pressures of this reversal, Clinton reacted quickly, firing off a letter to Attorney General Reno assuring her and the nation that "I find all forms of child pornography offensive and harmful, as I know you do, and I want the federal government to lead aggressively in the attack against the scourge of child pornography. It represents an unacceptable exploitation of children and contributes to the degradation of our national life and to a societal climate that appears to condone child abuse."[86] To further embarrass the attorney general, Clinton indicated that he agreed with those incensed Senators and others who had voiced support for their position on the intended scope of the child pornography law. He then ordered the attorneys in the Justice Department to "promptly prepare any necessary legislation," making sure that the federal laws would apply to all aspects of child pornography and exploitation.[87]

THE EXECUTIVE OFFICE AND THE SOCIAL AGENDA

In contrast to the *line* departments , responsible for implementing public policies, the president's *staff* agencies, with advisory functions, are located in the Executive Office of the President. In 1939, the President's Committee on Administrative Management indicated that the president "needed help" and recommended that President Roosevelt be given a limited number of assistants to assist in administering the executive branch. That year Roosevelt created the Executive Office of the President, which today contains fourteen units, including the Office of Management and Budget (OMB), the Council of Economic Advisers (CEA), and the National Security Council.

Agencies and Bureaus

Decision makers throughout the federal government also share authority with the chief executive. The heads of agencies and bureaus prepare budgetary increases each year, request new program authority, and pressure the chief executive to fill high-level appointments with people from their agencies. Civil servants interpret the meaning of statutes, lay down regulations, and make substantive policy decisions. In this way, the bureaucracy is able to make law just as Congress does. The strength of these agencies and bureaus can be seen in how most of them easily outlive presidents. Herbert Kaufman found, in fact, that 148 of the 175 agencies operating in 1923 were still in existence by 1973, fifty years later. [88] Moreover, it has been suggested that within these agencies about 125,000 career personnel have some input in the policymaking process, further dispersing this authority throughout the federal government and making it difficult for the president to control policymaking. Moreover, agencies frequently become the units for implementing and enforcing social policy.

As an example of this complex process, environmental policy often comes together after input from the Department of Interior, the Department of Energy, the Environmental Protection Agency, and the Federal Emergency Management Agency. From these agencies come rules, regulations, hearings, adjudications, and punishments for violations of regulations.

One of the most important of these noncabinet agencies dealing with environmental policy, of course, is the EPA, which was created by Richard Nixon in 1970 to protect and to safeguard both the public health as well as the environment. To accomplish these goals, the EPA enforces federal environmental laws and regulations and is responsible for public health as well as protecting the natural environment. In 1998, it had an annual budget of approximately $6.44 billion, with a staff of 18,045 persons.[89] Under Jimmy Carter, the EPA at times was responsive to public demands concerning environmental needs, but at other times was relatively neutral to these demands.[90] Under Ronald Reagan, the EPA rarely responded to public demands. Reagan discouraged public input on environmental concerns and made an effort to reduce EPA budgets while granting more protection to big business. Environmentalists were thus critical of the Reagan years, which seemed to give the polluters preferential treatment.

Another important agency that has helped to shape environmental policy is the Federal Emergency Management Agency, an agency that was established in 1979 to protect property from the national emergencies and disasters of all sorts. FEMA was staffed in 1998 with 4,888 persons and a budget of $3.698 billion.[91]

Environmental concerns led Dwight Eisenhower to move beyond the established cabinet and create a special Cabinet Committee on Water Resources Policy that would undertake a review of all aspects of water policy. The committee's main responsibility was to look for ways to strengthen, modernize, and clarify water policies. The Secretaries of Interior, Defense, and Agriculture also assisted the chair of the committee in this work.[92]

Ronald Reagan's campaign against federal law and the environment led him to appoint Anne Burford as the head of the Environmental Protection Agency. Here was an instance where Reagan used his authority of appointment to advance his conservative social agenda. He encouraged Burford to limit environmental funding, deregulate, limit the enforcement of federal rules, and be more supportive of business interests.

Clinton also showed he was serious in his attempts to make environmental policy an important part of his social agenda. The president insisted that all agencies of government incorporate guidelines of "environmental justice"— namely, that each agency was to develop strategies that would guarantee to all citizens the right to live in an untainted and unspoiled environment. Each agency was to identify and respond to any high and adverse health problem or environmental concerns in the low-income and minority populations. Each agency was to receive help in identifying these concerns from a newly created Interagency Federal Working Group on Environmental Justice whose task was to coordinate and provide guidance.[93]

An interesting addition to the Executive Office of the President under George Bush was Vice President Dan Quayle's Council on Competitiveness. This controversial advisory council was created as a part of the plea that President Bush made in his January 28, 1991 State of the Union address demanding of his cabinet that they issue no new federal regulations for ninety days until an extensive review could be conducted of all regulations. This was Bush's built-in structure that aided him in focusing in the values he wished to emphasize, and the main purpose of the council's activity was to remove those regulations that might interfere with business competitiveness.[94] The council was chaired by the vice president and had as regular members the director of the OMB, the secretaries of the treasury and of commerce, the chair of the Council of Economic Advisers, the chief of staff and the attorney general. In its short history it became a major deregulatory voice of the Bush administration involved in environmental issues,[95] including clean air policies, industrial safety laws, automobile emission laws, and food and drug regulations. As one critic suggested, the council left no "fingerprints" or "paper trail" that might justify its decisions.[96] Environmentalists were most unhappy with the council because it always favored business interests over the environment. The EPA found that despite the restrictions against pollution in the 1990 Clean Air Act, for example, the Bush Council on Competitiveness continued to protect those businesses and firms that would pollute by preventing them from having to report their excesses to the public.[97]

The council came to an abrupt and unceremonious halt under Bill Clinton, however , who quickly abolished it through executive order in his first full day in office.[98] Clinton established instead a scaled-down version that was more accessible to the public and more of a review process proposing that all written and oral communications between the White House and outside interests be written in the public record.

Presidents are frequently in a position to use the structure of government to further their own ends. Franklin Roosevelt's involvement with affirmative action was apparent when he told State Works Progress Administrators on June 17, 1935 that "we have to be extremely careful not to make any kind of discrimination. We cannot discriminate in any of the work we are conducting either because of race or religion or politics. Politics, so far as we are concerned, is out. If anybody asks you to discriminate because of politics you can tell them that the President of the United States gave direct orders that there is not to be any such discrimination."[99]

At times the president has established committees to share the workload. To support affirmative action, Roosevelt established the Committee on

Fair Employment Practice by executive order on June 25, 1941 to ensure that there was no discrimination in the labor force. The committee was also changed with investigating complaints of discrimination, carrying out appropriate ways to eliminate it, and writing policy rules to ensure it would not happen again.[100]

Harry Truman, supported Roosevelt's concerns about affirmative action, created a Committee on Civil Rights whose main function to report and study the problem of "federally secured civil rights." This committee was to be a source of legislative ideas as well as making recommendations to Congress concerning civil rights.[101]

Affirmative action was foregrounded for Jimmy Carter when workplace discrimination became an issue. Carter used the Civil Service Reform Act in 1978 to direct the Office of Personnel Management (OPM) to establish minority recruitment. As a result, all executive agencies were to "conduct a continuing program for the recruitment of members of minorities . . . in a manner designed to eliminate underrepresentation . . . within the Federal service."[102] To be considered underrepresented, a minority was to have a smaller percentage of persons in civil service employment than in the general labor force.[103]

A *presidential advisory commission* is an ad hoc advisory group appointed directly by the president and reporting to the public. In his extensive analysis of presidential advisory commissions from Truman to Nixon, Thomas Wolanin describes their five general functions in this way. Most presidential advisory commissions study a specific problem, assess existing efforts to solve it, and recommend an appropriate course of action. Other presidential advisory commissions serve as window dressing to persuade decision makers in Congress or the bureaucracy and the general public to support a proposal that already has the president's support. Still others respond to crisis. Although this is not generally how they are used, several have had this objective as a secondary purpose. Presidential advisory commissions, finally, can be used by a president to avoid an issue or to insulate an administration from having to take any meaningful remedial action on that issue.[104]

The issue-oriented presidential commissions that attracted the most controversy were those established to deal with pornography. Because these commissions had important consequences on presidential politics, it is useful to assess their impact.

The President's Commission on Obscenity and Pornography, also known as the Johnson Commission, was an eighteen person commission appointed in 1967 to study the distribution of obscene material and to see whether there was a link between antisocial behavior and obscenity. Staffed by attorneys and social scientists, the Johnson Commission was to analyze the laws that now monitor obscenity and to look at the volume of traffic in obscenity as well as assess the effect of pornography on the public, especially young people. Finally, the commission was to make administrative and recommendations for action to be taken.

When the final report came out in September 1969, commission members had not reached total agreement. The majority indicated that, based on their findings, (1) there was no evidence that would allow one to conclude that exposure to pornography encourages juvenile delinquency and criminal behavior; (2) repealing censorship laws would not increase the availability of pornographic material; (3) there was no evidence to suggest that exposure to sexual materials has any affect on moral attitudes; and finally, (4) those laws that prohibit the sale of pornographic materials should be repealed.[105] The 1969 Johnson Commission also recommended that state and local governments share in this responsibility to regulate and control the transmission of obscenity.

The Johnson Commission reported its findings during Richard Nixon's term in office. Nixon wanted it made quite clear that the findings of this report would not receive his administration's endorsement; in fact, he would do all he could to reject its findings. Nixon stated in no uncertain terms that he "categorically reject[ed] its morally bankrupt conclusions and major recommendations."[106] Nixon further stated in October 1970 that "pornography can corrupt a society and a civilization. The people's elected representatives have the right and obligation to prevent that corruption . . . Smut should not be simply contained at its present level; it should be outlawed in every State in the Union. And the legislatures and courts at every level of American government should act in unison to achieve that goal . . . I am well aware of the importance of protecting freedom of expression. But pornography is to freedom of expression what anarchy is to liberty."[107] Nixon further swore that "so long as I am in the White House, there will be no relaxation of the national effort to control and eliminate smut from our national life."[108] Nixon did not stop with these stern words but went on to enlist the services of a number of individuals in his administration—his vice president, his press secretary, and the postmaster general as well as several of his close advisors—to speak against the commission report. Blaming "radical-liberals" in the Democratic party for the report, these spokespersons made the report a major issue throughout the remainder of the 1970 off-year election campaign.

Nixon's rejection of the 1967 Johnson Commission report encouraged Ronald Reagan to establish a second pornography commission, the 1985 *Attorney General's Commission on Pornography* (also known as the Meese Commission, named after Edwin Meese, Reagan's Attorney General), that would ultimately determine that pornography *was* linked to antisocial behavior.[109] During 1984, Ronald Reagan had announced that his attorney general, Edwin Meese, would organize and staff a new president's commission to reexamine the effects of obscenity on society. In February 1985, Meese named the eleven-member commission, asking it to recommend measures that might control the distribution and production of obscene material. While the mandates for the two commissions were similar, the Meese commission was quite unlike the

1967 commission created by Lyndon Johnson. The two commissions were dissimilar in staffing,[110] in methods used to procure information,[111] and in budgetary and time constraints.[112] Findings of the 1985 commission focused on two main areas, child pornography and the pornography of sexual violence. As far as sex and violence were concerned, the commission drew one of the sharpest distinctions from its 1967 counterpart in concluding that "the available evidence strongly supports the hypothesis that substantial exposure to sexually violent materials . . . bears a causal relationship to antisocial acts of sexual violence and, for some subgroups, possibly to unlawful acts of sexual violence.[113] The certainty of its conclusions challenged the findings of the Johnson Commission on the effect of pornography on society. The Meese Commissions "assumed" a causal relationship, which it said was "significantly supported by the clinical evidence as well as by much of the less scientific evidence," as well as "common sense."[114]

Both Ronald Reagan and George Bush felt that the best way to deal with pornography was to use prosecutorial strength against the distributors and advertisers of this material, bringing indictments against individuals and companies in several jurisdictions. In 1988, for example, thirteen corporations and twenty individuals were indicted in eight states for using the mail to advertise and distribute presumed obscene materials through the mails.[115]

Organizations within the executive branch also helped George Bush reduce the spread of pornography that he believed would undercut family values. In 1988, the administration demanded that any film producer, book or magazine publisher, or photographer (some maintained that even sculptors and painters should be included) should be required to record the names, addresses, and ages of any person who appeared in any film or book that showed explicit sexual conduct, providing evidence that those persons involved were eighteen years and older. Any violations were to be handled by the FBI, the U.S. Customs, and the Postal Inspection Service. Not surprisingly, those most in opposition to this procedure included the American Library Association, the American Booksellers Association, Magazine Publishers of America, International Periodical Distributors Association, the American Society of Magazine Editors and the American Society of Magazine Photographers.[116] The strategy was indeed declared unconstitutional by the Supreme Court.

Bush was not dissuaded by this ruling, however. Instead, he saw from the numbers of convictions that occurred in 1990 that his approach was beginning to reap rewards, since in that year alone the FBI, U.S. Customs and the Postal Inspection Service had won 245 convictions against what he called "the smut merchants who deal in child pornography. These creatures have been put on notice. There is no place in America for this horrifying exploitation of children."[117] To the members of the Religious Alliance Against Pornography, President Bush shared his concerns about child pornography on October 10, 1991, when he said that: "it abuses, it degrades, and insults both women and men.

We've all heard the stories: innocent children drawn into the world of pornography, victimized by crimes whose consequences are beyond imagination. This horror must stop. Our administration, is committed to the fullest prosecution of obscenity and child pornography crimes. And as I have stated before . . . this will remain a priority."[118]

Bill Clinton explored a new area affected by child pornography, the Internet, by increasing the strength of existing law enforcement units. To handle the problem, the FBI and the Child Exploitation and Obscenity Section of the Justice Department increased their staffs handling the computer exploitation of minors by 50 percent under Clinton. During Clinton's years in office, the U.S. Customs increased its child pornography convictions from thirty-five in 1995 to ninety in 1996. Clinton's Attorney General's Advisory Committee also began to train prosecutors and law enforcement persons in the latest computer technology.[119]

FEDERALISM: THE STATES

Not only was the chief executive role used to staff and shape the administrations of these presidents, but a president exercising the chief executive role has been used to shape and redefine *federalism* as it relates to at least one of the social issues—environmental concerns. Social policymaking and its implementation occur at the subnational levels as well, further complicating the oversight activities of the president as chief executive. States and local areas have always served as laboratories for testing policy initiatives.[120] For Roosevelt, the concept of federalism changed from the pre–New Deal *dual* federalism, in which states were thought to possess equal sovereignty, to *cooperative* federalism, in which the states and local areas became almost extensions of the federal government in encouraging national priorities.[121] While Roosevelt centralized most environmental decisions, he was willing to work with the states on some problems, as he did in West Virginia, where the Forest Service, the CCC and the state conservation preserves helped restore trees that logging had denuded in the mountains

Clinton, similarly, was willing to work with states as partners on environmental policy as long as his administration found the state's proposals acceptable. In California for example, he successfully worked to allocate the water in San Francisco Bay to both agriculture and urban users; in Florida, the Army Corps of Engineers was sent to assist in the rehabilitation of the Florida Everglades. Not all states, to be sure, approved of the Clinton administration's proposals to "intrude" into state jurisdiction in the name of the environment. Clinton ran into the greatest opposition in the West over the plan to reintroduce the wolf into its natural habitat in such places as Yellowstone National Park. Two years after the wolves were introduced in 1995 to the Yellowstone area, Judge William Downes of the Federal District Court in Casper, Wyoming, ruled that the government's wolf recovery program was illegal and ordered the wolves removed from the park and from central Idaho. A stay of that order by the same Judge Downes and the appeals that followed have delayed any action on the judgment.[122]

If the states do not support the president's actions, various inducements can eventually guide states toward achieving purposes satisfying to the executive. These inducements might include funding, technical advice, and assistance to others. Rewards can be substantial if states and local areas will work with the chief executive or his designee. A 1999 program that came out of the Clinton-Gore administration, for example, involved $200 million dollars to be directed to clean rural water projects. These loans and grants were to go to more than 100 safe drinking water projects in some forty states. The distribution of these funds allowed the administration to state that it could achieve positive results in the environment while not neglecting the economy. As the administration's spokesperson stated: "These grants are another example of how we can continue to grow our economy without endangering our environment."[123]

Money also proved to be the major inducement of the Clinton administration's gun control program. Aimed toward putting an end to youth violence, Clinton's gun measure would select out fiftyfour communities to receive more than $100 million in what was called "Safe Schools\Healthy Students grants" designed to discover the best and most workable ideas to reduce youth violence in a community-based program with the federal government. Along with this program, Clinton hoped to encourage every student in the school system to sign a Student Pledge against Gun Violence, wherein students would swear an oath to never bring a weapon to school and never use a gun to settle disagreements. He stated that in 1998 some 1 million students had already signed the pledge and that he hoped many more would sign it in 1999.[124]

PRESIDENTIAL EXPERTISE

The chief executive's expertise gives the president some leverage with Congress in structuring a social agenda. However, the legislative branch lacks the capability to detail administrative regulations in highly technical areas and must seek advice from outside sources.

Information Sources

A president may not wish to use the information given him since it may be incompatible with his ideological preferences or may damage him politically with Congress, the bureaucracy, and the people. Furthermore, cross-cutting information may be too much for him to absorb and use. Aaron Wildavsky, in an early study, summed up the problem of diminishing returns this way: "There is a limit to the amount of information or advice that is useful for the President to have or on which he has time to act. After a while, the addition of new staff just multiples his managerial problems without giving him valuable service in return."[125]

For George Bush, for example, advice on the environment from the Department of Interior, the EPA, and the Department of Energy was weighed against broader political and economic concerns from other sources of information. On environmental issues, both Presidents Clinton and Reagan relied on their vice presidents as so-called pointmen on the initiatives relevant to the "managerial presidency," which were linked to environmental policy with Al Gore heading up the National Performance Review and Bush heading the Task Force on Regulatory Relief.

When all advice fails, a president may just give into his own feelings about what he thinks is the right thing to do regardless of what others may say. For Dwight Eisenhower, pornography had to be brought to a halt at any cost. While concerned with protecting free expression and the free flow of information and going against the advice of some, Eisenhower drew a limit when "indecency" was at issue. As he stated: "We have certain books we bar from the mails and all that sort of thing; I think that is perfectly proper, and I would do it now."[126]

CRISIS AND THE SOCIAL AGENDA

A domestic crisis augments the president's power to implement public policies because two clauses in the Constitution—those giving him "executive power" and those authorizing him to "take care that the laws be faithfully executed "—imply that initiatives may be taken to enforce the laws. The use of force by a president, moreover, is supported by Article 4 of the Constitution, directing the national government to protect every state "against Invasion . . . and against domestic Violence." Such use of federal power may be requested by a state's governor or legislature, although a president can refuse to send assistance. Conversely, a president may intervene in local disturbances when he believes that the state and local authorities are not enforcing federal laws.

Natural Disasters

The chief executive only infrequently experiences crisis in relation to shaping his social agenda. The two exceptions, however, are the environment and gun control. Every time a president declares or is asked to declare a climatic "disaster" within a state, the he does so as chief executive. In 1998 alone, from January 1 through December 31 there were sixty-two officially declared major disasters, including tornadoes, flooding, ice storms, drought, tropical storms, hurricanes, wildfires, a landslide, and a grain elevator explosion.[127] Once a declaration of emergency is established, the Federal Emergency Management Agency (FEMA) may work with as many as twenty-eight other federal agencies as well as the American Red Cross to get the assistance to the victims. Many presidents have been criticized either for not responding quick-ly enough to disasters or for responding too quickly. Although most appreci-ate FEMA, it is small in size and limited in funds. As has been suggested, FEMA lacks "regulatory authority, very limited mandating ability, relatively small budget and grant-issuance power, weak research capacity, profession-al and occupational conflicts (especially at the local level), inadequate agency self-evaluation, weak clientele support, [and] vacillating governor and state legislative support for emergency management."[128]

"Unnatural" Disasters

Gun control becomes an issue of concern each time an "unnatural" dis-aster with weapons results in the death of persons. It is particularly a concern when school violence results in the death of children, as occured on April 21, 1999, at Columbine High School in Littleton, Colorado, when two students killed themselves and thirteen others in the school.[129] Presidents and gun laws are then generally the focus of attention, demanding a president justify his administration's approach to gun control.

CONCLUSION

According to our framework of analysis, the location of the chief executive role at the midpoint of the power continuum suggests that both *authority* and *influence* are central to this role. The chief executive role is neither a president's strongest nor weakest role. Congress understands that the president must be responsible for the day-to-day management of government, but it is unwill-ing to abdicate its other powers to intervene in the affairs of constituency groups and/or special interests. A president can use his control over the ap-pointment process, the budget, and other managerial initiatives to encourage the adoption and/or initiation of social policy.

Although the role is normally weak, a number of presidents have learned to use the resources of the "managerial presidency" to advance their own social policy preferences. Roosevelt, Carter, Reagan, Bush, and Clinton all used the chief executive role to shape environmental policy as they saw fit. Moreover, they relied on different institutional tools to achieve their goals. Reagan and Bush provided regulatory relief and greater access for business in their concern for compliance costs. Carter and Clinton attempted to advance their environmental objectives by expanding participation and improving the regulatory review process. Clinton and two previous Republican adminis-trations experimented with more flexible approaches, using incentives rather than the so-called command-and-control regulation to expand control.

The chief executive role can affect a president's social agenda in major ways. As Jonathan P. West and Glen Sussman argued after examining the chief executive and environmental policy, when a president makes "wise use of existing tools and power resources of the 'managerial presidency' he can, when coupled with action in the president's other roles (e.g., legislative leader) and when circumstances permit, have far-reaching impacts, especially at the implementation stage of the policy process."[130] West and Sussman's conclusion applies equally to every other social policy in the president's social agenda that we have considered.

ENDNOTES

1. Court appointments are some of the president's most important staffing responsibilities in his chief executive role. A sampling of researchers who have recognized this fact includes Raymond Tatalovich and Byron W. Daynes, *Presidential Power in the United States* (Monterey, CA: Brooks/Cole, 1984), 241; Byron W. Daynes, Raymond Tatalovich, and Dennis L. Soden, *To Govern a Nation* (New York: St. Martin's, 1998), 185–87; James P. Pfiffner, *The Modern Presidency*, 2nd ed. (New York: St. Martin's, 1998), 12; *The Powers of the Presidency*, 2nd ed. (Washington, DC: Congressional Quarterly, 1997), 64; and Thomas Cronin, *State of the Presidency*, 2nd ed. (New York: Little Brown, 1980), 165.

2. See "1999-10-05 Statement by the President on Judge Ronnie White," White House Press Secretary, 5 October 1999. <www.pub.whitehouse.gov>.

3. See *Congressional Quarterly's Guide to the Presidency* (Washington, DC: Congressional Quarterly Press, 1989), 260.

4. U.S. President, "Remarks at the Swearing in Ceremony for Louis W. Sullivan as Secretary of Health and Human Services—March 10, 1989, "*Public Papers of the Presidents of the United States* (Washington, DC: Office of the Federal Register, National Archives and Records Service, 1990), 207–10.

5. "President Names Bill Lann Lee as Assistant Attorney General for the Civil Rights Division at the Department of Justice," *The White House: Office of the Press Secretary*, 12 June 1997, <www.pub.whitehouse.gov>. Accessed 13 June 1997.

6. Office of the Press Secretary, "Statement by the President," 21 July 1999. <www.pub.whitehouse.gov.> Accessed 22 July 1999.

7. "Senate Confirms Achtenberg to HUD Position," *New York Times*, 25 May 1995, A16.

8. "*Alumni Newsmaker*: James Hormel, JD'58, Appointed Ambassador to Luxembourg," *University of Chicago Magazine*, October 1999, 47.

9. David W. Dunlap, "Frank Lilly, a Geneticist, 65; Member of National AIDS Panel," *New York Times*, 16 October 1995, B7.

10. Jay Darling, who was originally appointed to head the Bureau of Biological Survey, grew disillusioned with FDR's approach to the environment and become one of his chief critics on the administration's wildlife conservation program.

11. Clinton's early staffing was plagued with missteps. The Senate rejected his first two appointees for attorney general (Zoe Baird and Kimba Wood); moreover, his choice for chief of staff, Thomas F. "Mack" McLarty III, was unable to do well in the position while his surgeon general appointee, Joycelyn Elders, proved too controversial to retain.

12. See Mark Dowie, "Friends of Earth—or Bill? The Selling (Out) of the Greens," *Nation* (18 April 1994), 514.

13. U.S. President, "Nomination for Posts at the Department of State—May 6, 1993, "*Public Papers of the Presidents of the United States* (1994), 468–72.

14. On July 20, 1995, for example, President Clinton announced his intention to appoint Eileen B Claussen as the Assistant Secretary for Oceans, Environment, and International Scientific Affairs for the State Department. "President Names Eileen Claussen to Serve as Assistant Secretary of State for Oceans, Environment, and International Scientific Affairs," Office of the Press Secretary, The White House, July 20, 1995, *Almanac Information Server* 19; 2 pages.

15. Jim Baca, who was Clinton's first Bureau of Land Management head, was another activist who later quit the administration, disillusioned with Clinton's decision-making style.

16. See M. Glenn Abernathy, Dilys M. Hill, and Phil Williams, *The Carter Years: The President and Policy Making* (London: Frances Pinter, 1984) 106–108; Herbert D. Rosenbaum and Alexej Ugrinsky, eds., *The Presidency and Domestic Policies of Jimmy Carter* (Westport, CT: Greenwood Press, 1994) 739; and John Dumbrell, *The Carter Presidency: A Re-Evaluation* (Manchester: Manchester University Press, 1993), 77.
17. See Jeffrey Rosen, "Mediocrity on the Bench," *New York Times*, 17 March 1995, A15; and Carl Rowen, "President Did Federal Bench a Disservice," *Salt Lake Tribune*, 5 April 1996, A19.
18. "Remarks by Telephone to Annual Convention of the Knights of Columbus in Chicago, Illinois, August 5, 1986." *Presidential Papers Infobase*, CDex Information Group, Lindon, UT, <e-mail, Cdex@autosim.com>.
19. Richard Regen, "Frontier justices," *Village Voice* (3 January 1989): 26.
20. Barbara Hinkson Craig and David M. O'Brien, *Abortion and American Politics* (Chatham, NJ: Chatham House, 1993), 174–78.
21. Nancy Maveety, *Justice Sandra Day O' Connor: Strategist on the Supreme Court* (Lanham, MD: Rowman and Littlefield, 1996), 18–19; also see "Hearings before the Senate Judiciary Committee on the Nomination of Judge Sandra Day O' Connor of Arizona to Serve as an Associate of the Supreme Court of the U.S.," 97th Cong., 1st sess. (1981), 125.
22. In 1988, the Supreme Court supported a president's power of removal when it stated that "the power of removal from office is incident to the power of appointment." See *Carlucci, Secretary of Defense, et al. v. Doe*, 488 U.S. 99 (1988).
23. *Carlucci, Secretary of Defense, et al. v. Doe*, 488 U. S. 94 (1988).
24. Michael Nelson, ed., *Congressional Quarterly's Guide to the Presidency*, 2nd ed. (Washington, DC: Congressional Quarterly, 1996), 507.
25. Nelson, *Congressional Quarterly's Guide to the Presidency*, 679.
26. Lyn Ragsdale, *Vital Statistics on the Presidency* (Washington, DC: Congressional Quarterly, 1996), chap. 7.
27. William Doyle, *Inside the Oval Office: The White House Tapes from FDR to Clinton* (New York: Kodansha International, 1999), 11.
28. J. Edward Kellough, *Federal Employment Opportunity Policy and Numerical Goals and Timetables* (New York, Praeger, 1989), 15.
29. Ruth P. Morgan, *The President and Civil Rights: Policy-Making by Executive Order* (Lanham, MD: University Press, 1987), 87–88.
30. U.S. President, "Statement by the President: Equal Opportunity Day—November 18, 1957," *Public Papers of the Presidents of the United States* (1958), 237.
31. See Norman C. Thomas and Joseph A. Pika, *The Politics of the Presidency*, rev. 4th ed. (Washington, DC: Congressional Quarterly, 1997), 267.
32. See Richard Lowitt, "Conservation, Policy On," in Leonard W. Levy and Louis Fisher, eds. *Encyclopedia of the American Presidency*, vol. 1 (New York: Simon and Schuster, 1994), 289.
33. U.S. President, "A Typical Executive Order (6910) on Withdrawal of Public Lands to Be Used for Conservation and Development of Natural Resources—November 26, 1934," *Public Papers and Addresses of Franklin D. Roosevelt* (New York: Macmillan, 1938), 477–79.
34. U.S. President, "Statement on Signing an Executive Order for the Control of Air and Water Pollution at Federal Facilities—February 4, 1970," *Public Papers of the Presidents of the United States* (1971), 78.
35. Office of the Press Secretary, "President Clinton and Vice President Gore: Clean Waters across America," The White House <www.pub.whitehouse.gov>. 14 August 1999. Accessed August 14, 1999.
36. U.S. President, "Remarks on the Federal Fleet Conversion to Alternative Fuel Vehicles—December 9, 1993, "*Public Papers of the Presidents of the United States* (1994), 2145–46.
37. Alison Mitchell, "President Designates a Monument across Utah," *New York Times, (*19 September 1996), B11.
38. *McLaughlin Report*, Public Broadcasting System, 22 September 1996.
39. Michael Kramer, "Reagan's Backdoor War on Abortion," *U.S. News and World Report* 103.7 (17 August 1987), 14.
40. U.S. President, "Proclamation 5761—National Sanctity of Human Life Day—January 14, 1988," *Public Papers of the Presidents of the United States* (1990), 42–43.
41. U.S. President, "Proclamation 5280—National Adoption Week—November 13, 1984," *Public Papers of the Presidents of the United States* (1986), 1827–82.
42. U.S. President, "Proclamation 5890—Pregnancy and Infant Loss Awareness Month, 1988—October 25, 1988," *Public Papers of the Presidents of the United States* (1990), 1384.

43. Glenn C. Graber, "Fetal Tissue Research Will Not Increase Abortion," in Charles P. Cozic and Jonathan Petriken, eds., *The Abortion Controversy* (San Diego: Greenhaven Press, 1995), 235.

44. Barbara Hinkson Craig and David M. O'Brien, *Abortion and American Polities* (Chatham, NJ: Chatham House, 1993), 354–55.

45. "Proclamation 5331—National Child Safety Awareness Month, 1985—April 29, 1985," *Presidential Papers Infobase.* CDex Information Group, Lindon, UT, <e-mail, cdex@autosim.com>.

46. Office of the Press Secretary, "National Day of Concern about Young People and Gun Violence, 1999," The White House <www.pub.whitehouse.gov>. 22 October 1999. Accessed 22 October 1999.

47. Office of the Press Secretary, "Protecting Children from Gun Violence, July 15, 1999," <www.pub.whitehouse.gov>. Accessed 16 July 1999.

48. In 1939, this practice ended when Congress established oversight procedures governing reorganizations. See Tatalovich and Daynes, *Presidential Power in the United States,* 203.

49. U.S. President, "Three Essentials for Unemployment Relief (CCC, FERA, PWA)—March 21, 1933," *Public Papers and Addresses of Franklin D. Roosevelt* (New York: Macmillan, 1938), . . . 80–84.

50. U.S. President, "Special Message to the Congress about Reorganization Plans to Establish the Environmental Protection Agency and the National Oceanic and Atmospheric Administration—July 9, 1970," *Public Papers of the Presidents of the United States* (1971), 578–86.

51. U.S. President, "Statement Announcing the Creation of the Environmental Quality Council and the Citizens' Advisory Committee on the Environment—May 29, 1969," *Public Papers of the Presidents of the United States* (1971), 186; Russell E. Train, "Environmental Record of the Nixon Administration," *Presidential Studies Quarterly* (Winter 1996); 186.

52. See Donald F. Kettl, "Did Gore Reinvent Government? A Progress Report," *New York Times,* 6 September 1994, A19.

53. Al Gore, *The Best Kept Secrets* (Washington, DC: Government Printing Office, 1996), 90.

54. Gore, *The Best Kept Secrets,* 17.

55. Office of the Press Secretary, "President Clinton and Vice President Gore: Growing Clean Energy for the 21st Century," <www.pub.whitehouse.gov>. 12 August 1999. Accessed 12 August 1999.

56. Office of the Press Secretary, "Executive Order: Developing and Promoting Biobased Products and Bioenergy," <www.pub.whitehouse.gov>. 1999-08-12 Executive Order on Developing Biobased Products, 12 August 1999. Accessed 12 August 1999.

57. U.S. President, "Remarks on Earth Day—April 21, 1993," *Public Papers of the Presidents of the United States* (1994), 468–72.

58. "Call for an Investigation into Activities of the Environmental Protection Agency," *Congressional Record-House,* 104th Congress, 1st Session, 9 May 1995, pp. H4609-H4616.

59. U.S. President"Annual Message to the Congress on the State of the Union," 12 January, 1961. *Public Papers of the Presidents of the United States* (Washington, DC: Office of the Federal Register, National Archives and Records Service, 1961), 913–31.

60. U.S. President, "Special Message to the Congress on Civil Rights—February 28, 1963," *Public Papers of the Presidents of the United States* (Washington, DC: Office of the Federal Register, National Archives and Records Service, 1964), 221–30.

61. U.S. President, "Equal Employment Opportunity Enforcement," Message to Congress Transmitting Reorganization Plan No. 1 of 1978—February 23, 1978, *Public Papers of the Presidents of the United States* (Washington, DC: Office of the Federal Register, National Archives and Records Service, 1979), 401.

62. U.S. President, "Memorandum for the Heads of Executive Departments and Agencies—July 20, 1977," *Public Papers of the Presidents of the United States* (1997–98), 1293.

63. U.S. President, "Memorandum on the Civil Rights Working Group—August 8, 1994." *Public Papers of the Presidents of the United States* (Washington, DC: Office of the Federal Register, National Archives and Records Service, 1995), 430–432.

64. U.S. President, "Memorandum on the Civil Rights Working Group—August 8, 1994."

65. The President of the United States, A Proclamation "National Day of Concern about Young People and Gun Violence, 1999," 21 October 1999. The White House <www.pub.whitehouse.gov>. Accessed 22 October 1999.

66. See the very fine studies of presidential leadership by Shirley Anne Warshaw, including *Powersharing: White House–Cabinet Relations in the Modern Presidency* (Albany: State Uni-

versity of New York Press, 1996) and her more recent *The Domestic Presidency: Policy Making in the White House* (Boston: Allyn and Bacon, 1997).

67. Department of Commerce, Economics and Statistics Administration, Bureau of the Census, *Statistical Abstract of the United States: 1998,* 118th ed. (Washington, DC) Department of Commerce, 1998), 353.
68. Richard Pious, *The American Presidency* (New York: Basic Books, 1979), 240.
69. U.S. President, "Special Message to the Congress Proposing Futher Legislation to Strengthen Civil Rights — April 28, 1966," *Public Papers of the Presidents of the United States* (1967), 461–69.
70. Gary L. McDowell, "Affirmative Inaction," *Policy Review* 48 (Spring 1989), 32–37.
71. Karen O' Connor and Lee Epstein, "Rebalancing the Scales of Justice," *Harvard Journal of Law and Public Policy,* (Fall 1984): 483–506.
72. U.S. President, "Executive Order 12902 — Energy Efficiency and Water Conservation at Federal Facilities — March 8, 1994," *Public Papers of the Presidents of the United States* (1995), 409.
73. *United States v. Lopez,* 514 U.S. 549 (1995).
74. U.S. President, "The President's Radio Address — April 29, 1995," *Public Papers of the Presidents of the United States* (1996), 610–11.
75. Office of the Press Secretary, "President Clinton Unveils Initiatives to Protect Our Communities from Gun Violence," 9 September 1999 <www.pub.whitehouse.gov>. Accessed 9 September 1999.
76. Donald Alexander Downs, *The New Politics of Pornography* (Chicago: University of Chicago Press, 1989) , 25.
77. U.S. President, "Remarks on Signing the Child Protection Act 1984 — May 21, 1984," *Public Papers of the Presidents of the United States:* Ronald Reagan (1985), 722.
78. Jim McGee, U.S. Crusade against Pornography Tests the Limits of Fairness," *Washington Post,* 11 January 1993: A1. IN 2113431/9 DIALOG (R) File 146: *Washington Post* Online (1997).
79. McGee, "U.S. Crusade against Pornography Tests the Limits of Fairness."
80. U.S. President, "The President's News Conference — August 29, 1962," *Public Papers of the Presidents of the United States: John F. Kennedy* (Washington. DC: Governmental Printing Office, 1963), 650.
81. Linda Greenhouse, "Supreme Court Roundup: Child Smut Conviction Vacated after U.S. Shift," *New York Times,* 2 November 1993, B7.
82. 32 F3d 733 (3rd, 1994); Cert. denied 513 U.S. 1109 (1995).
83. David Johnston, "Clinton Calls for Expansion of Child Pornography Laws," *New York Times,* 12 November 1993, A14.
84. Michaeli Isiokoff and Ruth Marcus, "Clinton Enters Child Pornography Dispute: Letter to Attorney General Orders Tougher Stand in Wake of Criticism," *Washington Post,* 12 November 1993, A4.
85. "Clinton Justice Department Errs in Diluting Child Pornography Law," *New York Times,* 8 January 1994, 22.
86. "Letter to Attorney General Janet Reno on Child Pornography — November 10, 1993," *Public Papers of the Presidents of the United States: Administration of William J. Clinton.* (Washington, DC: Government Printing Office, 1994), 1952.
87. David Johnson, "Clinton Calls for Expansion of Child Pornography Laws."
88. Herbert Kaufman, *Are Government Organizations Immortal?* (Washington, DC: Brookings Institution, 1976).
89. U.S. Department of Commerce, Economics and Statistics Administration. Bureau of the Census, *Statistical Abstract of the United States: 1998,* 118th ed. (Washington, DC: Department of Commerce, 1998), 353.
90. Cornelius M. Kerwin, *Rulemaking: How Government Agencies Write Law and Make Policy* (Washington, DC: Congressional Quarterly, 1994), 179.
91. U.S. Department of Commerce, *Statistical Abstract of the United States: 1998,* 353, 339.
92. U.S. President "Letter to Secretary McKay Establishing a Cabinet Committee on Water Resources Policy — May 26, 1954," *Public Papers of the Presidents of the United States* (1960), 122.
93. Executive Order 12898 — Federal Actions to Address Environmental Justice in Minority Populations and Low-Income Populations, 3CFR (1994) (11 February 1994): 859–63.
94. Elizabeth A. Palmer, "White House War on Red Tape: Success Hard to Gauge," *Congressional Quarterly Weekly Report,* 2 May 1992, 1155.

95. As its last political and ideological battle before the Clinton administration took over, the Quayle Council attempted to tackle one more environmental issue by redefining the meaning of "wetlands" in response to pressure by farmers and developers who wanted wetlands reduced in size. Had the council succeeded in its efforts, it would have preceded a congressionally sanctioned study by the National Academy of Sciences ordered to settle the scientific dispute over wetlands. See John H. Cushman, Jr., "Quayle, in Last Push for Landowners, Seeks to Relax Wetland Protections," *New York Times*, 12 November 1992, A8.

96. Kerwin, *Rulemaking*, 85, and Michael E. Kraft, *Environmental Politics and Policy in the 1990s* New York: HarperCollins, 1995), 19.

97. Kerwin, *Rulemaking*, 184.

98. The Clinton administration thought of creating its own instrument of oversight, but this time to protect environmental concerns rather than business interests. On February 24, 1993, Timothy Noah reported that proposed legislation circulating in the White House would grant the Environmental Protection Agency administrator increased powers to veto the action of any departmental or agency project that might damage environmental quality, public health, or welfare. Such action by the EPA could only be blocked by the president himself. Timothy Noah, "Proposed Legislation Would Give EPA Broad New Powers," *Wall Street Journal*, 24 February 1993, A3.

99. U.S. President, "Informal Extemporaneous Remarks to State Works Progress Administrators— June 17, 1935, " *Public Papers and Addresses of Franklin D. Roosevelt* (New York: Macmillan 1938), 262.

100. U.S. President, "A New Committee on Fair Employment Practice is Established, Executive Order No. 9346—May 27, 1943," *Public Papers and Addresses of Franklin D. Roosevelt* (New York: Russel and Russel, 1950), 228–29.

101. U.S. President, "Annual Message to the Congress on the State of the Union—January 6, 1947," *Public Papers of the United States* (Washington, DC: Office of the Federal Register, National Archives and Records Service, 1963), 1–12.

102. 92 Stat. 1152, 5 U.S.C. 7201(c)(1).

103. Andorra Bruno, "Affirmative Action in Employment," *Congressional Research Service, Report for Congress,* 17 January 1995, 95-165 GOV, 11.

104. Thomas R. Wolanin, *Presidential Advisory Commissions* (Madison: University of Wisconsin Press, 1975), chap. 2.

105. See Leslie W. Gladstone, "Pornography in the United States: A Brief Overview," *Congressional Research Service Report for Congress,* 19 August 1997, 95-759 GOV, 10–11.

106. U.S. President, "Statement about the Report of the Commission on Obscenity and Pornography—October 24, 1970," *Public Papers of the Presidents, 1970: Richard Nixon* (Washington D.C: Government Printing Office, 1971), 940.

107. U.S. President, "Statement about the Report of the Commission on Obscenity and Pornography—October 24, 1970."

108. U.S. President, "Statement about the Report of the Commission on Obscenity and Pornography—October 24, 1970."

109. Byron W. Daynes, "Pornography: Freedom of Expression or Societal Degradation," in Tatalovich and Daynes, *Social Regulatory Policy*, 55.

110. The Meese Commission was heavily staffed by law enforcement persons in contrast to the social scientists who had predominated on the 1967 commission.

111. The Meese Commission used some controversial methods to procure information, including sending some 8,000 letters to retail chain stores warning them that they were guilty of displaying popular soft-core-pornography if they sold magazines such *Playboy* and *Penthouse* and therefore might be identified as distributors of pornography. Playboy Enterprises and the American Booksellers Association immediately brought suit against the commission, charging it with attempting to suppress adult books and magazines and accusing it of harassment and blacklisting.

112. The 1985 commission was limited to a one-year period to budgetary constraints of $500,000, which, in the opinion of some panelists, "prevented us from commissioning independent research." See Robert Pear, "Panel Calls on Citizens to Wage National Assault on Pornography," *New York Times* 10 July, 1986, 10; also see Attorney General's Commission on Pornography, *Final Report*, vol. 1 (Washington, DC: Government Printing Office, 1986).

113. Attorney General's Commission on Pornography, *Final Report*, vol. 1, 326.

114. See U.S. Dept of Justice, "Charter of the Attorney General's Commission on Pornography,"

Attorney General's Commission on Pornography: Final Report (Washington, DC: Government Printing Office, 1986), 226.

115. Robert F. Howe, "U.S. Accused of 'Censorship by Intimidation' in Pornography Cases," *Washington Post*, 26 March 1990, A4.

116. Allan Parachini, "Administration to Fight Ruling on Child Porn Statute," *Los Angeles Times*, 18 July 1989, IN 01506072/9 DIALOG (R) File 630: *Los Angeles Times* Online (1997).

117. U.S. President, "Remarks to the National Association of Evangelicals in Chicago, Illinois—March 3, 1992," *Public Papers of the Presidents of the United States: George Bush* (Washington, DC: Government Printing Office, 1993), 368.

118. U.S. President, "Remarks on the Religious Alliance against Pornography—October 10, 1991." *Public Papers of the Presidents of the United States: George Bush* (1992), 1280.

119. "President, Vice President Announce Strategy for Family Friendly Internet, July 16, 1997," *1997-07-16 Fact Sheets on Internet Decency,* The White House, <www. pub.whitehouse. gov>. Accessed 4 October 1999.

120. See John DeWitt, *Civic Environmentalism: Alternatives to Regulation in States and Communities* (Washington, DC: Congressional Quarterly Press, 1994); Barry G. Rabe, *Beyond the NIMBY Syndrome: Hazardous Waste Facility Siting in Canada and the United States* (Washington, DC: Brookings, 1994); and William R. Lowry, *The Dimensions of Federalism: State Governments and Pollution Control Policies* (Durham, NC: Duke University Press, 1992).

121. Theodore J. Lowi and Benjamin Ginsberg, *American Government: Freedom and Power*, 2nd ed. (New York: Norton, 1992), 84–85.

122. Jim Robbins, "Ranchers Back Ruling on Wolves Out West," *New York Times*, 14 December 1997, sec. 1, p. 37 and William K. Stevens, "Wolves Are Establishing Strong Roots in the Rockies," *New York Times*, 1 June 1999, F3.

123. Office of the Vice President, "Vice President Gore Awards More than $200 Million for Clean Rural Water Projects," 13 July 1999. <www.pub.whitehouse.gov>. Accessed 13 July 1999.

124. Office of the Press Secretary, "National Day of Concern about Young People and Gun Violence, 1999," 21 October 1999. <www.pub.whitehouse.gov>. Accessed 22 October , 1999.

125. Aaron Wildavskys "Salvation by Staff: Reform of the Presidential Office," in Aaron Wildavsky, ed., *The Presidency* (Boston: Little, Brown, 1969), 697.

126. U.S. President, "The President's News Conference—June 17, 1953," *Public Papers of the President of the United States: Dwight D. Eisenhower,* (Washington, DC: Government Printing Office, 1954), 431.

127. FEMA, <http://www.fema.gov/library/diz98.htm> Accessed 1 November 1999.

128. Richard T. Sylves, "Ferment at FEMA: Reforming Emergency Management," *Public Administration Review* 543 (1993): 307.

129. "Gun Spree at Columbine High," *New York Times*, 21 April 1999, 22A .

130. Jonathan P. West and Glen Sussman, "Implementation of Environmental Policy: The Chief Executive," in Dennis Soden, ed., *The Environmental Presidency* (Albany, NY: SUNY Press, 1999), 106.

5

THE CHIEF DIPLOMAT/COMMANDER IN CHIEF AND THE SOCIAL AGENDA

INTRODUCTION

In contrast to the other presidential roles discussed in this book, the *chief diplomat* or *commander in chief*, is usually a strong position, concerned primarily with foreign and military relations rather than domestic politics—although domestic and international affairs may intersect, depending on the nature and scope of the issue. As chief diplomat, the president has been designated the "sole organ" of communication with foreign nations.[1] As commander in chief, the president serves as a civilian authority while presiding over a vast defense establishment.

The president as chief diplomat, is involved in the conduct of the country's foreign affairs in several ways, including participation in regional and international agreements, cooperative diplomacy, and regional and international organizations (e.g., the Organization of American States, the United Nations). As well, the United States through the president commits itself to fulfill agreements made through bilateral agreements, diplomacy, and discussions with the leaders of other countries.

The president as commander in chief, engages in myriad activities related to maintaining the country's security. In coordinating these activities, the president must balance the requirements of national security with other important national and international interests, such as public health, environmental quality, and human rights, among others. As the chief civilian military leader, the president must promote the country's interests but at the same time must take actions that might pose a direct and serious threat to the well-being of the environment or lead to dissension within the ranks of the military. For example, during the Vietnam War, in addition to the damage created by the tonnage of bombs dropped during the conflict, Agent Orange created serious public health and environmental problems; during the Persian Gulf War carried out by George Bush in his capacity as commander in chief, one outcome was the environmental threat posed by damage to numerous oil refineries. Also as chief civilian military leader, the president must ensure not only that the security interests of the country advanced and protected, but that the interests of the men and the women in the military establishment are promoted. Over the years, the latter have included equal opportunity for African Americans within the military ranks, abortion options for servicewomen on U.S. military bases on foreign territory, and the opportunity to serve and be promoted within the ranks of the military for homosexuals.

In conducting U.S. affairs in the international arena, most presidents have been focused primarily on national security issues, trade concerns, and the global economy's impact on the domestic economy and employment. Nonetheless, social issues that have had a considerable impact on domestic politics have also played a role in actions taken by the president as chief diplomat and commander in chief. At the same time, even though the president maintains considerable leverage in the conduct of the country's foreign relations, constraints on his ability to act remain. The Madisonian model of separation of powers as well as checks and balances establishes an external check on the ability of the president to carry out initiatives and actions as they pertain to foreign affairs.

In studying the president as chief diplomat and commander in chief, we find that roles can overlap and the president might use the power resources of yet another presidential role. In considering military personnel issues, the president might use also chief executive power—such as the executive order—as a means to make policy. During his presidential administration, Franklin Roosevelt established the Committee on Fair Employment Practices and included within its jurisdiction the full participation in the defense program of all persons, regardless of race, creed, or religion. Harry Truman was responsible for desegregation of the military—an act that preceded changes in the larger American society. The president as chief diplomat and commander in chief might also make use of executive orders in an attempt to stem the flow of firearms into the country. As one observer of the gun control issue has argued, "Domestic and international weapons issues are interwined."[2]

Basis of Authority

The president's authority to act as chief diplomat and commander in chief is found in Article 2, Section 2 of the Constitution, which states that the president has the authority to make treaties with other countries and act as

Commander in Chief of the United States armed forces. As such, the president "shall have the Power, by and with the Advice and Consent of the Senate, to make Treaties, provided two-thirds of the Senators concur." Although the president is in an important position constitutionally to set forth treaty commitments for the United States, the separation of powers ensures that the Senate also plays a formal role in the treaty-making process. Article 2, Section 2 also states that "the President shall be Commander in Chief of the Army and Navy of the United States, and of the Militia of the several States when called into actual service of the United States."

In addition to constitutional authority, the president's role in conducting the foreign affairs of the United States has also been influenced by historical precedent, traditions, and custom. As Tatalovich and Daynes argue, the stage was set for presidential preeminence in the conduct of foreign affairs by actions taken by the country's first president, George Washington, who "established customs that were inherited by his successors, thereby paving the way for the executive's preeminence in foreign affairs."[3] Thomas Jefferson, Washington's secretary of state, supported the preeminent position of the president when he stated: "The transaction of business with foreign nations is executive altogether. It belongs, then, to the head of that department, except as to such portions of it as are specifically submitted to the Senate. Exceptions are to be strictly construed."[4] The central role of the president as the primary actor in American foreign policy was also strongly supported by Alexander Hamilton, who argued that the president represents the country in its relationship with other nations "as the *power* which is charged with the execution of the laws, of which treaties form a part; as that which is charged with the command and disposition of the public force."[5]

For the framers of the Constitution, living at a time when the country was new and relatively weak, the responsibility for the security of the young nation was a most important issue. Consequently, the framers also argued over the distribution of powers associated with the war-making capability. Nonetheless, as Alexander Hamilton stated so clearly: "Of all the cares or concerns of government, the direction of war most peculiarly demands those qualities which distinguish the exercise of power by a single hand."[6] However, not all delegates to the Constitutional Convention accepted the president as sole authority. Elbridge Gerry argued that "freedom revolts at the idea, when . . . Despot may draw out his dragons to suppress the murmurs of the few."[7] Moreover, Patrick Henry declared: "If your American chief be a man of ambition and abilities, how easy is it for him to render himself absolute!"[8]

In an examination of the Founding Fathers and legislative-executive powers, Pletcher argues that "during the first forty years of national existence under the Constitution, the division of powers between Congress and the president in the conduct of foreign relations drifted steadily toward the president, giving him authority perhaps not contemplated by the members of the 1787 convention. . . . Nevertheless, the powers of these early presidents were still hedged by the ever-recurring need to go to the people or to Congress for confirmation of their policies."[9] Yet in the field of foreign affairs, political constraints did indeed exist that imposed on presidential prerogative. As Arthur Schlesinger, Jr., argues: "What restrained these early presidents was not only their respect for the Constitution. It was also that they saw Constitutional principles in political context and understood that there unwritten as well as written checks on unilateral presidential initiative in foreign affairs."[10]

Forrest McDonald's study of the relationship between the president and Congress regarding foreign affairs informs us that John Marshall, as a member of Congress (later chief justice of the Supreme Court) in 1800 and the Senate Committee on Foreign Relations in 1816, supported the president as the dominant actor in both diplomacy and its external relations.[11] Moreover, the preeminence of the president in foreign affairs was sustained in a major Supreme Court decision in 1936. Justice George Sutherland, writing for the Supreme Court in *U.S. v. Curtiss-Wright*, argued: "The broad statement that the federal government can exercise no power except those specifically stated in the Constitution, and such implied powers as are necessary and proper to carry into effect the enumerated powers is categorically true only in respect to internal affairs."[12] According to another observer of the *Curtiss-Wright* case, the Supreme Court argued that "the domestic and foreign policy powers of the federal government differed" such that "[*Curtiss-Wright*] did for the president's powers in foreign policy what . . . *McCulloch v. Maryland* did for the powers of the federal government."[13] In addition to the *U.S. v. Belmont* decision one year later, which sustained executive agreements, the Court's opinion that the president enjoys freedom to act in foreign affairs that the office lacks in domestic affairs strengthened the role of the presidency vis-a-vis Congress in foreign affairs.[14]

The United States is bound to other countries in its foreign relations through the use of several instruments including bilateral and multilateral international treaties, executive agreements, and statutory legislation. As "the sole organ of communication with foreign countries, commander in chief, and head of the foreign policy bureaucracy, presidents have been equipped with the means necessary to lead in most phases of the treaty making process."[15] As one observer of executive-legislative relations and international agreements argues, "although the Congress has participated in the making of many international agreements, major commitments . . . have been decided by the president alone."[16] Consequently, the Supreme Court decisions in *Curtiss-Wright* and *Belmont* put the president in a commanding position.

DETERMINANTS OF PRESIDENTIAL POWER

In addition to the constitutional authority upon which the president justifies action in the foreign policy arena, there are several other determinants of presidential power: decision making, public inputs, expertise, and crisis. Each in its own way affects the dynamics of presidential behavior as chief diplomat and commander in chief. In the president's capacity as diplomatic and military leader, several factors have had impact on the *decision-making* process. The debate over diplomacy and the war-making capability that took place among the framers of the Constitution centered on the role played by a single executive and a legislative body, comprised of many representatives of the people. The tug of war that can occur between the president and Congress can result in a problematic relationship, given the diverse interests and perspectives on diplomatic relations with other countries and of national security of the occupant of the White House and the people's representatives who work within the Capitol Building. While the president may not want his hands tied, members of the Congress do not want, for example, either to automatically support treaty commitments or endorse a president's proposed policy, or to be drawn into a conflict merely because the president sets the initiative. Moreover, when decision making occurs, the president might act on one hand as constitutional "dictator" or on the other consult with other important political officials and key advisors, including the vice president, the joint chiefs of staff, the secretaries of state and defense, and congressional leaders.

Public input into policymaking is a problematic factor in domestic politics generally and diplomacy and foreign policymaking in particular. On the one hand, polling the public's sentiments has become an institutionalized factor in American politics. On the other hand, public officials do not necessarily act in accordance with public opinion. Moreover, the public is not well informed about American domestic politics and is even less informed about foreign affairs.[17] The public is likely, therefore, to act deferentially to presidents' foreign policy initiatives. At the same time, despite the debate over the role public opinion should play in public policymaking, public sentiment is aggregated and articulated by interest groups, which can be very effective in the process of influencing members of Congress as well as the president. As far as social issues are concerned, organized interests have played an important role in American domestic politics and electoral politics; they have also exerted influence on issues that involve the president's role of chief diplomat and commander in chief. This influence can be seen, for instance, in the role played by pro-choice and pro-life groups debating the abortion issue as it relates to policymaking both domestically and internationally (e.g., funding United Nations family planning programs) as well as that played by environmental groups in the debate over the North American Free Trade Agreement (NAFTA).

Presidents can engage in diplomatic efforts by arguing that they have a mandate as a result of a previous election. As such, they are acting in the public interest as representative of the people. At the same time, presidents may feel compelled to take action in the international arena when they detect that public opinion is *strongly* in support of or in opposition to specific issues. Richard Nixon's environmental initiatives both domestically and internationally can be viewed in this perspective. On the other hand, presidents may also respond to the pressure exerted by organized interests. For example, in addition to feeling the heat from fellow Republicans, George Bush succumbed to pressure from business and industry when he worked to water down the Global Warming Treaty in 1992 in Rio de Janeiro as well as when he refused to sign the Biodiversity Treaty at the same conference. Consequently, Democratic presidential candidate Bill Clinton could appeal to electoral constituencies in 1992 in his criticism of Bush's actions (or failure to act) at the Earth Summit in Rio.

In the American political system the president acts as both leader of the people in the domestic arena as well as national representative of the citizenry in the international arena. In the domestic political arena, presidential actions are open to public debate because other actors (for example, members of the Congress) have alternative sources of information and the media provide yet another channel of information that may support or oppose the president's public position. In the foreign policy arena, however, presidential initiatives and actions are less likely to be subject to constraints since the president as chief diplomat and commander in chief has an advantage—namely, *expertise*—over other national institutions because of the monopoly in information. In this regard, the president has the power to "suppress the public's 'right to know,' Congress's 'need to know,' and the bureaucracy's 'desire to know.' Expertise, data manipulation, and classification and censorship techniques provided the president . . . with sources of power unavailable to him in his weaker roles."[18]

During times of *crisis* the president's leadership is initially supported by the public in conjunction with at least short term deference by members of the Congress. When the president is in the roles of chief diplomat and commander in chief, "crises usually require a president to confront a threat to our national interest, if not our very survival. In these roles, therefore, a crisis quickly mobilizes a consensus behind the need for decisive action."[19] For example, after the 1962 Cuban missile crisis, President Kennedy engaged in diplomatic efforts to reduce tensions with the Soviet Union. Kennedy was concerned about both the national security threat as well as the threat to public health and the environment posed by nuclear weapons.

The interrelationship between domestic and foreign affairs is also exemplified by gun violence in the United States. As a result of intense media coverage as well as public opinion strongly supportive of stricter restrictions on guns, President Clinton has made an effort to reduce the flow of weapons across national borders.

Although the Congress and the courts have the constitutional authority to exert influence over presidential actions, presidents have over the years—from Washington declaring neutrality to Jefferson's acquisition of the Louisiana territory to Franklin Roosevelt's Lend Lease Program—exercised their prerogative in the foreign policy arena. Presidential preeminence in foreign affairs occurred because the presidency is the only national office elected on a nationwide scale, the president's central position in the political system, the centralization of executive powers occurring in the twentieth century and the president's informational, communication, and bureaucratic resources.[20]

When involved in diplomatic efforts or acting in the capacity of a military leader, the president is confronted with an array of issues important to the United States. In addition to national security issues and the state of the global economy, presidents have been challenged with social issues that have transcended domestic affairs and intervened into the foreign affairs domain. Sometimes the president might act alone; at other times, the president might engage in bilateral or multilateral relations that can include several nations or regional or international organizations. The following discussion addresses four key areas involving the presidency and the social agenda—namely, matters involving military personnel, regional, and international agreements, the international flow of weapons, and international communication and cyberspace. Matters involving military personnel include equal opportunity in the military, abortions at U.S. military bases on foreign territory, and gays in the military. The discussion of regional and international agreements focuses primarily on bilateral and multilateral international environmental agreements. Our concern with gun control as a social issue addresses the international flow of weapons as a transboundary phenomenon. Finally, in the context of international communication and cyberspace we examine the "new" problem of pornography on the Internet—a social issue that involves the impact of new information technology.

THE MILITARY AND SOCIAL POLICY

The military has also played a part in presidents establishing their social agendas. Some presidents have dealt with the military as a separate and distinct society within the larger United States, either tailoring programs for the military alone or, as other presidents have done, insisting that the military comply with the will of the states wherein they are located.

Abortion has been an extremely divisive issue in American domestic politics, and it has also affected the presidents as commander in chief in terms of military personnel policies. In 1971, Richard Nixon issued a directive that changed a liberalized version of abortion policy at domestic military hospitals.[21] While personally opposed to abortions, Nixon did not seek to prohibit a woman's right to seek an abortion but rather directed that abortion policy in military hospitals conform to the laws of the state in which the hospital was located.

The issue gained increased prominence during the Reagan-Bush years, when both presidents opposed a woman's right to choose to have an abortion at a military hospital located outside the United States.[22] Up until 1988, women had access to an abortion at military hospitals on foreign territory. During the last years of Reagan's presidency, however, the administration imposed an abortion ban at all military hospitals abroad. Although George Bush continued the Reagan policy and used the veto power in 1992 to prevent legislation that would have lifted the ban, Bill Clinton reversed this policy very early in his first term in office.[23] However, the ban was reintroduced by the new Republican-controlled Congress in 1995.

Pornography was given added attention on military posts under Ronald Reagan, who at one time considered using an executive order to ban what he and his administration considered to be pornographic material from all of the military post exchanges (PXs). His close advisers, however, indicated that too many constitutional questions would come from such an order.[24] The prediction eventually proved accurate when Congress passed this measure in 1996 with the support of Bill Clinton, only to have it later declared unconstitutional.

As commander in chief, the president has the constitutional authority to become involved in military personnel policy. As Diller and Wirls have reported, "Presidents have usually taken the initiative in proposing changes in the size of the armed forces, the methods by which the ranks are filled, and where U.S. forces will be stationed."[25]

Although African Americans served in the military dating back to colonial times and the Revolutionary War,[26] substantive progress was not made until Franklin Roosevelt and Harry Truman used the power of their office — through the use of executive orders — to oppose discrimination and support equal opportunity for all citizens, both in the national civilian defense system and in the armed forces of the United States. Franklin Roosevelt's Executive Order 8802 issued June 25, 1941, put the power of the presidency in support of the "full participation in the Defense Program of all persons regardless of race."[27] In the ranks of the armed forces, the conditions of military service had been characterized by segregation and discrimination. During the few instances where African American and white soldiers fought side by side (e.g., the Battle of the Bulge during World War II), it was done out of expediency (the need for "manpower") rather than as a policy decision. During World War II, FDR approved the War Department's policy, which provided opportunities for African Americans to serve in all branches of the military as well as to train and serve as pilots.[28] Despite these War Department initiatives and the fact that African American fighting units had performed admirably in combat, U.S. military units still remained segregated by the end of the war.

The executive order addressing the relationship between the country's national defense program and equal employment opportunity was followed seven years later by Executive Order 9981, issued July 26, 1948, by Harry Truman, which led to the desegregation of the U.S. military.[29] Truman issued the order on the basis of his authority as commander in chief of the armed forces, establishing a committee to consult with the secretaries of State and Defense and the branches of the armed services to establish appropriate procedures in order to implement the order. As Kenneth O' Reilly characterized Truman's EO 9981 to abolish segregation in the armed forces: "As the Army clung to its ten-percent quota policy on black enlistments, Truman personally intervened with Secretary of the Army Gordon Gray. He ended up killing quotas and more."[30]

The impact of Truman's Executive Order 9981 was seen in both the Korean War and Vietnam War, when integration of the armed forces was put into practice. However, as one problem was resolved, another emerged when African Americans suffered increasing casualties and become overrepresented in the military.[31] As Butler reports, there was a noticeably high proportion of African Americans in the U.S. army during the 1980s and early 1990s, most notably during The Persion Gulf war.[32]

Affirmative action/equal opportunity in the military preceded the end of segregation in American society. Despite the existence of problems within the armed forces, opportunities have increased for African Americans as well as other minorities and women. However, the issue of gays in the military remains another divisive and controversial issue for American society in general and the U.S. armed forces in particular. George Bush was the president who campaigned against Democratic hopeful Michael Dukakis when homosexuality became an important issue in the campaign. Dukakis turned his back on the homosexual community when he indicated that if he were president he would refuse to sign an executive order banning discrimination in the military and federal government based on sexual preference.[33] Bush said little and as a result was less offensive to the homosexual community.

Military personnel policy captured center stage when Democratic challenger Bill Clinton indicated in his race for the presidency in 1992 that homosexuals should not be barred from service in the nation's military. In fact, gay PACs were among the largest financial contributors to Clinton's presidential campaign.[34] Candidate Clinton promised to end the ban on homosexuals serving in the military. In January 1993, President Clinton proposed issuing an executive order to fulfill his campaign promise and established his "Don't ask, don't tell" policy in the armed forces.[35] No other action a president took or has taken on social policy affecting the military resulted in such an outcry from both the public and the established military community. Although homosexuals have served in the armed forces over the years, it was the policy of the military establishment that "known" homosexuals would be discharged from service. According to military and political opponents of Clinton's proposal, the very fabric of military discipline and social relations was threatened by homosexuals serving in the armed forces.[36]

As Table 5.1 indicates, from Franklin Roosevelt to Clinton, homosexuals have generally had a difficult time in their effort to serve in the U.S. military. During the Roosevelt and Truman administrations in the 1940s and 1950s, homosexuality was considered a "mental disorder," homosexuals were considered a security risk, and the Uniform Code of Military Justice in 1951

Table 5.1   Presidential Administrations and Gays in the Military

Administration	Time Period	Homosexuality as a Military Problem	Action
Roosevelt	World War II	mental illness	discharge
Truman	late 1940s	security clearance	discharge
	1951	sodomy declared a criminal offense	discharge
Johnson	1966	psychological exams required	exam given prior to discharge
Carter	late 1970s	military reviews policies	no change
Reagan	early 1980s	homosexuality declared incompatible with military service	discharge
	1988	Pentagon study recommends lifting the ban	no change
Clinton	1990s	sexual conduct, privacy issues	"Don't ask, don't tell" policy

Source: Adapted from "Gays in the Military," *Los Angeles Times*, 31, January 1993: A23. (Original source: Senate Armed Services Committee, Congressional Research Service.)

made sodomy a criminal offense. Moreover, military psychiatrists compiled psychological tests that would be used to identify and then discharge homosexuals from the ranks of the military. While some homosexuals were "caught in the act, " others were identified by their peers or by officers due to "suspicious" behavior. Homosexual behavioral traits included acting in an" effeminate manner," having a "strong maternal attachment," "passivity," a "sense of superiority," and "fearfulness."[37]

Prior to becoming president, Franklin Roosevelt served as Secretary of the Navy during the Wilson administration. When allegations were made about "immoral" homosexual activity taking place at the Naval Training Station in 1919, Roosevelt referred to the behavior as "perverted" and "horrible practices."[38] When he became president, Roosevelt "as commander in chief, commuted the five-year prison sentence of a Navy officer who had just been convicted of homosexual activity, ordering his dismissal instead."[39]

When the Johnson administration began to escalate the U.S. military commitment in South Vietnam, homosexuals were required to take a psychiatric exam prior to their departure from the service. Although the military began to review its policies during the Carter administration, no substantive changes were made by the Defense Department. In the early years of the Reagan administration, homosexuality was still considered "incompatible with military service," and resulted in discharge. In the early 1990s, "gays in the military" because a salient issue when Bill Clinton campaigned for the presidency with a commitment to lift the ban that prohibited homosexuals from serving in the military. Although he was confronted with considerable political opposition, the Pentagon had recommended a similar course of action only a few years earlier.

Once in office, Clinton embraced the position that it was time to end restrictions on military service. President Clinton stated his position in a news conference in January 1993 when he said that "I believe that American citizens who want to serve their country should be able to do so unless their conduct disqualifies them from doing so."[40] The resulting debate divided the president, the military, and members of the Congress. Although opponents, including Senator Sam Nunn of Georgia, one of the most vocal adversaries, framed the issue in terms of "moral, religious, and civil rights," the fundamental issue appeared to be the extent to which lifting the ban would have a negative impact on "military morale and cohesion."[41]

As commander in chief, Clinton faced strong opposition from members of the Congress as well as the military. The Joint Chiefs of Staff, including its chair, General Colin Powell, and his predecessor, Admiral William Crowe, opposed Clinton's plan to lift the ban on military service among homosexuals.[42] According to a U.S. Army major opposed to Clinton's action, the military opposition to homosexuals serving in the military is that "once the Army presents evidence that there is a rational basis between excluding homosexuals and the maintenance of morale, good order, and discipline within the armed forces, the burden shifts to plantiffs. . . . Few plaintiffs have presented affirmative evidence in an effort to negate the Army's showing. . . . No plaintiff has yet attempted to show that homosexuality is compatible with military service."[43]

The debate over gays serving in the military was somewhat reminiscent of the effort to end segregation in the armed forces. Fifty years before, Senator Strom Thurmond of South Carolina argued against desegregating the military because it would be bad for morale; yet Thurmond brushed aside a similar question posed by reporters equating the debate about homosexual's military service to the debate about desegregating the armed forces, declaring that that issue (desegregation) had already been settled.[44] Nonetheless, some of the issues involved in the desegregation debate can be found in the current one. For example, from the military's point of view, morale and cohesiveness along with esprit de corps would be undermined if homosexuals and heterosexuals were compelled to work and associate in the close living conditions characteristic of life in the military.[45]

A study by Jones and Koshes about homosexuality and the military published in the *American Journal of Psychiatry* in 1995 examined the three primary arguments used by the military to exclude homosexuals from serving in the armed forces—that homosexuality was a mental disorder, homosexuals were a source of poor morale, and homosexuals were a security risk.[46] Using data from military archives, the two MDs concluded that homosexuals should not be barred from military service because there was no substantial body of evidence to support the military's concerns. The researchers acknowledged, however, that morale and fraternization remained issues to be addressed. Moreover, among the sixteen member states of the North Atlantic Treaty Organization (NATO), homosexuals are accepted in the military in fourteen.[47] Canada and Australia, which reversed their policy and lifted their ban on homosexuals serving in the armed forces, have not reported any significant problems.[48]

Organized interests also played an active role in this controversial issue. The Christian Coalition along with other religious and military organizations put pressure on Congress to oppose Clinton's plan.[49] On the other side, the Campaign for Military Service, for example, lobbied Congress in favor of Clinton's proposed plan of action. Moreover, the Gay, Lesbian, and Bisexual Veterans of America argued that "Mr. Clinton committed himself and we'll hold him to his promise."[50] Although the "Don't ask, don't tell" policy that eventually emerged was less than Clinton wanted, he accepted the compromise. Clinton argued that "as President of the American people, I am pledged to protect and to promote individual rights. As Commander in chief, I am pledged to protect and advance our security. In this policy, I believe we have come close to meeting both objectives."[51]

INTERNATIONAL DIPLOMACY, NATIONAL SECURITY, AND SOCIAL POLICY

The United States is a member of several regional and international organizations. Because this country is a member of the United Nations, for instance, the president must decide how its participation in a multilateral organization affects national policy.[52] Moreover, the U.S. Constitution and Supreme Court decisions provide an authoritative basis that puts the president in an important position when involved in the process of committing the country to regional and international agreements and supporting regional and international organizations.

Family planning practices have been promoted through international nongovernmental organizations (NGOs) such as the International Planned Parenthood Federation and the United Nations Population Fund. The politics involved in the abortion issue in the 1980s became so divisive that it affected U.S. funding efforts for both NGOs and United Nations population programs during the Reagan-Bush years.

Taking into consideration high fertility rates in developing countries, the Carter administration had taken the position that financial assistance could be employed in several ways, including an effort to reduce population growth; in contrast, the Reagan approach to foreign aid focused on economic growth only.[53] Reagan was less concerned about curbing the population explosion, which led to cuts in funding to NGOs whose policies might include family planning or abortion. In what became known as the "Mexico City Policy," the

"Reagan and Bush administrations prohibited the provision of funds to any non-governmental organization that was involved in abortion activities even if U.S. funds were not used for such activities."[54] Moreover, Reagan was concerned about the UN Population Fund's policy of providing assistance to countries where "coercive family planning practices" occurred. In the view of the Reagan administration, the program "either encouraged or permitted abortions in foreign countries."[55] Reagan's and Bush's primary concern was that the United Nations agency included China in its family planning program and China had been "condemned for its coercive abortion policy." [56] U.S. aid was all but eliminated from the UN Population Fund toward the end of Reagan's second term through the entire presidency of George Bush.[57] In fact, Bush threatened to make use of the veto if Congress attempted to restore the funding, and he used it when he opposed a 1989 foreign aid package which included assistance for the UN Population Fund.[58]

The election of Bill Clinton as president resulted in a reversal of the Reagan-Bush approach to international family planning. The Mexico City Policy was terminated and funding was restored to NGOs as well as to the UN Population Fund.[59] Clinton also provided financial assistance to foreign programs that included abortion as an option.[60]

The Global Environment and International Diplomacy

Although environmentalism has not been a major part of the political agenda of most presidents, several presidents have been engaged in regional and global efforts in support of environmental protection. Table 5.2 shows the proportion of international environmental agreements concluded by American presidents in relation to the total number of international agreements. A cursory assessment of international environmental agreements suggests that they constitute a rather small proportion of all agreements, ranging from a high of 28 percent to a low of 11 percent. Except for the Truman and Eisenhower administrations, when environmental agreements ranked fourth and third, respectively, out of the eight categories employed by Ragsdale, in each succeeding administration presidents have concluded more environmental agreements than in any other policy area except for defense and/or social welfare/civil rights.

All presidents from Roosevelt through Clinton have concluded environmental agreements either on a bilateral or multilateral basis. As Table 5.3 suggests, many of the earlier presidents signed agreements that focused on conservation and international marine interests. Franklin Roosevelt, for example, took several actions in support of conservation. During a campaign stop in West Virginia during the 1936 presidential campaign, Roosevelt considered it important to outline the accomplishments of his administration in wildlife conservation.[61] In order to ensure the safe passage of migratory birds in the northern hemisphere, the Roosevelt administration concluded the Migratory Bird Treaty with Mexico,

Table 5.2   Presidents and U.S. International Environmental Agreements[1]

Administration	Total International Agreements	International Environmental Agreements	Environmental Agreements as a Percentage of Total Agreements
Roosevelt	—	—	—
Truman	848	96	11.3%
Eisenhower	1,920	275	14.3
Kennedy	831	117	14.1
Johnson	1,112	247	22.2
Nixon	1,296	248	19.1
Ford	776	165	21.3
Carter	1,169	312	26.7
Reagan	1,251	350	28.0
Bush	1,011	186	18.4
Clinton	1,005	252	25.2

[1]According to Lyn Ragsdale, (1) the data include treaties, executive agreements, protocols, and conventions, and (2) environmental agreements include the following policy and program areas: energy, environment, transportation, communications, weather and navigation stations, land transfers, and space and aeronautics programs unrelated to defense.

Source: Adapted from Lyn Ragsdale, *Vital Statistics on the Presidency: Washington to Clinton* (Washington, DC: Congressional Quarterly Press, 1996), 318–21. Data for Clinton administration from Lyn Ragsdale, *Vital Statistics on the Presidency*, rev. ed. (Washington, DC: Congressional Quarterly Press, 1998), 329.

Table 5.3   The Presidency and International Environmental Diplomacy, Selected Agreements

Presidency	International Environmental Agreements
Roosevelt	Convention for the Protection of Migratory Birds and Game Animals, 1936 Protection of Halibut and Salmon Fisheries, 1936 Convention on Nature Protection and Wildlife Preservation in the Western Hemisphere, 1940
Truman	International Whaling Convention, 1946 Convention on Halibut Fishing Vessels, 1946 Treatment of Fur Seals, 1952
Eisenhower	International Convention for the Prevention of Pollution of the Sea by Oil, 1954 North Pacific Fur Seals Convention, 1957 Convention on Fishing and Conservation of the Living Resources of the High Seas, 1958
Kennedy	Protocol on North Pacific Furs, 1963 Limited Nuclear Test Ban Treaty, 1963

(Continued)

Table 5.3 (continued)

Presidency	International Environmental Agreements
Johnson	The King Crab and Fishing Operations Agreement, 1964 Harp and Hood Seals Agreement, 1966 Protocol on Northwest Atlantic Fisheries, 1966
Nixon	Treaty for the Conservation of Antarctic Seals, 1972 Convention on the Prohibition of the Development, Production, and Stockpiling of Bacteriological and Toxin Weapons, 1972 Convention on Trade in Endangered Species of Wild Fauna and Flora (CITES), 1973
Ford	International Convention Relative to Intervention on the High Seas in Cases of Oil Pollution Casualties, 1975 International Convention for the Prevention of Pollution by Ships, 1976 Conservation of Polar Bears Treaty, 1976
Carter	Great Lakes Water Quality Agreement, 1978 Convention on Long-Range Transboundary Air Pollution, 1979 Physical Protection of Nuclear Material, 1979
Reagan	Convention on the Conservation of Antarctic Marine Living Resources, 1980 Convention on the Conservation of Salmon in the North Atlantic Ocean, 1983 Montreal Protocol on Substances That Deplete the Ozone Layer, 1987
Bush	Agreement on the Control and Movement of Hazardous Waste, 1990 London Amendment to the Montreal Protocol on Substances That Deplete the Ozone Layer, 1991 Climate Change Convention, 1992[1]
Clinton	Convention on Biological Diversity, 1992[2] North American Free Trade Agreement, 1993 [Restored U.S. Aid to the United Nations Population Fund][3]

[1]Bush refused to sign the agreement until it was revised reflecting voluntary rather than mandatory emission reductions.

[2]Although Clinton signed the agreement (Bush refused to do so), the U.S. Senate refused to ratify it.

[3]The Reagan and Bush administrations had terminated funding because of concerns about abortion.

Source: Adapted from Peter M. Haas with Jan Sundgren, "Evolving International Environmental Law: Changing Practices of National Sovereignty," in Nazli Choucri, ed., *Global Accord* (Cambridge, MA: MIT Press, 1993), 420–29; Lamont C. Hempel, *Environmental Governance* (Washington, DC; Island Press, 1996), 170–72; Carolyn Long, Michael Cabral, and Brooks Vandivort, "The Chief Environmental Diplomat: An Evolving Arena of Foreign Policy," in Dennis Soden, ed., *The Environmental Presidency* (Albany, NY: State University of New York Press, 1999), 194–219.

which complemented a similar treaty concluded earlier with Canada. The rationale underlying Roosevelt's action was his commitment to conserving species for future generations. By the time Nixon assumed the presidency, endangered species were a global concern as well as oil pollution of the world's oceans and protecting the environment from the threat posed by nuclear weapons. Moreover, by the 1980s and 1990s, new global issues emerged, including stratospheric ozone depletion, acid rain, biodiversity, and global warming.

During the last two decades, the president has played an important role in several significant international agreements covering the new global environmental threats. Although Reagan is generally viewed as having an anti-environmental agenda, the one area where the United States used its influence in support of global environmental protection during the Reagan administration was the Montreal Protocol on Ozone Depletion of 1987. Scientific concern about the hole in the ozone layer and its consequences first arose in 1974. Although several countries, including the United States, imposed a ban on "nonessential chlorofluorocarbons (CFCs) (e.g., aerosol sprays) and the Vienna Convention for the Protection of the Ozone Layer of 1985 called on nations to take "appropriate measures to protect the ozone layer,"[62] substantive international action did not result until 1987. The Montreal Protocol required signatories to the agreement to work toward substantive reductions in the production of CFCs. In this case, the Reagan administration, in contrast to its domestic environmental agenda, supported the international effort to combat a global environmental threat. After encouraging Senate ratification of the protocol, Reagan signed the instrument of ratification in 1998, stating: "The Montreal Protocol is a model of cooperation. It is a product of the recognition and international consensus that ozone depletion is a global problem."[63]

Prior to the well-publicized Earth Summit in Rio de Janeiro, delegates at the United Nations World Climate Conference in 1990 met to discuss the global climate problem resulting of carbon dioxide emissions. Although most industrialized countries agreed to work toward the stabilization or reduction in the amount of carbon dioxide contributing to climatic change, political and business pressure on George Bush at home led to the United States' failure to join its global partners in the collaborative effort.[64] The Earth Summit of 1992, which took place in Rio once again, provided the opportunity for the president of the United States to provide global leadership concerning the environment. The fact that over a hundred delegates participated at the summit demonstrated that the environment had finally become a central part of the global agenda.[65]

Two major environmental issues at the summit were biodiversity and global warming. Although President Bush and campaigned that he would be the "environmental" president, his behavior at the summit indicated a clear reversal in his commitment to environmental priorities. Midway through Bush's presidency, inconclusive evidence about the global warming phenomenon among members of the scientific community played a role, in part, in his failure to join other delegates in signing the proposed global warming treaty.[66] In fact, Bush used his influence to alter the details of the agreement and pressure fellow international representatives to sign the new version. Specifically, he was able to persuade delegates to support his plan on global warming gases, which excluded binding timetables for reducing emissions or specific levels of emissions. [67] Moreover, Bush's refusal to sign the Biodiversity Treaty left the United States isolated among the host of international delegates.[68] Rather than providing leadership at the Rio convention, Bush exhibited an obstructionist approach. According to Susskind, Bush "held off deciding whether to attend until just a month before the conference" and when he did attend it was "for just three days."[69] Considering the tremendous importance of a convention where delegates from approximately 150 countries were in attendance, the United States was sadly isolated in the international community.

After winning the presidency in 1992, Bill Clinton signed the Biodiversity Treaty, but the international agreement was held up in the Senate. In addition to multilateral, international efforts to address global environmental problems, Clinton has also engaged in regional negotiations in an effort to promote environmental protection. Acid rain is a clear example of an issue that has been a source of tension between two countries—in this case, the United States and Canada. As a result of pollutants from Midwest power plants in the United States, for instance, Canadian lakes and forests have been degraded. In contrast to the global debate over stratospheric ozone depletion, the transboundary issue of acid rain between the United States and Canada did not receive the same level of attention or cooperation from President Reagan. Although the issue was addressed through direct meetings between Reagan and the Canadian prime minister or through American and Canadian envoys, it remained unresolved until George Bush assumed the presidency and signed an air quality agreement with Canada in 1991 as an important step in an effort to resolve the acid rain problem.[70] In fact, Canadian prime minister Brian Mulroney's anger about the U.S. role in producing acid rain and its negative impact on his country had caused him earlier to blast the Reagan administration for its "unacceptable" policy and argue that "the United States would be pretty upset with me if I were dumping my garbage in your backyard. That's exactly what is happening, except this garbage is coming from above."[71]

Also in 1991, George Bush was working in support of the regional North American Free Trade Agreement (NAFTA). In addition to citing the economic benefits of free trade between the United States and Mexico, Bush highlighted his position that "prosperity offers the surest road to worker safety, public health, and indeed, environmental quality."[72] Bill Clinton eventually signed the NAFTA agreement into law in 1993, arguing that the legislation would provide both regional economic development and environmental protection.

National Security.   The president serves as commander in chief during routine times as well as periods of conflict. One area of vital importance is that of national security. To ensure that the country is secure, the president sits atop a vast defense establishment. At the same time, national security interests come into conflict with other national interests, including environmental quality. War making, for example, has a devasting impact on the environment. "The environment," according to Nietschmann, "has been both a military target and a casualty of war."[73] Environmental destruction is directly related to military action because of the consumption of resources that could be used for other purposes; the direct impact on the environment from the employment of weaponry; and the pollution that results from war preparation.[74]

The United States, like other countries, is no stranger to war. Two recent examples of presidential war making—Vietnam and the Persian Gulf War—illustrate the devastating impact of war on the environment. During the U.S. military involvement in Vietnam, Presidents Johnson and Nixon ordered massive bombing campaigns of such proportion that tremendous destruction of the countryside occurred. According to one estimate, the use of a herbicide defoliant—Agent Orange—destroyed 50 percent of coastal habitat and 80 percent of all forestland.[75] Moreover, environmental destruction resulted from landmines, bulldozing, metal fragments among other threats to the natural habitat.[76]

The Persian Gulf War in the early 1990s provides another example of the environment as a casualty of presidential war making. While George Bush had the support of a new sense of patriotic pride, "electronic espionage wizardry," "well-trained combat forces," and "smart weaponry" that was "spectacularly demonstrated in the Persian Gulf war,"[77] the damage to the environment remained a minor consideration. One study reports that hundreds of oil wells burned for weeks and perhaps months, the coastline of the Persian Gulf was polluted by oil spills, and marine life was decimated.[78] As commander in chief, George Bush succeeded in his mission to drive Saddam Hussein out of Kuwait. Yet in the process the environment was victimized.

Intended and unintended consequences occur during presidential war making. Of the Persian Gulf War, one student of international politics argues:

> If unintended environmental degradation was not bad enough, 1991 witnessed the sad spectacle to humankind's first calculated attack on the atmosphere. . . . The 1991 war in the Middle East showed that conventional war can also bring environmental havoc. Iraq set fire to some oil facilities and others were set ablaze by allied military action. Not only was a huge reservoir of a valuable natural resource wasted, but the conflagration billowed immense amounts of CO_2 into the atmosphere, adding to the thermal blanket forming around the earth. Even worse, the Iraqis opened oil pipelines and emptied tankers, spewing a black tide of crude petroleum into the Persian Gulf. . . , by far the single greatest man-made environmental catastrophe in human history.[79]

The nuclear arms race provides another example of the competition between maintaining the preeminence of national security interest and the potential threat to the environment. One outcome of the huge nuclear arsenals amassed by the United States and the Soviet Union was the need to engage in testing nuclear weapons and the placement of nuclear weapons at strategic sites. Four treaties that included the United States and the Soviet Union demonstrate the capacity of political leaders in general, and the American president as chief diplomat and commander in chief in particular, to demonstrate a conviction toward both arms control and protecting the environment. The Antarctic

Treaty, signed in Washington in 1959; the Nuclear Test Ban Treaty, signed in Moscow in 1963; the Outer Space Treaty, signed in Washington, Moscow, and London in 1967; and the Seabed Treaty, signed in Washington, London, and Moscow in 1971, were indicative of a diplomatic and collaborative effort to defuse the nuclear threat and protect the environment (see Table 5.4).[80]

By the mid-1950s, there was an increasing international concern about the dangers posed by nuclear weapons testing. After a nuclear explosion in the South Pacific by the United States, the crew of a Japanese fishing vessel, the *Lucky Dragon*, was exposed to radioactive fallout and became severely ill. This incident only added to international concern about radioactive debris resulting from nuclear testing. Although Soviet and American leaders were encouraged to take action, they were unable to agree on appropriate procedures for a viable test ban. According to President Eisenhower, "A simple agreement to stop H-bomb tests cannot be regarded as automatically self-enforcing on the unverified assumption that such tests can instantly and surely be detected."[81]

Table 5.4   Presidential Administration, Nuclear Weapons, and the Environment

Administration	International Agreement	Action
Eisenhower	Antarctic Treaty, 1959	Article V: "Any nuclear explosions in Antarctica and the disposal there of radioactive waste shall be prohibited."
Kennedy	Limited Test Ban Treaty, 1963	Article II: "Each of the Parties to this Treaty undertakes to prohibit, to prevent, and not to carry out any nuclear weapons test explosion . . . in the atmosphere, beyond its limits, including outer space; or under water, including territorial waters or high seas."
Johnson	Outer Space Treaty, 1967	Article IV: "Parties to the Treaty undertake not to place in orbit around the Earth any objects carrying nuclear weapons or any other types of weapons of mass destruction, install such weapons on celestial bodies, or station such weapons in outer space in any manner."
Nixon	Seabed Treaty, 1971	Article I: "Parties to this Treaty undertake not to emplane or emplace on the seabed and the ocean floor . . . any nuclear weapons or any other types of weapons of mass destruction as well as structures launching installations . . . designed for storing, testing or using such weapons."

Source: Data drawn from the U.S. Arms Control and Disarmament Agency, *Arms Control and Disarmament Agreements* (Washington, DC: Government Printing Office, 1996), 11–18, 24–44.

Although the Eisenhower administration was unable to conclude a nuclear test ban with the Soviet Union, it did take action on a regional basis when it worked toward the denuclearization of Antarctica. The Antarctic Treaty of 1959 sought to ensure cooperative scientific exploration of Antarctica among the signatories to the treaty. It also included a prohibition again nuclear explosions in the region as well as storage of radioactive waste. An important consideration in this early and first step toward reducing the security and environmental threat posed by nuclear weapons, Article IX committed the signatories to work toward the "preservation and conservation of living resources in Antarctica." Four decades after the Antarctic Treaty was signed, one student of international law characterized the status of the treaty in the following way: "In the 1980s, the partners were headed towards the exploitation of resources. . . . Now they've reversed direction . . . for conservation and environmental protection."[82] Moreover, the signatories to the treaty signaled new progress as they agreed to refrain from the exploration of minerals and work toward the protection of biodiversity until the middle of the twenty-first century.[83]

After the grave threat posed by the U.S.-Soviet nuclear standoff that occurred during the 1962 Cuban missile crisis, President John Kennedy spoke for the nation when he worked to establish the 1963 nuclear test ban. On the advice of his science advisor Jerome Wiesner, Kennedy became better informed about the environmental dangers posed by nuclear fallout. According to Theodore Sorenson, Kennedy was concerned about both national security and the environmental and public health impact resulting from nuclear weapons explosions. As Sorenson explains, Kennedy was "genuinely concerned about fallout: the airborne radioactive debris produced by all atmospheric explosions which emitted tissue-damaging rays into human bodies and food."[84]

The Nuclear Test Ban Treaty ratified by the United States, United Kingdom, and the Soviet Union prohibited nuclear explosions in the atmosphere, under water, and in outer space. The treaty was a step toward the ultimate goal of banning nuclear weapons testing altogether. The three signatories to the treaty agreed to a common goal: "an end to the contamination of man's environment by radioactive substances."[85] A joint United States–United Kingdom statement announced on the one-year anniversary of the test ban treaty was unequivocal in its message; "This treaty moved our planet toward a further strengthening of peace. It helps restrict the arms race. It gives all men and women confidence that they and their children will be breathing purer air and living in a healthier, a less contaminated world."[86]

On the basis of agreements made earlier regarding Antarctica and the nuclear test ban treaty, the signatories to the Outer Space Treaty in 1967 recognized that the placement of nuclear weapons in outer space or celestial bodies might result in both security and environmental risks as a result of the competition in this new frontier. The major stumbling block concerned the scope of the treaty. The United States, which focused only on celestial bodies, eventually accepted the Soviet view, which encompassed the entire outer space environment.[87] Consequently, President Johnson committed the United States to this treaty, which forbade the placing of nuclear weapons in orbit around the earth or on celestial bodies and the testing of such weapons in outer space. Moreover, the Seabed Treaty, signed shortly thereafter in 1971, prohibited the parties to the treaty from placing nuclear weapons on the ocean floor. Although several problems, including the issue of verification, delayed progress in moving the treaty negotiations forward, negotiators were eventually able to complete their task. When the participants' concerns about aspects of the treaty were resolved, agreement was achieved. As president, Richard Nixon helped to ensure the peaceful exploration of the oceans and access to resources on and under the ocean floor.

Over the last two decades, presidents have presided over a military establishment in which plans were made to implement all-out nuclear war that would have two devastating effects on the environment—namely, the catastrophic impact resulting from multiple, simultaneous nuclear explosions and the phenomenon known as "nuclear winter."[88] In preparing for war, the president as commander in chief has the capability to set into motion global climatic and environment disaster.

In addition to the impact of war making, the environment-national security debate also includes the value conflicts between environmental protection and a country's access to vital resources. On several occasions, George Bush referred to this dilemma facing the nation. Although he spoke about his concern for environmental protection, he also indicated his commitment to maintaining access to energy resources to ensure the security of the United States. In a 1989 interview, Bush argued, for instance, in favor of "prudent development" of the Arctic. He indicated that "we can find a balance between environmental interests and national security interests" with regard to Arctic oil and gas resources.[89] Bush reiterated this position two months later when he argued that his administration supported environmental protection "while assuring energy requirements and national security requirements are being met."[90]

Cooperative diplomacy has also played a role in presidential foreign relations, national security, and social issues and can be seen as a bilateral means to foster better relations with, and influence the behavior of, political leaders. Given the American identification with Boris Yeltsin, it is not surprising that during the Clinton administration cooperative diplomacy was an important instrument employed in U.S.-Russian relations. For instance, in discussing his aid package to Russia in 1993, Bill Clinton argued that financial assistance to promote a "healthy democracy," "healthy economy," and "healthy environment" in Russia was a means to ensure U.S. national security.[91] At a summit meeting in September of the following year, President Clinton and Russian President Boris Yeltsin once again showed their cooperation in support of environmental quality in the Arctic region in light of Russian problems in the processing and storage of nuclear waste.[92]

The International Flow of Weapons

As chief diplomat, the president plays an important role in the country's affairs in foreign relations. However, the president also has "rights, duties and obligations growing out of the Constitution itself, our international relations, and all the protection implied by the nature of government under the Constitution."[93] Consequently, as Bledsoe, Bosso, and Rozell argue, the implied powers of the president suggest that "presidents theoretically can undertake any action deemed necessary to carry out their constitutional duties, to provide for the nation's defense, or to protect the common good."[94] One could argue, therefore, that the prohibition on the importation of guns, assault weapons among others is subsumed under the larger category of the "common good." The president's use of the executive order, an "offspring of the implied powers doctrine,"[95] thus becomes a tool for the chief diplomat and commander in chief in foreign commerce and protecting and ensuring the safety of American citizens.

The gun control issue is a good example of the intersection between domestic and international affairs. The president has dual responsibilities—namely, maintaining the security and safety of the people at home and ensuring the safety of the country's borders. Yet Robert Spitzer has argued that the president's role in the gun control debate has been marginal because Congress has been the primary actor in the gun control legislative process.[96] From Roosevelt through Clinton, presidents have directed their attention to other issues, although gun control measures were supported by Roosevelt early in his first term, Lyndon Johnson after the assassination of John Kennedy, and more recently Bill Clinton.

On the domestic front, Congress passed and Roosevelt signed into law two gun control measures in the 1930s—the National Firearms Act of 1934 and the Federal Firearms Act of 1938—yet both were primarily concerned with domestic politics. Moreover, while the National Firearms Act was basically limited to submachine guns— "gangster weapons"—the enforcement procedures in the subsequent Federal Firearms Act were relatively weak since the Treasury Department and its enforcement agency, the Internal Revenue Service, had little interest in the issue.[97]

But the 1950s, imported firearms had increased to the point the Massachusetts Senator John Kennedy introduced legislation—which eventually failed—to end the influx of these weapons.[98] However, the gun control issue remained a minor issue at a time when the nation was enjoying the prosperity of the early postwar period and was most concerned with the Cold War and its relationship with the Soviet Union. Nonetheless, gun control measures were still being advocated by members of Congress when Lyndon Johnson took up the cause in the 1960s as a result of the assassination of President John Kennedy.

In 1968, Congress passed and Lyndon Johnson signed into law the Federal Gun Control Act. Title I of the legislation included provisions related to foreign commerce. As such, "surplus military firearms" could no longer be imported. Although the legislation was the first major alteration in existing gun control measures since 1938 and included new provisions, it remained modest in its scope since it was less than what Johnson had asked for during his campaign for effective gun control legislation.[99] Although the federal role in gun control expanded, enough exceptions were included in the legislation to provide ample opportunity for the continued importation of guns and gun parts.[100] For example, guns could still be imported if they were for "scientific or research purposes," were "unserviceable as a curio or museum piece," and were "generally recognized as particularly suitable or readily adaptable to sporting purposes."[101]

Gun control advocates continued in their quest to establish viable and effective gun control measures in Congress, but they were confronted by roadblocks established by other legislators opposed to gun control measures as well as effective lobbying by the National Rifle Association. During the 1980s, gun control advocates were challenged by a Reagan administration that has no intention or interest in backing domestic gun control legislation or prohibiting the importation of guns into the United States. However, the climate began to change when George Bush became president and first opposed, then supported, efforts to address at least one important aspect of the gun control debate — namely, the role of imported semi-automatic assault weapons and their use in violent acts in communities around the country.

Although President Bill Clinton embraced the gun control issue beginning in his first term, his predecessor George Bush set the stage for presidential action on the importation of semi-automatic weapons. Although Bush initially held the position that he would not take action against the influx of these weapons into the United States, within a month of making this statement he reversed himself and issued an executive order in March 1989 that temporarily banned the importation of semi-automatic rifles, including AK47s and Uzis carbines, among other types of assault weapons.[102] This order prohibited the importation of weapons from several countries, including China, Belgium, Austria, and Israel. By taking this action, President Bush was ensuring that the law (Gun Control Act of 1968) was faithfully executed because the administration concluded that the weapons covered by the executive order no longer fit the definition of "sporting purposes."[103] At this time, although continuing to defend a citizen's right to own a firearm for legitimate purposes, former president Ronald Reagan irritated gun groups, including the NRA, when he stated that "I do not believe that an AK-47, a machine gun, is a sporting weapon."[104] Bush as chief diplomat and commander in chief had ensured the "common good" (i.e., safety of American citizens) through executive action via foreign commerce (i.e., prohibiting the importation of assault rifles into the United States).

Bill Clinton embraced the gun control issue, an integral part of his overall public agenda. Although most of the focus on the firearms issue concerned domestic-made weapons, the importation of firearms remained a controversial element in the debate on the issue. Although passage of the Brady Bill was essential to Clinton, he was also concerned about the continuing export of firearms from other countries that found their way into the United States. Clinton issued two executive orders in 1993 that imposed additional limitations on the firearms trade. Although bypassing the domestic-made weapons market, Clinton ordered an immediate ban on assault-style handguns (e.g., Uzis) that expanded on Bush's earlier executive order prohibiting the importation of assault-style rifles.[105]

Up to this point, we have concentrated on the role of the president as chief diplomat and commander in chief in foreign commerce and the importation of deadly assault guns and rifles. The issue of gun control also includes the transfer of "small arms," which include handguns and assault weapons on one hand and machine guns, grenades, mortars and antitank missiles on the other hand.[106]

The United States has been in the business of arms transfer of small and large weapons for decades. From the Nixon-Ford era through the Bush administration, rifles and carbines among other weapons were provided to the opposition forces in Angola as well as the government of Zaire.[107] During the Reagan-Bush administrations, tens of thousands of pistols, revolvers, rifles, shotguns, submachine guns, and assault weapons were exported to forty-seven countries.[108]

In this October 1995 address to the United Nations General Assembly, President Clinton argued in support of "standards that will reinforce and strengthen national laws that prohibit illegal arms transactions beyond national borders."[109] Clinton emphasized that "no one is immune . . . where drug traffickers wielding imported weapons have murdered judges, journalists, police officers, and innocent passers by."[110]

Although much of this chapter is limited to Clinton's first term in office, it is important to note that on April 18, 1998, well into his second term in office, President Clinton joined other hemispheric partners in supporting new regulations aimed at improved regulation of arms transfers. The agreement concluded at the Summit of the Americas held in Santiago, Chile, was an effort to deal more effectively with the widely accepted threat posed by the increasing flow of weapons that end up in the hands of terrorists and the drug trade. This treaty amended the International Traffic in Arms Regulations along with revised "licensing practices" in an effort to improve monitoring of the firearms export.[111] In November of the same year, U.S. Secretary of State Madeleine Albright stated: "The culprit is not the legitimate international trade in arms, nor the individual sale of weapons to sportsmen, collectors, businesspeople, and homeowners. The problem is the unregulated and illegitimate sale of . . . weapons. . . . That is why the Clinton administration has taken significant steps to strengthen controls over the export . . . of small arms."[112]

On June 8, 1999, Bill Clinton submitted to the U.S. Senate the Inter-American Convention against the Illicit Manufacturing of and Trafficking in Firearms, Ammunition, Explosives, and Other Related Materials, signed by thirty-one member states of the Organization of American States, including the United States, the previous November. This convention was the first multilateral instrument established to organize an effective collaborative effort to stop the flow of firearms, among other light weapons, which tend to wind up in the hands terrorists and individuals involved in the transnational drug trade.[113]

Although several governments, including the United States under President Clinton, have moved toward greater cooperation in addressing the illegal flow of firearms, the legitimate transfer of light arms remains a focal point for debate. American diplomats have articulated an American position that opposes the continued illegal flow of firearms. Yet in 1996 alone, "$500 million worth of small arms and shotguns" and "50,000 assault rifles" were either sold or given away by the Pentagon or Departments of State and/or Commerce.[114]

According to one observer of the small arms trade:

> The fact that military-style weapons today are in the hands of guerrilla groups, criminal enterprises, and other nonstate actors has heightened the concern of Northern governments. But these weapons are also a menace in the hands of many state security forces. Assault rifles, in particular, are a principal tool of repression used by police, internal security forces, and allied militias to crush opposition movements, eliminate dissidents, and terrorize populations.[115]

An argument can be made that American diplomacy lacks the moral high ground since its focus has been primarily on illicit trafficking in firearms while "legitimate" small arms sales and transfers of guns, rifles, assault weapons, and the like continue as they have done for decades. As one critic of current policy under the Clinton administration argues, "'Guns don't kill people—people kill people.' This kind of bumper-sticker diplomacy now guides U.S. diplomacy."[116]

During the first term of the Clinton administration, legal small arms transfers continued as thousands of assault rifles and/or carbines were sold to at least twenty-five different countries.[117] Moreover, the NRA and other gun groups took their fight to the global arena because they "fear that those who advocate controls on small arms and light weapons internationally are also likely to advocate stronger national controls."[118] Given the history of legal and illegal small arms transfers, along with past and present American diplomatic efforts, there is no reason to expect the flow of weapons to discontinue in the near future.

Having said this, in an attempt to "insure domestic tranquility" that has been increasingly threatened by escalating gun violence, both George Bush and Bill Clinton used the power resources available to them as president to address at least one aspect of the domestic gun violence crisis. In doing so, they issued executive orders that prohibited firearms manufactured in foreign countries from crossing the border into the United States.

Cyberporn

Compared with the other issues addressed in this book, pornography is perhaps least salient for the chief diplomat and commander in chief roles. While pornography has gained the attention of several presidents involved in domestic politics, the chief diplomat and commander in chief roles have usually come into play (1) when pornographic materials cross the border into the United States and the U.S. Customs Service or the U.S. Postal Service intercept the material, (2) or when pornography becomes an integral feature of the international flow of information. As President Clinton stated in 1996: "The more open our borders are, the more freely our people can travel, the more freely money can move and information and technology can be transferred, the more vulnerable we are to people who would seek to undermine the very fabric of civilized life."[119] The view from the Clinton White House is clear—namely, that the United States faces many external dangers, including that posed by computers and the Internet, which can be viewed as a threat to our national security both by countries and groups, and by individuals who disseminate pornography on the information highway.[120]

The Truman administration entered into several international agreements regarding pornography. In 1950, Harry Truman signed an agreement with Austria, Ceylon, Finland, Rumania, and Switzerland that amended an earlier agreement to stop the flow of obscene materials established in 1910 during the Taft administration.[121] The revised agreement transferred the functions of the agreement from the original signatories to the United Nations, which provided a forum where any member nation could also sign the agreement.[122] The Truman administration also engaged in bilateral agreements that banned the exchange of articles of obscene or immoral nature.[123] Truman signed and ratified one agreement with Yugoslavia in 1950 and entered into agreements the following year with the Gold Coast Colony and the Netherlands West Indies.

Other than these few instances of a presidential effort to stop the flow of pornographic material across national borders, the issue received scant attention by modern presidents. By the 1990s, however, the importance of communication in cyberspace began to demonstrate that new challenges were on the horizon for the president as chief diplomat and commander in chief. Presidential decision making in the future may well be influenced to a large degree by the new challenge of *cyberporn*, which may include the issues of privacy, "community standards," illegal conduct on the Internet, and new strategies for federal agencies in a "war on cyberporn."

Although privacy is considered a fundamental "right" in the United States that allows citizens to gain access to a variety of materials within the confines of their homes, individual privacy and First Amendment freedoms run head-on into the legal jurisdictions of every country in the world. In 1995, for instance, CompuServe terminated service to its four million subscribers in over 200 transnational locations because a federal prosecutor in Munich, Germany, along with the Bavarian police declared that the pornography laws of the country were being violated by the dissemination of explicit sexual discussion groups.[124]

As mentioned in an earlier chapter, the *Miller v. California* Supreme Court decision in 1973 attempted to clarify what constituted free speech under the First Amendment and applied the principle of "community standards" as a test of obscenity. The issue of community standards in cyberspace raises a new challenge for the president as chief diplomat, given the frequency of pedophilic and paraphilic imagery on the Internet in some 2,000 cities throughout the world.[125]

As the last president of the twentieth century, Bill Clinton declared that he was committed to stemming the flow of pornography, particularly child pornography. In addressing illegal conduct on the Internet, Clinton signed the Communications Decency Act in 1996 (although it was eventually struck down by the Supreme Court) and the Child On-Line Protection Act, which is intended to protect children from pornography on the Internet. In 1999 he also issued Executive Order 13133, which established a "Working Group on Unlawful Conduct on the Internet" to address several issues, including the illegal sale of guns and the dissemination of child pornography.[126] Notwithstanding the domestic focus of the legislation and Clinton's role in signing it, the domestic and international context of these efforts is self-evident since the Internet has a global reach.

In an effort to deal with new challenges from the new technology, the president and federal agencies have had to enhance their enforcement of laws and develop new strategies to combat the international flow of pornographic materials. For example, as a result of a crackdown by the U.S. Customs Service, the number of convictions for using the Internet to disseminate child pornography almost tripled during the last year of Clinton's first term in office.[127] Since 1985, the U.S. Customs Service and more recently the Federal Bureau of Investigation (through its Operation Innocent Images initiative which began in 1995) have organized units to combat child pornography on the Internet in an effort to prosecute individuals and groups.[128] Given the increase in international pornography rings, the purpose is to reduce the flow of pornographic materials moving across the U.S. border. Furthermore, in an effort to strengthen the investigation and prosecution of those involved in international child pornography, the U.S. Departments of State and Defense have had department officials trained by federal law enforcement authorities with the goal of establishing a "global exchange of information."[129]

Given the domestic and international dimension of the Internet, the president may be called upon to defend U.S. interests in the communication of information in the international community. Since each country has rules, regulations, and national priorities, Eli M. Noam has argued that it is unlikely that the Internet will remain unregulated since countries will act on matters that they care about.[130] Consequently, the potential for international conflict over future global communication suggests that the president as chief diplomat and commander in chief will become involved in future information conflicts, including a "war on cyberporn" in cyberspace.

PARTISAN DIFFERENCES

As chief diplomat and commander in chief, the president can take action with more discretion than he can in domestic politics. Congress is less likely to constrain the president and the public will generally be supportive of the president when he is engaged in issues related to the international community, as least in the short term.

As far as social policy is concerned, several of the issues discussed here have a longer history than the others. Once presidents decided to act on an issue, however, they used the power resources available to them as chief diplomat and commander in chief (sometimes with the instruments of power from other roles, such as the executive order) in order to exert their influence in a specific policy area. Sometimes they were successful, as was Harry Truman when he desegregated the military. Other times they were unsuccessful, as in Bill Clinton's battle with the Congress and the military over gays in the military.

In the role of chief diplomat and commander in chief, Democratic presidents have promoted affirmative action/equal opportunity, abortion rights, gay rights, and gun control. In the arena of military and defense affairs, Franklin Roosevelt and Harry Truman used executive orders to create opportunities for all Americans in the defense industry and within the ranks of the military. Bill Clinton embraced the controversial issue of homosexuality during the 1992 compaign for the presidency. After winning the support of electoral constituencies concerned about gay rights by promising that he would terminate the ban on homosexuals serving in the armed forces, Clinton was prepared to issue an executive order to implement his campaign promise. However, he ran head on into a maelstrom of political and military opposition. Clinton also took on the gun control issue both domestically and internationally. At home he supported the Brady Bill and he used executive orders in an effort to stop the flow of firearms across U.S. borders. Moreover, he attended regional and international meetings to work toward collaborative efforts to address the flow of illegal weapons across national borders.

Among Republicans, Ronald Reagan and George Bush were most likely to use their power as chief diplomat and commander in chief as it related to social policy. Reagan and Bush used their resources to influence the policies of international organizations and NGOs about family planning practices because of their concern about abortion. Funding to the United Nations

Population Fund was terminated until Bill Clinton assumed the presidency and reversed their policy. Moreover, while acting cautiously, George Bush also became involved in the international firearms issue. Although resisting involvement at first, he eventually reversed himself and worked to stop the spread of firearms from abroad into the United States. Although Bush's action were incremental in scope, his action helped pave the way for Democrat Clinton to work on this problem as well.

The environment as a policy area is the one issue where most, if not all, of the presidents were involved to some extent in bilateral, regional, or multilateral agreements. Tables 5.2 and 5.3 illustrate the importance of the environment for Democratic as well as Republican presidents. Ronald Reagan is an interesting case because he characterized by his anti-environment domestic agenda. Yet in the international arena, Reagan was willing to join the international community in signing several important agreements, including the Montreal Protocol on Ozone Depletion.

CONCLUSION

As chief diplomat and commander in chief, the president is in a stronger position in the policymaking process compared to the other roles because of fewer constraints on this role. As the "sole organ" of communication or head of the defense establishment, the president has a commanding advantage in exercising power. As Michael Genovese argues, "The presumption of presidential leadership in foreign affairs gives the president a wide range of opportunities to take the initiative and act. It is less likely that Congress will challenge the president's authority in foreign than in domestic affairs."[131] Although the "gays in the military" issue proved to be a divisive instance of institutional relations in which the president was confronted by congressional assertion of power and military intransigence, the president has generally been successful in exercising presidential power, if he chooses to do so, when engaged in diplomatic or defense endeavors regarding social policy. The extent to which the president as chief diplomat and commander in chief becomes involved in social policy may change in the future as presidents face new challenges from old issues (e.g., military personnel policy and illegal firearms trade) as well as from the international community.

ENDNOTES

1. *U.S. v. Curtiss-Wright Export Corp.* 299 U.S. 304 (1936) and *U.S. v. Belmont* 301 U.S. 324 (1937).
2. Natalie J. Goldring, "The NRA Goes Global," *Bulletin of the Atomic Scientists 55* (January/February 1999): 62.
3. Raymond Tatalovich and Byron W. Daynes. *Presidential Power in the United States* (Monterey, CA: Brooks/Cole, 1984), 260.

4. Tatalovich and Daynes, *Presidential Power in the United States*, 260.
5. Tatalovich and Daynes, *Presidential Power in the United States*, 261.
6. *The Federalist Papers*, no. 74 (New York: Modern Library, 1941), 482.
7. Quoted in Warren W. Hassler, Jr., *The President as Commander in Chief* (Menlo Park, CA: Addison-Wesley, 1971), 7.
8. Hassler, *The President as Commander in Chief*, 7.
9. David M. Pfletcher, "What the Founding Fathers Intended: Congressional-Executive Relations in the Early American Republic," in Michael Barnhart, ed., *Congress and United States Foreign Policy* (Albany, NY: State University of New York Press, 1987), 135.
10. Arthur Schleslinger, Jr., *The Imperial Presidency* (Boston: Houghton Mifflin, 1973), 33.
11. Forrest McDonald, *The American Presidency* (Lawrence, KS: University Press of Kansas, 1994), 382.
12. Justice Sutherland quoted in Sidney M. Milkis and Michael Nelson, *The American Presidency: Origins and Development, 1776–1998* (Washington, DC: Congressional Quarterly Press, 1999), 275.
13. Lawrence Margolis, *Executive Agreements and Presidential Power in Foreign Policy* (New York: Praeger, 1986), 59.
14. McDonald, *The American Presidency*, 275–76, 405.
15. Stephen H. Wirls and Daniel C. Diller, "Chief Diplomat," *Powers of the Presidency*, 2nd ed. (Washington, DC: Congressional Quarterly Press, 1997), 135.
16. Loch Johnson, *The Making of International Agreements* (New York: New York University Press, 1984), 158.
17. Charles W. Kegley, Jr., and Eugene R. Wittkopf, *American Foreign Policy*, 2nd ed. (New York: St. Martin's Press, 1982), 272–73.
18. Tatalovich and Daynes, *Presidential Power in the United States*, 353.
19. Tatalovich and Daynes, *Presidential Power in the United States*, 23.
20. Barbara Kellerman and Ryan J. Barilleaux, *The President as World Leader* (New York: St. Martin's Press, 1991), 41.
21. "Statement about Policy of Abortions at Military Base Hospitals in the United States—April 3, 1971," *Public Papers of the Presidents of the United States: Richard Nixon* (Washington, DC: Government Printing Office, 1972), 500.
22. "Retreating Rights Backers Vow Early Return in Next Session," *Congressional Quarterly Weekly Report* (10 October, 1992), 3163; "Court, House Abortion Votes Revive Emotional Debate." *Congressional Quarterly Weekly Report* (25 May, 1991), 1377.
23. "Clinton Reverses Directives, Battle Begins Anew," *Congressional Quarterly Weekly Report* (23 January, 1993): 182.
24. "Clinton Reverses Directives, Battle Begins Anew."
25. Daniel C. Diller and Stephen H. Wirls, "Commander in Chief," in *Powers of the Presidency*, 2nd ed. (Washington, DC: Congressional Quarterly Press, 1997), 199.
26. John Sibley Butler, "Affirmative Action in the Military," in *The Annals of the American Academy of Political and Social Science* 523 (September 1992): 198–99 and Jack D. Foner, *Blacks in the Military in American History* (New York: Praeger, 1974), 43.
27. Executive Order 8802, "Reaffirming Policy of Full Participation in the Defense Program by all Persons, Regardless of Race, Creed, Color, or National Origin and Directing Certain Action in Furtherance of Said Policy," 25 June, 1941: 3 CFR; 1938–1943, 957.
28. Martin Binkin and Mark J. Eitelberg with Alvin J. Schexnider and Marvin M. Smith, *Blacks and the Military* (Washington, DC: Brookings Institution, 1982), 19.
29. Executive Order 9981, "Establishing the President's Committee on Equality of Treatment and Opportunity in the Armed Forces," 3 CFR 1943–1948, 722.
30. Kenneth O'Reilly, *Nixon's Piano: Presidents and Racial Politics from Washington to Clinton* (New York: Free Press, 1995), 160–61.
31. Gerald Astor, *The Right to Fight: A History of African-Americans in the Military* (Novato, CA: Presidio Press, 1998), 436–37.
32. Butler, "African-Americans in the Military," 203–04.
33. Raymond Tatalovich and Byron W. Daynes, *Moral Controversies in American Politics: Cases in Social Regulatory Policy* (Armonk, NY: M. E. Sharpe, 1998), 107.
34. David Gergen, "The Commander's First Minefield," *U.S. News and World Report*, 30 November, 1992, 32.
35. Tatalovich and Daynes, *Moral Controversies in American Politics*, 108.

36. Clyde Wilcox and Robin M. Wolpert, "President Clinton, Public Opinion, and Gays in the Military," in Craig A. Rimmerman, ed., *Gay Rights, Military Wrongs* (New York: Garland Press, 1996).

37. Garry L. Rolison and Thomas K. Nakayama, "Defensive Discourse: Blacks and Gays in the U.S. Military," in Wilbur J. Scott and Sandra Carson Stanley, eds., *Gays and Lesbians in the Military* (New York: Aldine De Gruyter, 1994), 125.

38. Allan Berube, *Coming Out under Fire: The History of Gay Men and Women in World War Two* (New York: Free Press, 1990), 134.

39. Berube, *Coming Out under Fire.*

40. "The President's News Conference," *Weekly Compilation of Presidential Documents* (1, February, 1993): 108.

41. Caroll Doherty, "Heated Issue Is Off to Cool Start as Hearing on Gay Ban Begins," *Congressional Quarterly Weekly Report* (3 April, 1993): 851.

42. Chuck Alston, "Clinton's Rough Start with the Hill: Minor Slip or Serious Flaw?"*Congressional Quarterly Weekly Report* (30 January, 1993): 203.

43. Melissa Wells-Petry, *Exclusion: Homosexuals and the Right to Serve* (Washington, DC: Regnery Gateway, 1993), 57. For another military critique of Clinton's plan, see Col. Ronald D. Ray, "Lifting the Ban on Homosexuals in the Military: The Subversion of a Moral Principle," in Wilbur J. Scott and Sandra Carson Stanley, eds., *Gays and Lesbians in the Military* (New York: Aldine De Gruyter, 1994), 87–101.

44. David Lauter, "Clinton Orders Steps to Lift Ban on Gays in the Military," *Los Angeles Times*, 31 January, 1993, A18.

45. Christine Lawrence, "Ban on Homosexuals to End in Two Steps, Frank Says," *Congressional Quarterly Weekly Report* (23 January, 1992): 187 and David Gergen, "The Commander's First Minefield," 32.

46. Franklin D. Jones and Ronald J. Koshes, "Homosexuality and the Military," *American Journal of Psychiatry* 152 (1995): 16–21.

47. Gergen, "The Commander's First Minefield," 32.

48. B. D. Gellman, "Clinton Says He'll 'Consult' on Allowing Gays in the Military: Advisors Warn of Likely Repercussions," *Washington Post*, 13 November, 1992, 1.

49. Caroll J. Doherty, "Emotions on Both Sides," *Congressional Quarterly Weekly Report* (3 April, 1993): 852.

50. William A. Henry III, "Clinton's First Fire Fight," *Time*, 30 November, 1992, 42.

51. Denise Bostdorff, "Clinton's Characteristic Issue Management Style: Caution, Conciliation, and Conflict Avoidance in the Case of Gays in the Military," in Robert E. Denton, Jr., and Rachel L. Holloway, eds., *The Clinton Presidency* (Westport, CT: Praeger, 1996), 196.

52. Wirls and Diller, "Chief Diplomat," 146.

53. "Overview of U.S. Policy: Population Assistance and Family Planning," *Congressional Digest* 76 (April 1997): 100.

54. "International Population Assistance: U.S. Support for Family Planning and Reproductive Health," *Congressional Digest* 76 (April 1997): 99.

55. Steven K. Wisensale, "Family Policy during the Reagan Years: The Private Side of the Conservative Agenda," in Eric J. Schmertz, Natalie Oatlof, and Alexej Ugrinsky, eds., *Ronald Reagan's America* (Westport, CT: Greenwood Press, 1997), 264.

56. "Cold War's Demise Shapes $26.3 Billion Spending Bill," *Congressional Quarterly Weekly Report* (10 October, 1992): 3178.

57. "Cold War's Demise," 128.

58. John T. Rourke, *International Politics on the World Stage*, 3rd ed. (Guilford, CT: Dushkin, 1991), 555.

59. Rourke, *International Politics on the World Stage*, 555.

60. Richard J. Tobin, "Environment, Population and the Developing World," in Norman J. Vig and Michael E. Kraft, eds., *Environmental Policy in the 1990s*, 3rd ed. (Washington, DC: Congressional Quarterly Press, 1997), 282.

61. "Campaign Address at the Mountain States Forest Festival, Elkins, West Virginia, October 1, 1936," *The Public Papers and Addresses of Franklin D. Roosevelt*, vol. 2 (New York: Random House, 1938), 396–400.

62. Richard Elliot Benedick, *Ozone Depletion: New Directions in Safeguarding the Planet*, enlarged edition (Cambridge, MA: Harvard University Press, 1991), 24.

63. U.S. President, "Statement on Signing the Montreal Protocol on Ozone-Depleting Substances—April 5, 1988," *Public Papers of the Presidents of the United States: Ronald Reagan* (Washington, DC: U.S. Government Printing Office, 1990), 420–21.

64. Marvin S. Soroos, "From Stockholm to Rio: The Evaluation of Global Environmental Governance," in Vig and Kraft, *Environmental Policy in the 1990s*, 313–14.

65. Philip Shabecoff, "Shades of Green in the Presidential Campaign," *Issues in Science and Technology* 9 (1992): 73–79.

66. Mark K. Landy, Marc J. Roberts, and Stephen R. Thomas, *The Environmental Protection Agency*, expanded ed. (New York: Oxford University Press, 1994), 291–94.

67. Landy, Roberts, and Thomas, *Environmental Protection Agency*, 295.

68. Rudy Abramson, Norman Kempster, and James G. Zang, "Bush Will Not Sign Wildlife, Habitat Treaty," *Los Angeles Times*, 30 May, 1992 and Russell Mittermeier and Peter Seligmann, "U.S. Should Take a Stand on Biodiversity," *Christian Science Monitor*, 17 July 1992.

69. Lawrence E. Susskind, *Environmental Diplomacy* (Oxford and New York: Oxford University Press, 1994), 39–40.

70. U.S. President, "Remarks by the President and Prime Minister Brain Mulroney of Canada at the Air Quality Signing Ceremony in Ottawa—March 13, 1991," *Public Papers of the Presidents of the United States* (Washington, DC: Government Printing Office, 1991), 254–57.

71. Quoted in *New York Times*, 25 April, 1988, A10.

72. U.S. President, "Remarks at a Meeting with Hispanic Business Leaders in Houston, Texas—April 8, 1991," *Public Papers of the Presidents of the United States: George Bush* (Washington, DC: Government Printing Office, 1991), 345–48.

73. Bernard Nietschmann, "The Ecology of War: Battlefields of Ashes and Mud," *Natural History* 99 (November 1990): 34.

74. Daniel Deudney, "The Case against Linking Environmental Degradation and National Security," in Ken Conca and Geoffrey D. Dabelko, eds., *Green Planet Blues: Environmental Politics from Stockholm to Kyoto* (Boulder, CO: Westview Press, 1998), 306.

75. E. W. Pfeiffer, "The Ecology of War: Degreening Vietnam," *Natural History 99* (November 1990): 37–40.

76. Charles H. Southwick, *Global Ecology in Human Perspective* (New York and Oxford: Oxford University Press, 1996), 316–17.

77. McDonald, *The American Presidency*, 423.

78. Southwick, *Global Ecology in Human Perspective*, 318.

79. John T. Rourke, *International Politics on the World Stage*, 3rd ed. (Guilford, CT: Dushkin, 1991), 577.

80. *Treaties and Alliances of the World: An International Survey Covering Treaties in Force and Communities of States* (New York: Charles Scribner's Sons, 1974), 37–40.

81. U.S. Arms Control and Disarmament Agency, *Arms Control and Disarmament Agreements* (Washington, DC: United States Arms Control and Disarmament Agency, 1996), 25.

82. Colin Woodard, "Endless Detente," *Bulletin of the Atomic Scientists 55* (January/February 1999): 11.

83. Woodard, "Endless Detente," 11.

84. Theodore C. Sorenson, *Kennedy* (New York: Harper and Row, 1965), 621.

85. U.S. Arms Control and Disarmament Agency, *Arms Control and Disarmament Agreements* (Washington, DC: Government Printing Office, 1996), 24.

86. Keesing's Research Report, *Disarmament: Negotiations and Treaties, 1946–1971* (New York: Charles Scribner's Sons, 1972), 324.

87. U.S. Arms Control and Disarmament Agency, *Arms Control and Disarmament Agreements* (1996), 35.

88. Paul R. Ehrlich, Carl Sagan, Donald Kennedy, and Walter Orr Roberts, *The Cold and the Dark* (New York: W.W. Norton, 1984).

89. U.S. President, "Interview with Gerald Boyd of the *New York Times* and Katherine Lewis of the *Houston Post*—April 25, 1989," *Public Papers of the Presidents of the United States: George Bush* (Washington, DC: Government Printing Office, 1990), 13–15.

90. U.S. President, "Remarks at the Swearing-In Ceremony for James D. Watkins as Secretary of Energy—March 9, 1989," *Public Papers of the Presidents of the United States: George Bush* (Washington, DC: Government Printing Office, 1990), 193–95.

91. U.S. President, "Remarks on Earth Day—April 21, 1993," *Public Papers of the Presidents of the United States: William Jefferson Clinton* (Washington, DC: Government Printing Office, 1994), 468–72.

92. U.S. President, "Joint Announcement on Environmental Protection in the Arctic—September 28, 1994," *Public Papers of the Presidents of the United States: William Jefferson Clinton* (Washington, DC: Government Printing Office, 1995), 1654.

93. *In re Neagle*, 135 U.S. 1 (1890).

94. W. Craig Bledsoe, Christopher J. Bosso, and Mark J. Rozell, "Chief Executive," in *Powers of the Presidency*, 2nd ed. (Washington, DC: Congressional Quarterly Press, 1997), 41.

95. Bledsoe, Bosso, and Rozell, "Chief Executive," 41.

96. Robert Spitzer, *The Politics of Gun Control* (Chatham, NJ: Chatham House, 1995), 169.

97. Carol Skalnik Leff and Mark H. Leff, "The Politics of Ineffectiveness: Federal Firearms Legislation, 1919–1938," *Annals of the American Academy of Political and Social Science* 455 (May 1981): 52–57.

98. Franklin E. Zimring, "Firearms and Federal Law: The Gun Control Act of 1968," *Journal of Legal Studies* 4 (January 1975): 144.

99. Spitzer, *The Politics of Gun Control*, 144–47.

100. Zimring, "Firearms and Federal Law," 155–56.

101. "The Gun Control Controversy," *Congressional Digest* 65 (May 1986): 134.

102. R. W. Apple, "The Search for an Issue," *New York Times*, 16 March, 1989, A1; David Hoffman, "Bush Vows Action on Assault Rifles," *Washington Post*, 23 March, 1989, A1; Charles Mohr, "U.S. Bans Imports of Assault Rifles in Shift by Bush," *New York Times*, 15 March, 1989, A1.

103. Michael Isikoff and David Hoffman, "Administration Bans Assault-Gun Imports," *Washington Post*, 15 March, 1989, A1 and Charles Mohr, "Federal Agency to Begin a Survey on Use of Semiautomatic Weapons," *New York Times*, 23, March 1989, A22.

104. Quoted in Osha Gray Davidson, *Under Fire: The NRA and the Battle for Gun Control* (Iowa City, IA: University of Iowa Press, 1998), 201.

105. Douglas Jehl, "Clinton Undertakes His Drive on Guns and Crime," *New York Times*, 12, August 1993, A20 and Ruth Marcus and Michael Isikoff, "Clinton's Anti-Crime Package: More Police, Curb on Pistol Imports," *Washington Post*, 12 August, 1993, A16.

106. Michael Renner, *Small Arms, Big Impact: The Next Challenge of Disarmament* (Washington, DC: Worldwatch Institute, 1997), 10 and United Nations Institute for Disarmament Research, *Small Arms Management and Peacekeeping Southern Africa* (Geneva: UNIDR, 1996), 8.

107. Lora Lumpe, Federation of American Scientists, "Monitoring the Diffusion of Light Weapons: A Campaign of the Arms Sales Monitoring Project: U.S. Policy on Small/Light Arms Exports," paper prepared for the American Academy of Arts and Sciences, December 11–12, 1997, Washington, DC. <http://www.fas.org/asmp/light_weapons/AAAS.htm> Accessed 17 June, 1999.

108. Lumpe, "Monitoring the Diffusion of Light Weapons."

109. U.S. Arms Control and Disarmament Agency, "Small Arms Issues: U.S. Policy and Views," 11 August, 1998. <http://www.usia.gov/abtusia/posts/IN1/wwwh11b.html> Accessed 17 June, 1999.

110. Lora Lumpe, "In Focus: Small Arms Trade," *Foreign Policy in Focus* 3 (May 1998). <http://www.foreignpolicy-infocus.org/brief/vol3/v3n10arms.html> Accessed 19 June, 1999.

111. U.S. Arms Control and Disarmament Agency, "Small Arms Issues: U.S. Policy and Views."

112. "U.S. Initiatives," *Bulletin of the Atomic Scientists* 55 (January/February 1999): 30–31.

113. "Message to the Senate Transmitting the Inter-American Convention against the Illicit Manufacturing of and Trafficking in Firearms, Ammunition, Explosives, and Other Related Materials with Documentation," *Weekly Compilation of Presidential Documents* 34 (15 June, 1998): 1085.

114. Lora Lumpe, "The Leader of the Pack," *Bulletin of the Atomic Scientists* 55 (January/February 1999): 29.

115. Lumpe, "In Focus: Small Arms Trade."

116. Dan N. Nelson, "Damage Control," *Bulletin of the Atomic Scientists* 55 (January/February 1999): 56.

117. Lumpe, "Monitoring the Diffusion of Light Weapons."

118. Goldring, "The NRA Goes Global," 62.

119. Quoted in "Responding to Emergency International Crime Threats," <http://www2.whitehouse.gov/WH/EOP/NSC/html/documents/iccsviii.html> Accessed 13 October, 1999.

120. "Responding to Emergency International Crime Threats."
121. See "George Washington to Woodrow Wilson. *Obscenity and Pornography*, 1911-29-8. "*CIS Index of Presidential Executive Orders and Proclamations*, Part 1, *April 30, 1789, to March 4, 1921* (Bethesda MD: Congressional Information Service, 1987).
122. "Multilateral Protocol on Obscene Publications, Ratification Proclamation," *CIS Index of Presidential Executive Orders and Proclamations.* Part 2: *March, 1921 to December 31, 1983,* "Warren Harding to Ronald Reagan, *Obscenity and Pornography*, 1950-29-11. (Bethesda, MD: Congressional Information Service, 1986), 880–81.
123. See *United States Treaties and Other International Agreements*, vol. 2, part 2. (Washington, DC: Government Printing Office, 1952), 1511–23, 1861–75, 2079–115.
124. See John Markoff, "The Media Business: On-Line Service Blocks Access to Topics Called Pornographic," *New York Times*, 29 December, 1995, 1 and "Bavarian Police Probe Sparked CompuServe's On-Line Censorship," *San Francisco Examiner*, 30 December, 1995, A12. America Online, which also conducts business in Germany, became concerned about being prosecuted for something that it does not completely control.
125. May Rimm, "Marketing Pornography on the Information Superhighway: A Survey of 917, 410 Images, Descriptions, Short Stories, and Animations Downloaded 8.5 Million Times by Consumers in over 2,000 Cities in Forty Countries, Provinces, and Territories," Carnegie Mellon, <http://trfn.pghpa.us/guest/mrtext.html>.
126. "Executive Order 13133—Working Group on Unlawful Conduct on the Internet," *Weekly Compilation of Presidential Documents*, 9, August 1999, <http://web4.infotrac.galegroup.com/itw/i ...0_A56056758&dyn=4!sw_aep=viva_odu> Accessed 13 October, 1999.
127. "A 'Family Friendly' Internet," <http://www2.whitehouse.gov /WH/News/Ratings/index/html> Accessed 13, October 1999.
128. "Responding to Emergency International Crime Threats."
129. "Responding to Emergency International Crime Threats."
130. Eli M. Noam, "An Unfettered Internet? Keep Dreaming." *New York Times*, 11 July, 1997, A21.
131. Michael A. Genovese, *The Presidential Dilemma* (New York: HarperCollins, 1995), 94.

6

Conclusion:
Presidents and the Social Agenda

Introduction

American presidents devote most of their attention, skills, and resources to domestic, economic, foreign, and national security policies. At the same time, the intrusion of social issues into the political process has become an aspect of concern to American politics. As we have seen, some issues have received little, if any, consideration while others have gained a considerable amount of the president's attention. Some presidents have practiced avoidance, while others have felt that it was appropriate to embrace at least in a symbolic way some aspect of the social agenda.

The Relationship between the Presidency and the Social Agenda

Presidential involvement in social policy has varied over the years. The differences can be explained, in part, by presidential roles. Each role, though possessed of a different power potential, can be used to shore up a social agenda if the president is particularly skilled in its use. Although the opinion\party leader is recognized as a weak role, a president can make public policy by fulfilling the promises made in party platforms at presidential conventions and can establish relationships with the public and organized interests through a variety of major and minor speeches in which the president can take a stand on an issue. A president also has resources, albeit limited, as legislative leader that provide opportunities for guiding the legislative agenda through the Congress. As chief executive, a president can influence government policymaking by executive orders, the appointment process, reorganization efforts, and proclamations. Finally, for those issues having a transnational impact, the president as chief diplomat and commander in chief can influence social policy in the international community.

The Supreme Court in its 1973 *Roe v. Wade* decision nationalized the abortion issue, which has resulted in a formal battle between contending forces that each seek to influence public policy. Since then, American presidents have been challenged to take a position on the issue—some have taken a pro-choice position, other presidents have promoted a pro-life orientation, and still others have avoided the issue. A potential dilemma for presidents is when their personal beliefs about abortion might be in opposition to their public position. Jimmy Carter, as an example, refused to take action that would weaken abortion rights despite his personal opposition to abortion as a family planning choice. Among the eleven presidents beginning with Franklin Roosevelt, Ronald Reagan was the one who most strongly embraced the issue as he sought support from constituency groups that saw abortion as a defining issue in American politics. In his campaign for the presidency, Reagan's successor, George Bush, continued in the effort to court electoral support of the opponents of abortion rights.

Affirmative action/equal opportunity has affected the president's relationship with Congress, the public, and state governments. Among the issues most important to the Roosevelt and Truman administrations was the struggle to promote equality of opportunity for all Americans. In the process of issuing an executive order to terminate segregation in the armed forces, for instance, Truman incurred the wrath of members of Congress, the public, southern state governments, and the military. Although using the power of the presidency to integrate universities in southern states, President Kennedy's actions were tempered by his narrow presidential victory and the ideological composition of Congress, where he was opposed by conservative southern Democrats.[1] For some, Kennedy embodied the presidency as a basis of moral support for affirmative action/equal opportunity;[2] for others, Kennedy's approach was either too cautious or was based on strategic electoral considerations.[3] Lyndon Johnson's Great Society and War on Poverty were indicative of his personal concern and his desire in having a positive impact on social relations in the United States. Much of Johnson's attitude and sensitivity to these issues can be traced to his early political career.[4] It is not surprising that he among the modern presidents spoke most often about the issue of affirmative action/equal opportunity.

Jimmy Carter and Bill Clinton are also proud of their efforts to open doors to all members of American society.[5] They can point to the success of their administrations compared to others in terms of the number of women and minorities appointed to high-level government positions. In contrast, Ronald Reagan and George Bush criticized the use of quotas and timetables, resulting in fewer opportunities for minorities in their administrations. As Barker and Jones observed: "The Reagan administration continued to push its position that under affirmative action each beneficiary must be required to establish that he/she was an actual victim of discrimination."[6]

Overall, despite the variety of actions taken by modern presidents for and in behalf of affirmative action—executive orders by Roosevelt and Truman, Johnson's activism, appointments of minorities and women by Carter, Reagan, Bush, and Clinton—Earl O. Hutchinson asserts that given the nature of the times, the actions of the various Congresses, and federal-state relations, presidents have exhibited "symbolic rather than substantive" leadership in support of affirmative action/equal opportunity.[7] Moreover, in another recent book on the presidency and civil rights, Kenneth O'Reilly argues that among the modern presidents, only Lyndon Johnson used the power of the presidency in support of racial equality and social justice.[8]

Presidents have responded to the environment in a slightly different way. Despite partisanship, presidents have generally acted in favor of environmental measures. Given the consistent support for environmental protection among the American electorate as demonstrated in public opinion polls, presidents can only gain by supporting environmental priorities. For six decades, more often than not Democratic and Republican presidents have publicly endorsed and worked for pollution control and conservation efforts. Where they have differed has been in assigning the level of government—federal or state—to assume primary responsibility for environmental policy. The two exceptions were Presidents Reagan and Bush, whose actions in the legislative process, bureaucratic arena, and the international arena belied their public statements about concern for the environment. Reagan's "administrative presidency" employed appointment and budget powers to reverse previous bipartisan progress on the environment.[9] George Bush used the power of the presidency to ensure passage of the Clean Air Act amendments in 1990, yet his role at the Earth Summit in Rio in 1992 was disappointing since he only signed the global warming treaty after it had been watered down. Moreover, Bush stood alone at the international forum in his refusal to sign the biodiversity treaty.

On gun control measures, presidents as well as members of Congress have felt the political pressure and economic power of the National Rifle Association as it has mobilized its members and resources in an effort to thwart gun control initiatives. Still, the death of John F. Kennedy in 1963, along with those of Martin Luther King, Jr., and Senator Robert Kennedy in 1968, encouraged Lyndon Johnson to speak out in favor of restrictions on handguns and encouraged Congress to pass gun control legislation as a means to impose federal control over the violent consequences associated with firearms. Although Ronald Reagan opposed gun control even after being shot early in his presidency, once he left office he spoke in favor of the Brady Bill gun control legislation. George Bush also changed positions, from initially opposing gun control measures to withdrawing from the National Rifle Association and also issuing an executive order that banned the importation of several types of semi-automatic weapons.

Bill Clinton has long been committed to putting the power of the presidency behind gun control. He has responded to public perceptions about crime in the United States, the escalation of shootings taking place in America's schools, and the easy access to handguns and other types of firearms. Clinton's support for the Brady Bill and further restrictions on assault weapons resulted in strong opposition from the NRA as well as from private citizens who opposed the intrusion of the federal government into the private sphere.

While most presidents have avoided the issue of homosexuality as a social issue, Bill Clinton's position on the issue as it related to military service became the focal point of the national media, attracting criticism from both the military and civilian sectors. Clinton's effort to open up access to the military erupted into a national debate and divided members of the Congress, including Clinton's Democratic partisans. Moreover, since the "gays in the military" issue occurred early in his term in office, during the so-called honeymoon period, it diverted attention away from other issues and caused problems for Clinton since his leadership was called into question.

Presidents Johnson, Nixon, Reagan, Bush, and to a lesser extent President Clinton have used the presidency to address the issue of pornography. Richard Nixon, who inherited the report of the pornography commission established by his predecessor Lyndon Johnson, disagreed with the report and made public his differences with it. Despite a second commission established by Ronald Reagan to study the impact of pornography on society, most of Nixon's successors focused their attention primarily on a politically safer aspect of pornography—on ridding society of child pornography.

THE IMPACT OF OTHER EVENTS ON THE PRESIDENCY AND THE SOCIAL AGENDA

Several domestic, economic, and foreign policy issues prominent during respective administrations perhaps diverted attention away from shoring up presidents' social agendas. Franklin Roosevelt, of course, was most concerned about helping the American people in their struggle during the Great Depression and World War II, while Harry Truman assumed responsibility for bringing to a conclusion a global conflict and its aftermath. Dwight Eisenhower presided over postwar prosperity and the early stages of the Cold War, while Kennedy and Johnson were challenged by domestic and foreign policy constraints. At home, John Kennedy was confronted by stubborn Southern Democrats on the affirmative action/equal opportunity issue while he was dealing with the threat of Cuba and the Berlin situation. Although Johnson's domestic agenda was bolstered by the prospect of increased numbers of moderate to liberal Democrats in Congress as a result of the 1964 election, his administration was eventually consumed by the war in Vietnam.

Despite Richard Nixon's social activism during his first term in office, in foreign affairs he was involved with the continuing conflicts in Southeast Asia and in achieving detente with the Soviet Union and the People's Republic of China. By his second term, Nixon's administration was beset by the Watergate scandal and its consequences. Jimmy Carter's presidency was successful in bringing peace between Israel and Egypt; at the same time, however, his administration suffered the impact of high inflation and high interest rates, Americans held hostage in Iran, and the Soviet invasion of Afghanistan. While Ronald Reagan tried to use the power resources of the presidency in support of his social agenda, it is clear that economic and budget issues were his priority. Moreover, by his second term, he was struggling with the Iran-Contra scandal. Although attempting to continue the Reagan legacy, George Bush was more interested in foreign policy issues that received prominence in his years in office, including personal conflict with Manuel Noriega of Panama and Saddam Hussein of Iraq as well as the Persian Gulf War. Finally, despite his public statements and political commitment to gun control, abortion rights, and gay rights, Bill Clinton centered his first term priorities on the economy, the budget, and passage of his health care package.

SUMMARY: PROPOSITIONS AND GENERALIZATIONS INVOLVING THE AMERICAN PRESIDENCY AND THE SOCIAL AGENDA

Why might presidents act differently in implementing social policy? As the central figure in the political system, the president can focus the attention of the nation on specific issues including the social agenda. Yet presidents are also constrained by political necessities. Presidential behavior is influenced by constitutional authority, symbolic power of the office, and personal capacity. To what extent is a president a "facilitator of change" or a "director of change"?[10] Do presidents provide bold leadership, or do they act symbolically, primarily reflecting public preferences?

Presidential differences may be based on three main factors. Presidential action may be based upon *personal predisposition*, as when the president strongly supports the social agenda. Yet the officeholder must also take into consideration "the risk of alienating support against his conviction about what must be done and his desire to put it into practice."[11] Presidential action may be the result of *partisanship*, in which Democrats and Republicans are divided over politicized social policy disputes.[12] *Political opportunism*, finally, may explain presidential action. Presidents are political animals and seek out political opportunities that provide both personal rewards and favorable public outcomes.

In short, domestic as well as foreign policy issues have frequently superseded a president's interest in his social agenda. As this study has demonstrated, however when presidents have asserted themselves even symbolically, they have been able to make use of the resources associated with the various presidential roles and have been able to influence and shape social policy. The following propositions, then, both summarize our findings on the presidency and the social agenda and provide an agenda for future research.

> **Proposition 1:** The social agenda has a tendency to divide the American polity and is characterized by different types of presidential action and policy outcomes.

Presidential involvement in social policy is a risky venture because it tends to be highly politicized and divisive. Once the president becomes involved, however, he can be either assertive or passive. The type of role the president relies on provides a different type of political authority and resource, allowing and encouraging the president to use personal skills and to achieve the goal at hand.

To better understand presidential behavior regarding the social agenda, we created a classification scheme that focuses on presidential action (Table 6.1). The first dimension— *level of involvement*— concerns the extent to which the president plays a role in social policy. In this case, the president can be *assertive* in his involvement, taking an active role in support of or in opposition to the dynamics of the social issue. Ronald Reagan, as an example, spoke frequently about the "unborn child" and the need for a Human Life Amendment; Bill Clinton strongly supported the Brady Bill in an effort to reduce the violence associated with firearms. Presidents can also choose to be involved in a *passive* way or can avoid the issue all together by ignoring it or rejecting it. The second dimension— *policy outcome*—concerns whether a *tangible* or *nominal* result occurs. Harry Truman, as an example, issued an executive order to integrate the U.S. armed forces, which produced a tangible policy change. By contrast, despite Ronald Reagan's outspoken position on abortion, a Human Life Amendment never resulted.

Table 6.1   Presidential Action and Policy Outcome

		Level of Involvement	
		Assertive	*Passive*
Policy Outcomes	*Tangible*	Activism	Avoidance
	Nominal	Symbolic action	Rejection

The purpose of the social agenda framework is to develop presidential *types* based on how assertively or passively each president has acted and whether there has been a tangible or nominal outcome. The classification scheme has four categories: activist, symbolic, avoidance, rejection. An *activist* type is characterized by an assertive president who achieves a tangible outcome. The *symbolic* presidential type represents an activist president with no substantive outcome. The *avoidance* type is a president who refuses to become involved with the issue, yet a tangible outcome occurs as a result of the action of another political actor, such as Congress or the Supreme Court. The *rejection* type describes the president who has no interest in getting involved in the issue and, since no other political actors have tackled the issue, there is no tangible outcome.

> **Proposition 2a:** Presidents do not generally provide decisive leadership on the social agenda.

Although the president is a central figure in American politics, competing institutions are involved in public policymaking. Moreover, organized interests play an active role in their attempt to influence social policy. These interests have ample opportunities to be effective in persuading policymakers to respond to their position. For instance, the National Rifle Association has been quite effective in lobbying to convince members of Congress and the president that gun control is an inappropriate means to deal with crime and violence.

Since other political actors tend to be involved in social policymaking as well, the president must decide whether and to what extent he should become involved with the issue and at what cost. The nature of the issues, divisive and sometimes explosive, raise the question of why any president would decide to spend political capital on issues which lack consensus and sometimes threaten domestic tranquility. For example, presidents have usually avoided the issue of homosexuality, believing that there is little to gain from becoming involved. When Bill Clinton decided to change social policy by terminating the ban on gays in the military, he was confronted with a firestorm of opposition and was forced to compromise on the issue. Clinton became the target of political opponents and also incurred the wrath of members of the gay community, who felt that the president had not done enough for them and had even betrayed them in compromising on the issue.

Although it has been relatively safe for the president to avoid involvement in social policy, different presidents have decided to use the power resources of the office for different reasons. Truman's decision to desegregate the armed forces changed the military establishment forever and also set the stage for social changes throughout society. The bipartisanship among presidents on behalf of environmental protection has resulted in important legislation passed by Congress and signed by the president, in the structuring of executive agencies, in the creation of the Environmental Protection Agency, and in the preservation of vast tracts of public land set aside for future generations. John Kennedy's dual theme underlying the decision to end above-ground nuclear weapons testing stands as a testament to presidential leadership in the role of chief diplomat and commander in chief. For Kennedy, prohibiting nuclear testing was an important step in arms control; it was also a significant step in protecting public health and the environment.

As legislative leader, Lyndon Johnson played a key role in encouraging the passage of civil rights legislation and in stressing the importance of affirmative action/equal opportunity. Johnson put the struggle for social justice and racial equality at the forefront of his administration. Moreover, it was Johnson, as chief executive, who issued the executive order establishing affirmative action in support of equal opportunity that shaped U.S. social policy for the next three decades.

Richard Nixon ensured that the 1970s would be the decade for environmental awareness. He used his office to support passage of the National Environmental Protection Act, the creation of the EPA, and the passage of more pieces of environmental legislation than any other modern-day president. Nixon was aware of public opinion in support of environmental quality and felt compelled to use the power resources of the presidency on behalf of the environment. Although he received credit for several environmental initiatives, he was not necessarily a bold innovator but rather an astute politician. Moreover, by supporting environmental proposals, Nixon could blunt the 1972 presidential campaign of Senate Edmund Muskie of Maine, who had strong environmental credentials. Several years later, in the same policy arena, George Bush, as legislative leader, helped to pass the 1990 Clean Air Act amendments. According to Sussman and Kelso, without Bush's involvement it is less likely that the legislation would have passed.[13]

> **Proposition 2b:** Presidents have been passive or practiced avoidance on social issues either because the issues were not yet politicized at the federal level or because other national or state institutions were already involved with the issue or because involvement in the issue carried too much risk for the president.

In many instances, political actors other than the president have tended to be the major players in social policy. Congress, the Court, and state governments have dealt with social policy longer than have presidents, who have tended to practice avoidance. Once issues became politicized, however, several presidents were compelled to use their office in pursuit of influencing the social agenda. The assassination of John Kennedy turned the attention of the nation to the consequences of gun violence and made the public aware that even the most visible figure in the country was vulnerable to violence. This awareness encouraged Johnson to lobby for gun control legislation in 1968.

The Supreme Court has been a major actor involved with abortion policy ever since *Roe v. Wade* in 1973. This decision nationalized the issue. Moreover, other important decisions set forth by the Court including the *Webster* case in 1989 and the *Planned Parenthood of Pennsylvania* decision in 1992, returning the focus on abortion to the states.[14] Nonetheless, once the issue was nationalized, presidents became involved. It was the rare president who could avoid involvement. Ronald Reagan embraced the abortion issue, arguing against abortion rights and vigorously supporting the rights of the "unborn." While George Bush continued Reagan's agenda, Bill Clinton used his presidency in support of the pro-choice position.

In the environmental arena, most of the progress in this area has not been made through presidential action. Although Eisenhower spoke in favor of environmental protection, he viewed it as a responsibility of state and local governments. However, where some states assumed a "green" approach to the environment, other states became centers of heavy industry and pollution ranging from the automobile industry in Michigan to chemical plants in Louisiana. Although the two Roosevelts set examples for presidential involvement with conservation measures, over the years, efforts to protect the environment have usually centered in the Congress.

Similarly, even though Franklin Roosevelt supported two gun control bills in the 1930s, few other actions occurred in support of gun control until Lyndon Johnson's support of his legislation in 1968, followed later in the 1990s, with Bill Clinton's support for the Brady Bill.

> **Proposition 3a:** Although it is a weak role, opinion/party leadership has been used by presidents to explain their positions on social policy and to educate and mobilize the electorate.

The roles used by the president when taking action on social policy may provide the necessary authoritative basis and resources they need. Some roles, however, lack the support required for effective presidential action and require the president to rely more on personal skills.

As opinion/party leader, the president can attempt to implement the electoral commitments made by the party and can make an effort to build a bridge between the presidency and the electorate through direct and indirect personal contact. Yet the role lacks formal authority and has few built-in resources. Modern presidents have tried a number of ways to engage the American public in an effort to make their case. They have used the important State of the Union message to emphasize social policy because these speeches provide a vehicle where the president can reach out to a national audience. Both Truman and Eisenhower used this message to discuss their views about conservation. Kennedy and Johnson emphasized their commitment to affirmative action/equal opportunity in communication with the public and Congress. Ronald Reagan made numerous references to his social agenda in his State of the Union messages, maintaining his connections to specific constituency groups and shoring up his electoral base.

Minor speeches have also played an important role, since every president beginning with Franklin Roosevelt addressed the public and interest groups about affirmative action/equal opportunity and the environment. The frequency of references to affirmative action/equal protection in minor speeches indicates the importance presidents have placed on these issues.

The other four issues did not become politicized until the 1960s and 1970s. Nixon, Carter, and Ford used a variety of media and public outlets in expressing their views about abortion, but the level of their activity paled in comparison to that of Reagan and Bush, who spoke more often in support of the pro-life position that any other president. Clinton, who spoke less frequently on the issue than his two predecessors, bolstered the pro-choice constituencies when he did speak to the issue.

Johnson, Reagan, Bush, and Clinton also relied on their access to the public to inform and educate citizens about their position on gun control. While Reagan and Bush presented their opposition to restrictions on guns, Johnson and Clinton made their case to the American public in favor of more restrictions on firearms.

Pornography has long been subject to state and local laws and court decisions, allowing most presidents to avoid the issue in a public forum. However, Nixon and Reagan used the State of the Union message to explain their concerns about the issue, and Reagan, Bush, and Clinton employed their opinion/party leadership to focus specifically on child pornography.

Proposition 3b: As legislative leader, the president is in a weaker role, lacking the authority to force Congress to act; yet the president can employ several legislative tools in dealing with social policy.

The veto can be a very powerful tool, but it must not be used too frequently since it is then viewed as a sign of weakness. Kennedy and Johnson used the veto to protect First Amendment rights from becoming weakened through restrictions in antipornography legislation that tended to threaten the free flow of information. Reagan and Bush employed the veto to prohibit the expenditure of public funds for abortions. Bush also applied the veto to blocking financial support for the United Nations Population Fund because of concerns that international family planning programs included abortion as an option. Clinton used the veto on several occassions to protect what he saw as a Republican assault on the environment.

In contrast to presidential leadership by veto, successful legislative leaders have relied on their personal skills and creative strategies. For example, presidents have put their position before the Congress in nationally televised addresses and special messages. Roosevelt and Clinton used national addresses to focus on environmental priorities, while Johnson did the same for affirmative action/equal opportunity. Nixon and Reagan used speeches before joint sessions of the Congress to mobilize action on pornography. Reagan also used this forum to encourage congressional action in support of a Human Life Amendment.

As legislative leaders, presidents have also employed creative activities to influence Congress. Where Nixon proclaimed 1970 the "year of the environment" after signing clean air legislation, George Bush signed an environmental agreement at the Grand Canyon. Clinton used his weekly radio addresses to lobby for those social issues he considered important.

The personal skills of presidents can make or break their efforts to shape social policy. Lyndon Johnson was the consummate legislative leader, a president who understood the dynamics of the legislative process and the need to court legislative leaders in the House and in the Senate. By contrast, Jimmy Carter, viewed by many as aloof to Congress, preferred to speak to a televised audience in his efforts to influence members of Congress. This approach, coupled with failure to engage in personal consultation and vigorous lobbying, contributed to the defeat of what might otherwise have been successful ventures.

While presidents might prefer to work with a Congress with a partisan majority, many presidents have presided over divided government. Still, the experience of Carter indicates that unified government is no guarantee that Congress will work with the president. When Carter decided to terminate nineteen water projects in several Western states, he incurred the wrath of his fellow Democrats as well as Richard Russell, the powerful chair of the Senate Finance Committee, who saw these projects as "pork" for their constituents.[15]

If the president appreciates the milieu in which he is operating and has the requisite personal skills and creativity, he can overcome constraints and be moderately successful in his relationship with the Congress.

> **Proposition 3c:** Sitting at the midpoint of the power continuum, the chief executive role is a rather modest one in which presidents must successfully employ the resources of the "managerial presidency" in order to carry out their social policy agenda.

The size and complexity of the federal government makes it increasingly difficult for the president to manage the bureaucracy. Additionally, constraints on the president, including specific grants of power to Congress and fragmented control in the hands of the bureaucracy, can frustrate presidential priorities. Nonetheless, the president has powers as chief executive that can be useful regarding his social agenda preferences.

Executive orders and proclamations are important tools of the chief executive. Executive orders carry the force of law and, though they are less powerful, proclamations can also be used to shape social policy. Roosevelt used the executive order to open up employment opportunities in the defense industry. While Kennedy issued an executive order to establish the Equal Employment Opportunity Commission, Johnson employed the tool as a means to establish "affirmative action" in the hiring of minorities seeking employment involving federal contractors. Both Bush and Clinton used the instrument to stop the international flow of firearms into the country.

In the mid-1980s, Reagan issued a proclamation encouraging Americans to speak out against child pornography, while Bush and Clinton did the same to acknowledge Earth Day. Perhaps one of the more interesting proclamations was Clinton's establishment of the Grand Staircase–Escalante National Monument. In one sweeping action, by the authority vested in him by the 1906 Antiquities Act, he set aside some two millions acres of public land in Utah.

Important federal agencies have been established or have had their missions revised as a result of reorganization plans of the chief executive. The Environmental Protection Agency, the Environmental Quality Council, and the Citizens' Advisory Committee on the Environment were all created by Richard Nixon. John Kennedy changed the focus of the Civil Rights Commission, making it an even more effective instrument for affirmative action/equal opportunity. The Reagan administration set up a special unit in the Justice Department to put pressure on producers and distributors of pornography. Both Johnson and Reagan established presidential commissions to investigate the impact and threat posed by pornography.

As chief executive, the president has the power of appointment, allowing him to staff and shape policy. Ronald Reagan's appointment of James Watt as secretary of the interior stands in stark contrast to Clinton's selection of environmentalist Bruce Babbitt. Moreover, Clinton's selection of A1 Gore as Vice President and the appointment of Carol Browner as head of the EPA were positive signals to the environmental community that this president believed the environment was a worthwhile social issue on which to focus. Lyndon Johnson showed his interest in affirmative action by appointing the first African American, Thurgood Marshall, to the U.S. Supreme Court. Two decades later Ronald Reagan broke precedent and selected Sandra Day O'Connor as the first woman justice on the Supreme Court.

The president as chief executive can be successful if he uses personal skills and managerial tools effectively. Yet he can also be frustrated in his efforts. Where Reagan's "administrative presidency" used budget and appointment powers to shape environmental policy and the composition of the judiciary (and hence its influence on social policy), Bill Clinton confronted a Republican Senate Judiciary Committee after the 1994 Congressional elections that thought his judicial appointments were too liberal or gave too much support to affirmative action/equal opportunity.[16]

Proposition 3d: Chief diplomat and commander-in-chief are the president's strongest roles, but he relies on them less frequently to support a president's social agenda.

These two roles have a strong authoritative base in the Constitution, statutory laws, customs, and tradition, all of which provide substantial resources for the president if he chooses to act. Among the six social issues in this study, this role has been used primarily with abortion, the environment, and gun control; while homosexuality received attention during Bill Clinton's first term when he made gay members of the military issue of consequence.

Presidents Reagan and Bush used this role as a means to influence global population policy when they decided to end financial contributions for the UN Population Fund and non-governmental organizations involved in family planning practices because they were concerned that abortion was included among the options. Moreover, Reagan and Bush chose to oppose a woman's right to choose to have an abortion at military hospitals whether at home or abroad.

The environment has been an important area for the president in this role because the president has been engaged in both environmental diplomacy and also issues that relate to national security and environmental protection. Every president from Franklin Roosevelt through Bill Clinton has signed important bilateral or multilateral agreements in support of environmental measures. Several of these agreements, including the 1959 Antarctic Treaty and the 1963 Nuclear Test Ban Treaty, attempted to protect the environment, which was put at risk as a result of the nuclear arms threat. At the same time, environmentalists have been disappointed when, for instance, Bush refused to sign the Biodiversity Treaty at the 1992 Earth Summit. Environmentalists have also been surprised when, for example, Ronald Reagan (whose domestic environmental agenda was criticized) signed the important Montreal Protocol on Ozone Depletion.

In an effort to ensure domestic tranquility and the security of the people from an external threat, both Bush and Clinton used the chief diplomat role in conjunction with that of the resources of the chief executive to issue executive orders to stop certain firearms from entering the country.

> **Proposition 4:** Presidential roles matter because they control the resources that allow a president to be assertive in shaping social policy.

As Table 6.2 indicates, presidential roles do matter in terms of the president's level of involvement in specific social issues. We have seen that although roles other than the chief diplomat and commander in chief are considered moderate to weak, presidents have been able to assert themselves using the power resources available to them. Moreover, by the force of individual skills and personal commitment to influencing social policy, several presidents have made profound changes that have affected American society, while other presidents have remained passive in their response to social issues.

Presidents have been assertive in each of the roles examined in this book regarding abortion, affirmative action/equal opportunity, the environment, and gun control. As opinion/party leader, the president has asserted himself through State of the Union messages, speeches to

Table 6.2 Presidential Roles and the Social Agenda

	Presidential Roles			
Social Agenda	Opinion/ Party Leader	Legislative Leader	Chief Executive	Chief Diplomat and Commander in Chief
Abortion	+	+	+	+
Affirmative action/ Equal opportunity	+	+	+	+
Environment	+	+	+	+
Gun control	+	+	+	+/−
Homosexuality	−	−	−	+/−
Pornography[1]	−	+	+	[1]

(+) represents presidential assertiveness.

(−) represents presidential passiveness.

(+/−) represents moderate or symbolic action by the president.

[1]The challenges posed by pornography on the Internet in the future may increasingly involve this role in negotiations with other nations on international "community standards" as well as protecting the security of the country in a "war on cyberporn."

constituency groups, and town meetings. He has used legislative power by special messages to the Congress, signing legislation, and vetoing it. As chief executive, the president has influenced and shaped social policy through the power of appointment, reorganizing government and the creation of executive agencies, and issuing executive orders and proclamations. As the sole organ of communication with the international community and as military leader, the president has negotiated treaties and shaped military personnel policy.

Presidents have, overall, been rather passive in these roles when it has come to the issues of pornography and homosexuality. More often than not, when presidents have decided to act on a pornography issue, they have relied on their legislative leader, chief executive, or opinion/party leader roles to stop the production and distribution of pornography. It is much more difficult for a president to speak in support of the social value of pornographic literature or even to support First Amendment concerns about restricting literature, since a moderate to liberal president would be putting himself at risk with an American public opposed to pornography. The extent to which the president as chief diplomat and commander in chief becomes increasingly involved in addressing the issue of global pornography remains to be seen. Given the scope and pervasiveness of the Internet, the president may well become assertive on this issue since different nations have different customs, rules, and regulations and the need to create international community standards may well arise. Moreover, the proliferation of international pornography rings may also encourage the president to take an assertive stance in devising ways to control cyberporn.

Most presidents have chosen to remain passive on homosexuality, the quintessential controversial issue in American society. Until Clinton as opinion/party leader took on the issue of open access to military service, little had been done by any president for the gay community.

> **Proposition 5:** Although a president's attention to the social agenda has focused on domestic politics, the increased transparency of national borders may encourage new challenges for presidents in the future.

When presidents have chosen to be assertive regarding social policy, it has usually been within the American domestic arena. Once the Supreme Court nationalized the abortion issue, presidents felt compelled to take a position on this divisive domestic issue as it related to American women's access to abortion as a family planning option. Roosevelt, Truman, Kennedy, Johnson, Carter, and Clinton responded to race relations in the domestic area by using resources and skills to improve equal access and equal opportunity for all Americans. Gun control also encouraged an essentially national focus in the 1990s. The modern environmental movement, born in the mid-1960s, has also had primarily a domestic focus. The exercise of presidential power first centered on conservation measures, followed by pollution controls to improve the quality of the environment in the United States.

Many of these issues easily can have a transnational effect with an increasingly international impact. Presidents Reagan and Bush addressed the issue of abortion on a global scale when they employed their power to prohibit U.S. funds for international and nongovernmental organizations. Since the global population is increasing at an alarming rate—recently surpassing 6 billion people—future presidents may feel even more compelled to address family planning practices in the international community because of increasing global poverty, disease, stress on the environment, and unstable conditions leading to war.

The president not only represents an important position in American politics but is also a central figure in the international community, as Woodrow Wilson recognized long ago. As such, he must recognize that the activities of individual nations have consequences on a regional and international scale. The problem of acid rain, addressed during the Reagan administration, is a good example of how the actions of one nation (i.e., United States) impinge on the quality of life in another country (Canada). The debates over stratospheric ozone depletion and global warming show the interconnections between countries. The disappearance of the ocean's fish resources has involved many nation's well-being. The prospect of war over access to resources (e.g., water) always remains a dangerous prospect and may constitute new challenges for the president as chief diplomat and commander-in-chief, since global environmental issues quite possibly will dominate the twenty-first century.

The international flow of firearms will continue to be a problem for U.S. presidents. Given the debate over gun control within the United States, the NRA and other gun organizations have appealed globally in their effort to prevent further restrictions on firearms. Although Presidents Bush and Clinton used executive orders to stop the flow of weapons across national borders, bilateral agreements and multilateral conventions already in place may serve as models for presidential involvement in this issue in the international community.

Presidential actions on restricting pornography have usually been restricted to the domestic arena. Yet, pornography is an international industry and Americans are major consumers of the product. Concerns over any perceived threat to this country's "standards" can demand presidential attention to this issue.

> **Proposition 6:** Presidents can exert assertive policy leadership over the social agenda, but they must do so in a supportive political and social climate.

Where party, ideology, Congress, and public opinion have been supportive of a president's actions, several presidents have exerted both activist as well as symbolic leadership on social policy. Presidents have, on occasion and despite the obstacles, sailed against the wind and used their power of persuasion to promote social policy.

Lyndon Johnson, supported by a Democratic-controlled Congress, used his influence to secure passage of the 1968 gun control act. The assassinations of political figures in the 1960s, and a new Congress in 1964 along with a supportive public, enabled him to assert his role as legislative leader in support of social policy.

Richard Nixon as chief executive, chief legislator, and opinion/party leader became the modern environmental president. His impressive legislative record, along with the establishment of important executive agencies and the declaration of the 1970s as the decade of the environment, was fully supported by the public climate of the times, including public opinion and the impact of the first Earth Day in 1970.

Even though Nixon and Reagan had to contend with a Democratic Congress (for Reagan, a Democratic Senate during his last two years), conditions appeared right for these presidents to maximize their leadership on the issue of pornography. In contrast to Kennedy and Johnson, Nixon and Reagan as conservatives were less bothered by First Amendment concerns and the restriction of access to the flow of information. Nixon and Reagan could be outspoken about the issue because public opinion was compatible with their positions.

As commander in chief, Truman and Clinton became involved in military personnel policy, which had different results. Despite opposition within his own party and from the military, Truman felt that the time was right to desegregate U.S. armed forces. Truman's decision paved the way, if only indirectly, for the Supreme Court's decision in *Brown v. Board of Education* in 1954. By contrast, Bill Clinton promised during his 1992 campaign for the presidency that he would use his power as president to end the barriers to military service for homosexuals. Faced with strong congressional and military opposition, Clinton failed to issue his promised executive order and was forced to compromise his stand in support of gays in the military.

> **Proposition 7a:** Modern presidents from Franklin Roosevelt to Clinton represent different presidential types on the six social issues in this study.

Table 6.3 presents an overall assessment of the eleven presidents examined in this study. In some instances, presidents were activist types and used the power of the presidency to shape social policy. In other cases, depending on the role they relied on, presidents became symbolic types, using their power but without achieving a tangible outcome. At still other times, presidents avoided the issues altogether.

Reagan, Bush, and Clinton were the most active presidents on the abortion issue, although their action was partisan in nature. Reagan and Bush were conservatives who used their power as opinion/party leader, chief executive, and legislative leader in support of the pro-life position. By contrast, Bill Clinton was a liberal activist strongly in support of a woman's right to choose abortion as a family planning option. As opinion/party leader, he used the bully pulpit in support of this position; as legislator leader, he lobbied Congress in support of abortion clinic safety; and as chief diplomat, he reversed the Reagan-Bush ban on funding of abortion for the United Nations Population Fund.

Seven of the eleven presidents were activist types on affirmative action/equal opportunity. Although Lyndon Johnson has been characterized as the president most committed to creating a society where all citizens enjoyed equal opportunity, Roosevelt, Truman, and Kennedy before him used their power as chief executive and/or legislative leader to begin the process of institutionalizing affirmative action/equal opportunity in American society. Later, Carter and Clinton used their appointment power as chief executive to appoint women and minorities to high-level governmental positions.

Among the early modern presidents, Franklin Roosevelt was an activist on environmental issues. As opinion/party leader, he included environmental priorities in his State of the Union message . As legislative leader, he included environmental funding in his budgets. As chief executive, he created several offices which fostered environmental protection. Among the late modern presidents, Nixon was the most successful in promoting environmental priorities. Nixon relied on all of the presidential roles to advanced environmental interests. Although he was unable to create a new Department of Natural Resources, he established the Environmental Protection Agency and signed into law the National Environmental Protection Act. These two environmental initiatives, in conjunction with other environmental actions, make Nixon the activist environmental president.

Table 6.3 Presidential Types and the Social Agenda

President	Abortion	Affirmative Action/Equal Opportunity	Social Agenda — Environmental	Guns	Homosexuality	Pornography
F. Roosevelt	avoidance	activism	activism	avoidance	avoidance	avoidance
Truman	avoidance	activism	symbolic action	avoidance	avoidance	avoidance
Eisenhower	avoidance	symbolic action	symbolic action	avoidance	avoidance	symbolic action
Kennedy	avoidance	activism	symbolic action	avoidance	avoidance	symbolic action
Johnson	avoidance	activism	symbolic action	activism	avoidance	activism
Nixon	symbolic action	symbolic action	activism	avoidance	avoidance	activism
Ford	symbolic action	avoidance	symbolic action	avoidance	avoidance	avoidance
Carter	symbolic action	activism	activism	avoidance	avoidance	avoidance
Reagan	activism	activism	activism	activism	avoidance	activism
Bush	activism	symbolic action	activism	activism	avoidance	symbolic action
Clinton	activism	activism	activism/ symbolic action	activism	activism	symbolic action

Nixon's successors—Carter, Reagan, Bush, and Clinton to a lesser degree—also used their power to shape environmental policy. In addition to his effort in energy conservation, Jimmy Carter signed into law the Superfund Act and also supported preserving public land in Alaska. Reagan was an activist type but used his power as chief executive to reverse environmental progress in support of development over preservation. As legislative leader, George Bush assisted Congress in passing the 1990 Clean Air Act, but he began to reverse himself on other environmental priorities after feeling the pressure from business and fellow Republicans in the Congress. As chief executive, Clinton appointed several environmentalists to important positions including heads of the EPA and the Department of the Interior, as well as setting aside 2 million acres of land in Utah as a new national monument. Yet as legislative leader, Clinton had a record that was disappointing to environmentalists. The only major piece of legislation passed during his first term in office was the 1994 California Desert Protection Act.

Most presidents have avoided the gun issue. Although two bills were passed during the Roosevelt administration, these bills were geared toward organized crime weapons and enforcement of the legislation was problematic. As legislative leader, Johnson took action in 1968, after three political assassinations, to oppose access to guns. His successors Reagan and Bush, while representing anti–gun control positions, did make exceptions—to support the Brady Bill, in Reagan's case, and to support a ban on foreign semiautomatic weapons imports. Among the modern presidents, Clinton has used all to the presidential roles in support of gun control. He has spoken on behalf of the Brady Bill and other restrictions, signed the Brady Bill into law, and issued executive orders to restrict the importation of firearms.

Clinton stands alone among the modern presidents to take a formal stand on homosexuality. Though painful, given the vigorous opposition to his stance, Clinton's activism on gays in the military may lead future presidents to argue once again in favor of creating a system of open access for military service if the political and social climate is right.

CONCLUSION

Presidential roles are important and when presidents choose to act they can achieve tangible outcomes. This effect can be seen especially in the activist presidential types—represented by Roosevelt, Truman, and Johnson on affirmative action/equal opportunity, Nixon on the environment, Reagan and Bush on abortion, and Clinton on gun control.

> **Proposition 7b:** Given the important position of the president in the political system, even symbolic leadership can be helpful in furthering a social agenda.

By taking a stand in shaping social policy, the president is challenging Congress, mobilizing organized interests, and educating and informing the public. By taking an activist position, the president is either encouraging fellow politicians and the electorate to support him or creating the conditions that cause opposition forces to line up against him.

Presidential involvement in the social agenda is important for several reasons. First, social policies have affected the linkage between presidents and social constituencies. Lyndon Johnson's support for equal opportunity strengthened his relationship with African Americans, just as Ronald Reagan found increased support from the pro-life movement as a result of his strong pro-life stance. Moreover, social policies have influenced presidential action indirectly since constituency groups pressure the Congress which in turn supports, constrains, or modifies a president's agenda.

Second, presidents and the role they assume can make a difference in public policymaking. The role assumed by the president can lead to the pursuit or avoidance of social policies, and these policies in turn can have a profound impact on the exercise of presidential power. At the same time, however, the president must recognize the political and social context. For example, Democrats Truman and Clinton could use the chief executive role to open up opportunities in the armed forces. Although both presidents faced a hostile environment, Truman issued an executive order that desegregated the military, while Clinton refrained from issuing his promised executive order and settled instead on the "Don't ask, don't tell" policy on gays in the military. The environment was addressed quite differently by Republicans Nixon and Reagan. Where Nixon saw a political opportunity in supporting environmental initiatives, Reagan pursued a developmentalist, anti-environment approach. Both Nixon and Reagan used the chief executive and legislative leader roles, for example, but in contrasting ways. Nixon used the executive order and signed legislation to promote environmentalism. Reagan used budget and appointment powers and the veto to thwart environmentalism. Likewise, partisans Reagan and Clinton used the opinion/party role in contrasting ways regarding abortion. Republican Reagan spoke on behalf of the "unborn child," whereas Democrat Clinton publicly supported a woman's right to choose to have an abortion.

Third, the president has been forced to respond to social issues because of the emergence of "culture wars"—social conflicts that gained prominence since the 1960s but had their roots in political activism of the pre-1960s. *Culture conflict* is what James Davison Hunter calls "political and social hostility rooted in different systems of moral understanding . . . . the range of issues debated . . . . can be traced ultimately and finally to the matter of moral authority . . . . . It is the commitment to different and opposing bases of moral authority and the world views that derive from them that creates the deep cleavages between antagonists in the contemporary culture wars."[17] In describing the opposing sides as cultural conservatives or moral traditionalists versus cultural progressives or liberals, Hunter argues that "on political matters one can compromise; on matters of ultimate moral truth, one cannot."[18]

The social issues discussed in this book can be viewed within the context of the larger social movements affecting American politics and society, including the women's movement, the right-to-life movement, the gay rights movement, and the Christian Coalition, among others, which have imposed new demands on the political system and on presidents. These movements have benefited from the fragmentation and decentralization of government, which provides numerous access points to exert political pressure, as well as from the technological advances that have made it easier to disseminate information. Susan Tolchin suggests that the "anger common to this era . . . focuses on distinct themes all rooted in social values" resulting in "serious frictions within society."[19] Furthermore, the social change taking place in post-industrial America suggests continuing political conflict over social issues between contending forces. For some, the conflict has arisen because of the change from a materialist to postmaterialist value orientation among the public, which places greater emphasis on noneconomic issues (world peace, environmental protection).[20] Or political conflict might be characterized by ideological social cleavages, where a liberal agenda (pro-choice on abortion, support for gay and women's rights) confronts a conservative agenda that emphasizes a pro-life, anti-gay and anti-women's rights orientation.[21]

Fourth, domestic, economic, foreign and national security policy have included social issues, making the social agenda deserving of systematic treatment as it applies to the American presidency. For example, abortion is a salient domestic issue but it also affects U.S. policy regarding the United Nations, foreign countries, and family planning. The environment is increasingly viewed as an important consideration in national security issues, given the military impact on environmental quality. Pornography has been considered primarily as a domestic issue although cyberporn raises new challenges for the United States and the president as chief diplomat and commander in chief.

As we have seen, activist presidents have shaped social policy in many ways. At the same time, many presidents have practiced avoidance at some time during their tenure in office. Still, whenever presidents used the power resources of their office, either actively or symbolically, their social agenda has been strengthened. While the activist president seeks results, the symbolic president has taken action that is significant in various sectors of the political system even if the results have been nominal. It is meaningful when the president as opinion/party leader talks about an issue on the campaign trail or when he is out among the public during his term in office. It is important when the president as legislative leader lobbies Congress in the face of potential defeat of a bill which the president supports.

The president occupies an important position within the Madisonian model of government. He may head a divided or unified government. He must work with a decentralized Congress and know which players to court and when to court them. As chief executive, he must deal with a fragmented bureaucracy. As opinion/party leader, he can inform and educate the voters, yet he lacks formal authority to do so. As chief diplomat and commander in chief, the president has an authoritative base and more resources at his control, but he is less likely to rely on this role to shape social policy.

For a president to maximize strength from his stance, he must use the authority and resources available to him in each of his roles to establish a social agenda. He must also use his personal skills and be creative. Moreover, he must also be supported by a political and social climate that is favorable to him. When these conditions are met, the social agenda is secured. Unfortunately, this complete scenario occurs only rarely. Conflict over social policy is consequently likely to continue to challenge the American political system and the president as its most visible figure.

ENDNOTES

1. Donald W. Jackson and James W. Riddlesperger, "John F. Kennedy and the Politics of Civil Rights," in James W. Riddlesperger and Donald W. Jackson, eds., *Presidential Leadership and Civil Rights Policy* (Westport, CT: Greenwood Press, 1995).
2. Arthur Schlesinger, Jr., *A Thousand Days: John F. Kennedy in the White House* (New York: Fawcett Crest, 1965), 843–92.
3. Mark Stern,"John F. Kennedy and Civil Rights: From Congress to the Presidency," *Presidential Studies Quarterly* 19 (1989): 797–823.
4. Robert Mann, *The Walls of Jericho: Lyndon Johnson, Hubert Humphrey, Richard Russell, and the Struggle for Civil Rights* (New York: Harcourt Brace, 1996).
5. David O'Brien, "Clinton's Legal Policy and the Courts," in Colin Campbell and Bert A. Rockman, eds., *The Clinton Presidency: First Appraisals* (Chatham House, NJ: Chatham House, 1996), 137.
6. Lucius J. Barker and Mack H. Jones, eds., *African Americans in the American Political System,* 3rd (Englewood Cliffs, NJ: Prentice-Hall, 1994), 118.
7. Earl Ofari Hutchinson, *Betrayed: A History of Presidential Failure to Protect Black Lives* (Boulder, CO: Westview Press, 1996), 8.
8. Kenneth O'Reilly, *Nixon's Piano: Presidents and Racial Politics from Washington to Clinton* (New York: Free Press, 1995).
9. Richard Nathan, *The Administrative Presidency* (New York: Wiley, 1983).
10. George C. Edwards III, "The Presidential Pulpit: Bully or Baloney?" in James P. Pfiffner and Roger H. Davidson, eds., *Understanding the Presidency* (New York: Longman, 1997), 327.
11. Rexford G. Tugwell, *The Democratic Roosevelt* (Garden City, NY: Doubleday, 1957), 231.
12. Raymond Tatalovich and Byron W. Daynes, eds., *Moral Controversies in American Politics: Cases in Social Regulatory Policy* (Armonk, NY: M. E. Sharpe, 1998), 262.
13. Glen Sussman and Mark Kelso, "Environmental Priorities and the President as Legislative Leader," in Dennis Soden, ed., *The Environmental Presidency* (Albany, NY: SUNY Press, 1999), 119–25.
14. See *Webster v. Reproductive Health Services,* 492 U.S. 490 (1989), and *Planned Parenthood of Southeastern Pennsylvania v. Casey,* 112 S. Ct. 2791 (1992).
15. See James David Barber, *The Presidential Character: Predicting Performance in the White House,* 4th ed. (Englewood Cliffs, NJ: Prentice-Hall, 1992), 437–38 and Charles O. Jones, *Separate but Equal Branches: Congress and the Presidency* (Chatham, NJ: Chatham House, 1995), 153.

16. O'Brien, "Clinton's Legal Policy and the Courts," 143.

17. Jeffrey Davison Hunter, *Culture Wars: The Struggle to Define America* (New York: Basic Books, 1991), 42–43.

18. Hunter, *Culture Wars*, 46.

19. Susan J. Tochin, *The Angry American: How Voter Rage Is Changing the Nation* (Boulder, CO: Westview Press, 1999), 85.

20. Ronald Inglehart, *The Silent Revolution: Changing Values and Political Styles among Western Publics* (Princeton, NJ: Princeton University Press, 1977).

21. Scott C. Flanagan, "Changing Values in Industrial Societies Revisited: Towards a Resolution of the Values Debate," *American Political Science Review* 81: 1301–319.

Appendix: Presidents as Legislative Leaders and Major Social Legislation

President	Abortion	Affirmative Action	Environment	Gun Control	Homosexuality	Pornography
Franklin D. Roosevelt 1933–1945		National Labor Relations Act; PL 74-198 Fair Labor Standards Act of 1938; PL 75-718	Tennessee Valley Authority Act of 1933; PL 73-16 Fish and Game Sanctuaries Act; PL 73-120 Conservation of Wildlife Act; PL 73-121 Migratory Bird Conservation Act; PL 73-124 Emergency Conservation Work; PL 74-82 Soil Conservation and Domestic Allotment Act; PL 74-461 Insect and Pest Control, Appropriations; PL 75-26			

(continued)

Appendix: Presidents as Legislative Leaders and Major Social Legislation (*Cont.*)

President	Abortion	Affirmative Action	Environment	Gun Control	Homosexuality	Pornography
Franklin D. Roosevelt *continued*			Wildlife Restoration Projects; PL 75-415 Water Conservation, etc.; PL 76-398 Bald Eagle; PL 76-567			
Harry S Truman 1945–1953			Water Pollution Control Act; PL 80-845 Water Pollution Control Act, extension; PL 81-579			
Dwight D. Eisenhower 1953–1961		Veterans Benefits Acts; PL 83-695 and PL 83-698 School Milk Program; PL 84-465 Civil Rights Act of 1957; PL 85-315	Submerged Lands Act; PL 83-31 Bill Amending the Water Facilities Act; PL 83-690 Agricultural Act of 1954; PL 83-690			

	Social Security Amendments; PL 85-840 Civil Rights Commission Extension; PL 86-383 Civil Rights Act of 1960; PL 86-449	River and Flood Control Act of 1954; PL 83-780 Rivers and Harbors Bill; PL 85-500 Water Pollution Act Amendments of 1956; Fish and Wildlife Act of 1956; PL 84-1024			
John F. Kennedy 1961–1963	Manpower Training Act Amendment of 1964; PL 88-214	Federal Water Pollution Control Act; PL 87-88			
Lyndon B. Johnson 1963–1969	1964 Civil Rights Act; PL 88-352 Voting Rights Act; PL 89-110 Immigration Act of 1965; PL 89-236 Fair Housing Act; PL90-284	1964 Wilderness Act; PL 88-577 Establish Land and Water Conservation Fund; PL 88-578 Water Resource Planning Bill; PL 89-80 Bill to Strengthen Control over Water Pollution; PL 89-234			Omnibus Crime Control and Safe Streets Act of 1968; PL 90-351 Gun Control Act of 1968; PL 90-618

(continued)

Appendix: Presidents as Legislative Leaders and Major Social Legislation (*Cont.*)

President	Abortion	Affirmative Action	Environment	Gun Control	Homosexuality	Pornography
			Clean Water Restoration Act; PL 89-753 National Water Commission Act; PL 90-515			
Richard M. Nixon 1969–1974	Family Planning Legislation; PL 91-572 FY 1975 Labor-HEW Appropriations Bill; PL 93-517	1972 Equal Employment Opportunity Act; PL 92-261 Civil Rights Commission Extension and Expansion Bill; PL 92-496 The Rehabilitation Act of 1973; PL 93-112	Water Quality Improvement Act; PL 91-224 Air Pollution Bill; PL 91-604 Water Clean Up Bill; PL 92-611 1972 Marine Mammal Protection Act; PL 92-522 Federal Water Pollution Control Act Amendments of 1972 (by a congressional override veto); PL 92-500 Endangered Species Act; PL 93-205	Organized Crime Control Act of 1970; PL 91-452		

(continued)

President				
(continued from previous page)		Clean Air Deadlines Legislation; PL 93-319 Additional Funding for National Park System; PL 93-477 Additional Wilderness Areas; PL 93-622		Protection of Children against Sexual Exploitation Act; PL 95-225
Gerald R. Ford 1974–1977	Age Discrimination Act of 1975; PL 94-135			
Jimmy Carter 1977–1981	The Civil Service Reform Act of 1978 PL 95-454	Establish a National Advisory Committee on Oceans and Atmosphere; PL 95-63 Clean Air Act Amendments of 1977; PL 95-95 Fish and Wildlife Improvement Act; PL 95-616 National Parks and Recreation Act; PL 95-625		

Appendix: Presidents as Legislative Leaders and Major Social Legislation (*Cont.*)

President	Abortion	Affirmative Action	Environment	Gun Control	Homosexuality	Pornography
			1980 Alaska Lands Act; PL 96-187 1980 Comprehensive Environmental Response, Compensations, and Liability Act; PL 96-510			
Ronald Reagan 1981–1989		Fair Housing Act (the President endorsed this bill under pressure from Vice-President Bush); PL 100-430	Water Projects Bill; PL 99-89 Harbors and Waterways Bill; PL 99-662 Clean Water Act (passed over Presidential Veto); PL 100-4			Child Pornography Bill; PL 98-292

George H. W. Bush 1989–1993	Departments of Labor, Health and Human Services and Education and Related Agencies Appropriations Bill Fiscal Year 1990; PL 101-517	Civil Rights Reauthorization Act; PL 101-180 Americans with Disabilities Act of 1990; PL 101-336 Civil Rights Act of 1991; PL 102-166 Bilingual Ballots; PL 102-344	Clean Air Act Amendments of 1990; PL 101-549 North American Wetlands Conservation Act; PL 101-223	Crime Control Act of 1990; PL 101-647		A Bill Making Appropriation for the Departments of Labor, Health and Human Services, and Education, and Related Agencies; PL 101-106 900 Number Regulations; PL 102-556
William J. Clinton 1993–present	National Institutes of Health Reauthorization Act of 1993; PL 103-43 Abortion Clinic Access Bill; PL 103-259		California Desert Protection Act; Pl 103-433 Safe Drinking Water Act; PL 104-182	Brady Handgun Violence Protection Act of 1993; PL 103-159	Defense of Marriage Act; PL 104-199	Communication Decency Act of 1996; PL 104-104

INDEX